Discourse and Genre

Analysing Language in Context

Stephen Bax

palgrave
macmillan

The author and publishers would like to thank the following for permission to reproduce copyright material: Christian Aid, for Illustration 4.1, an excerpt from a Christian Aid fundraising text (2007), and also for Illustration 4.2, an excerpt from a fundraising leaflet. Every effort has been made to trace all copyright-holders, but if any have been inadvertently overlooked the publishers will be pleased to make the necessary arrangement at the first opportunity.

The author has asserted his right to be identified as the author of this work in accordance with the Copyright, Designs and Patents Act 1988.

First published 2011 by
PALGRAVE MACMILLAN

Palgrave Macmillan in the UK is an imprint of Macmillan Publishers Limited, registered in England, company number 785998, of Houndmills, Basingstoke, Hampshire RG21 6XS.

Palgrave Macmillan in the US is a division of St Martin's Press LLC, 175 Fifth Avenue, New York, NY 10010.

Palgrave Macmillan is the global academic imprint of the above companies and has companies and representatives throughout the world.

Palgrave® and Macmillan® are registered trademarks in the United States, the United Kingdom, Europe and other countries.

ISBN 978–0–230–21796–6 hardback
ISBN 978–0–230–21797–3 paperback

This book is printed on paper suitable for recycling and made from fully managed and sustained forest sources. Logging, pulping and manufacturing processes are expected to conform to the environmental regulations of the country of origin.

A catalogue record for this book is available from the British Library.

A catalog record for this book is available from the Library of Congress.

10 9 8 7 6 5 4 3 2 1
20 19 18 17 16 15 14 13 12 11

Printed and bound in Great Britain by
CPI Antony Rowe, Chippenham and Eastbourne

To my family, for their patience

Contents

Figure, Tables and Illustrations

Figure

Tables

Illustrations

Series Editors' Preface

The first three books to be published in the Perspectives on the English Language series (Jeffries, *Discovering Language*: Chapman, *Thinking About Language*; and Clark, *Studying Language*) together formed the first wave of what will ultimately be a comprehensive collection of research-based text-books covering the wide variety of topics in English Language studies. These initial three books provide the basics of English Language description, theory and methodology that students need, whether they are specialists in English Language or taking only one or two modules in the subject. The idea was that these books would be used differently by such different students, and indeed they have already proved useful to postgraduate students as well as undergraduates.

Now we are beginning the process of adding to the series the envisaged set of higher-level textbooks that will build on the core books by bringing together the latest thinking in a range of topics in English Language. This 'second wave' comprises books written by current researchers in the field, and far from simply providing an overview or summary of work so far, these books are distinctive in making the latest research available to a student audience. They are not 'dumbed down', but are written accessibly, with exercises and questions for the reader to consider where relevant, and for the higher education teacher these books provide a resource that s/he can use to bring out the best in students of all abilities.

The book you are holding will ultimately be part of a large series of topic-based books in English Language, and we are confident that you will find them useful and interesting. Although this series was begun with only one series editor, the rate of production of the second wave calls for more help in editing and proofreading. We look forward to surfing this second wave together!

LESLEY JEFFRIES
DAN McINTYRE

Introduction

This book is part of a series whose earliest volumes offered a 'foundation in descriptive apparatus, theoretical background and research skills' for the study of language (Jeffries, 2006:2), In her volume, entitled *Discovering Language: The Structure of Modern English*, Jeffries described and discussed elements of the language system, including phonology, lexis and syntax, and pointed out that later volumes in the series – of which this is one – would seek to build on those foundations so as to explore language in context.

When language is discussed not as a system, in terms of its phonology, its lexis and grammatical patterning, but in terms of how it is used in various settings in order 'to enact activities and identities' (Gee, 2005:7), it is often referred to as *discourse*, and its study is termed *discourse analysis*. This terminology is used partly to make it clear that the analyst is interested not only in the language system in itself, but also in a host of other factors which contribute to the impact of the discourse in various contexts. As Johnstone puts it:

> [c]alling what we do '<u>discourse</u> analysis' rather than 'language analysis' underscores the fact that we are not centrally focused on language as abstract system. We tend instead to be interested in what happens when people draw on the knowledge they have about language, based on their memories of things they have said, heard, seen, or written before, to do things in the world. (Johnstone, 2002:3, emphasis in original)

Discourse is important because it enters into virtually every human domain, including human relationships, work, politics, the media, buying and selling, study, and numerous others besides. It is also complex, since users of discourse manipulate a host of factors, including their knowledge of the context, of language forms, of gestures and body language, in highly intricate ways, in order to achieve various goals.

1

This book, then, examines the phenomenon known as discourse, namely language in context and in use. It has three main aims:

(i) To raise awareness of the nature of discourse in general;
(ii) To offer insights into specific types of discourse, and
(iii) To set out an approach to researching discourse systematically.

My approach in this book is based on a number of principles derived from my experience of teaching discourse and discourse analysis. These can be summarised as follows.

Firstly, the study of discourse is most motivating when we can connect it with the real language we experience all around us. This book will therefore focus on a wide range of genuine examples of discourse in action, drawn from internet discourse, political discourse, discourse in the law courts, discourse in the media, jokes, sports commentary and other areas of current interest.

Secondly, in seeking to explain discourse this book adopts a broadly *inductive* approach. *Induction* and *deduction* are terms sometimes used to refer to research processes (see Chapman, 2006) but here they refer to a manner of presenting information pedagogically. This means that instead of presenting theory and then illustrating it with examples, which would be a traditional *deductive* way of presenting a topic, my approach here is the opposite, since each section will typically begin with short examples which are then examined and discussed, with key theoretical principles emerging through the discussion. In my experience this approach tends to lead to clearer insights into the ways in which discourse theory and terminology connect with the reality of actual texts.

When researching discourse we often look out for patterns which can help to explain our responses. If certain sorts of drama make us cry, for example, we tend to see a pattern and then group them as 'tragedies'; if they make us laugh we see a different pattern and call them 'comedies'. In other words, as we seek to explain how discourse operates we frequently identify common features in texts and then group the texts accordingly. *Genre* is a term which is used to refer to patterning of various features in texts, and since *genre features* can offer a useful entry point to understanding texts, this book examines genre and genre features closely, as well as other ways in which texts seem to be patterned, so as to help us to understand how discourse operates.

Finally, this book also has a practical, 'enabling' ambition. Anyone working through the book should by the end be enabled to understand and also to analyse more systematically a range of types of discourse. To help in this endeavour, Chapter 5 sets out a broad heuristic approach to the analysis of discourse, based on three central questions, *what, how* and *why*:

- *What* does the particular text under analysis do or achieve?
- *How* does it achieve it?
- *Why* does it seek to do so?

This broad approach is then exemplified and elaborated in Chapters 6 to 9, and expanded in Chapter 10 into a fuller approach to studying discourse systematically.

Structure of the book

The book begins, in Chapter 1, by considering language in context from the reader's and listener's point of view, through a series of short texts. The aim of this is to see how discourse draws on areas of knowledge which we all share, knowledge not only of lexis, grammar and phonology, but also of the wider world, of society, and particularly of texts and how texts are structured and patterned.

Chapter 2 expands on this by looking in more detail at discourse, what it means and how it can be defined and approached. Two key ways in which discourse is patterned relate to *genre* and *discourse mode*, so these are described and defined in Chapters 3 and 4 respectively.

Since one aim of discourse analysis, as noted above, is to identify patterns in discourse, these concepts serve as useful entry points into the analysis of discourse in general, and therefore come into the discussion in Chapter 5, which sets out a broad 'heuristic', namely a relatively practical way by which to approach a text or texts with a view to analysis.

This broad approach to discourse analysis is taken up in Chapters 6 to 9, in which a range of texts are analysed. These include examples taken from legal contexts, from online games, 'lonely hearts' advertisements, news reports, sports commentary, political speeches and so on. The main aim of these chapters, besides exemplifying the analytical procedure and examining interesting texts, is to build a 'toolkit' for analysis, identifying a range of approaches and techniques which could be used in the analysis of other texts in future.

This 'toolkit' is then more fully assembled in Chapter 10, where the techniques, approaches and perspectives encountered through previous chapters are brought together and summarised as part of a more substantive approach to researching and analysing discourse in context. This approach is based on the three central questions *what, how* and *why*, and the heuristic in Chapter 5, but they are expanded to take account not only of single texts but also of larger discourse research projects.

1 How do we Understand Texts?

As language users we encounter a host of spoken and written texts every day, in a range of contexts. On the whole we deal with them speedily and effectively, without paying much attention to their grammar or lexis, their structure or form. However, if we are to understand how discourse operates, it is useful to unpack these comprehension processes to some extent, which is the aim of the first part of this chapter.

In particular it is interesting to examine the various kinds of knowledge which we draw on as we try to understand language in use, including knowledge of grammar and lexis, but also other sorts of knowledge. Discourse analysis concerns itself in particular with the knowledge which users have at the level of *text*, and this is the focus of the second part of the chapter.

However, in accordance with the broadly inductive approach to discourse outlined in the introduction, I begin not with a theory or concept or definition, but instead with a sample text, or at least a tiny piece from the beginning of the text:

A:

Is it possible to deduce from this alone what kind of text this will be? Even though the evidence is scanty, we might guess that the full text could be a *dialogue* of some sort, because we have seen other examples of dialogues in which a single letter signifies one character about to speak. We could perhaps then predict that the next line might start with the character B. We draw on our *prior knowledge*, in this case on our knowledge of texts or genres, and can therefore make a small but useful start on interpreting the text. This is how the text continues:

A: It's cold with that window open.

Our suspicion is confirmed, as this does seem to be part of a dialogue, partly because the style seems relatively informal (*it's* instead of *it is*), and the language seems to refer to an everyday situation of some sort (a place with windows and weather). In making these assumptions and guesses, we draw quickly and largely subconsciously on areas of knowledge we already possess, about types of texts, about how we use language, about people and so on. As we continue to read, we then draw on *knowledge of the world* to make other guesses about the situation. Who is the speaker? Is it a man or a woman, young or old? Where is it taking place? What is she or he aiming at?

In respect of this last question we would probably guess that the speaker wants something. Although the language is framed as a statement of fact, simply that 'it is cold with the window open', our previous linguistic and social knowledge may suggest to us that it is in fact a *request* or *instruction* meaning 'please close the window'. What is noteworthy is that in the language itself there is nothing to tell us this. A visitor from Mars, we might imagine, who had learned English grammar and lexis from an interplanetary phrasebook, might justifiably take the utterance as a simple statement of fact about the temperature. So why is it that humans would typically take it to mean more than that, a request or instruction?

The reason is that when interpreting a text we naturally draw on years of experience not only of words and grammar but also of how language is *used* in real situations. We draw on this knowledge to interpret the *function* of the utterance as a request of some sort, and we also know that the function of language can be quite different from its *form*. From this prior knowledge we quickly see in this case that the speaker is not simply telling us something, but also *wants* something. This then helps us to interpret the next part of the dialogue:

A: It's cold with that window open.
B: Yes it is (*reading the paper*).

Our imaginary visitor from Mars might consult its grammar book and interpret this as cooperative agreement, simply because B says 'yes'. However, from our experience of language in use, we realise that B is probably not behaving cooperatively at all. Unlike the Martian, we see that although the *form* of the utterance resembles a statement, the *function* is probably a request, perhaps to shut the window. So we now suspect that B is deliberately failing to comply. In other words, although – like our imaginary Martian – we use our knowledge of *grammar* and *lexis* in order to guess that B seems to be agreeing, we also use our knowledge of language in the world, in particular our knowledge of linguistic *function*, to understand that this is not in fact so. We might then ask ourselves, why did B respond like this? Again drawing on our knowledge of the world and of people we notice that B is reading a 'paper', and we might take this as a possible explanation for B's behaviour – perhaps he or she is distracted? Perhaps that 'paper' is a newspaper?

As we read or hear language we are all the time constructing scenarios in this way; 'mental scenes' which help us to understand the language itself. Of course we do it so quickly that we are barely conscious of it, which is why it is sometimes illuminating to unpack the process gradually as we have done here, so as to raise it to our awareness. If we return to the example, we might now be wondering a number of things, for example where might this conversation take place? Are the speakers men or women? Is A male or female? Previous readers who have discussed this text with me almost always offer the same interpretation: A is probably a woman, and B is probably a man, and the 'paper' is perhaps a newspaper. They may be married, or in some way related, and are probably at home, perhaps in the kitchen or sitting room. Here is the rest of what we can call the 'Window' text, and the characters have now been given names:

> Ann: It's cold with that window open.
> Brian: Yes it is (*reading the paper*).
> Ann: Well, could you close it?
> Brian: Yes, I could (*still reading*).

When readers see this text in full, they frequently report that it confirms their initial assumptions. Brian is a man, not happy to be interrupted, as he is reading a newspaper. Ann perhaps thought at first he had simply not heard her, but now she is sure he is being difficult deliberately. He *could* shut the window but will not do it.

How and why do readers draw these conclusions even when they have seen only a small part of the text? Several features are of interest here, for example the issue of gender. Why do almost all readers see the first speaker as a woman and the second as a man? This may have something to do with the indirect form of the request, which some researchers on language and gender have suggested might be a more 'female' request strategy, but it could also derive from our social expectations and even our personal experience about how people actually behave. Some readers report that in their culture it is men who predominantly sit and read newspapers in domestic settings while it is women who tend to be more active!

The larger question for us here is: how do readers come to such conclusions about texts, for example about the speakers, their intentions and so on? The reason, of course, is that we do not simply depend on the text in comprehension. As we read or listen, we draw extensively, automatically and rapidly on large stores of *knowledge about the world* which we have already acquired, about human relationships, including stereotypes of gender relations, about texts and genres, about how sentences link together and about words and syntax, and we then combine all of this previous knowledge with the information which we draw from the text, and thereby *construct* an interpretation of what is happening.

Here is a second text, part of a famous piece of research by Bransford and Johnson (1972) into discourse processes. Readers in their experiment were asked if they could understand this passage:

> The procedure is actually quite simple. First you arrange items into different groups. Of course, one pile may be sufficient depending on how much there is to do. If you have to go somewhere else due to lack of facilities that is the next step; otherwise, you are pretty much set. It is important not to overdo things. That is, it is better to do too few things at once than too many. In the short run this may not seem important but complications can easily arise. A mistake can be expensive as well. At first, the whole procedure will seem complicated. Soon, however, it will become just another facet of life. (Bransford and Johnson, 1972:722)

What is this text about? Gardening? Fishing? From the point of view of the lexis alone, the text appears not to offer any serious problems, so why is it so difficult to understand in practice?

This can be explained again by the fact that an understanding of the syntax and lexis alone is not enough for comprehension, partly because the text contains many items (such as 'procedure', 'items', 'pile', 'things', 'facilities') which are deliberately chosen so as to refer potentially to a number of different things. In order to understand their meaning the reader needs more information. In this case, if we are given a title for the text, for example 'Washing clothes', we can then interpret the 'items' as pieces of clothing, perhaps divided into 'piles' according to colour, perhaps taken to a laundry because we lack the 'facilities', a washing machine, at home and so on.

This in fact is the correct key to the text. It serves to demonstrate that in order to understand discourse we draw on far more than simply *language* knowledge; we draw on a range of knowledge which we could say is above or beyond the level of syntax and lexis, in this case, knowledge about washing machines and human domestic activity.

The aim of discussing these texts in such detail is to bring out the kind of processes and the kinds of knowledge which we use in comprehension. In the next section these kinds of knowledge will be set out in diagrammatic form, so it is useful at this point to summarise some of the key points raised so far.

1. Texts themselves are only one factor in comprehension.
2. In trying to achieve comprehension we draw extensively on our *prior knowledge*, as part of a highly creative, constructive process.
3. One reader's or listener's interpretation is necessarily to some extent different from another's (since, for one thing, my prior knowledge is not exactly the same as yours).
4. In comprehension we also draw on elements of the *context*, and if we do not have contextual clues we construct mental scenarios to help us towards a suitable explanation.

1.1 A framework for understanding comprehension

In considering the 'Window' text and the 'Washing clothes' text, it was pointed out that we make use of a wide range of knowledge in coming to our interpretations, including knowledge of lexis, syntax, types of texts, aspects of the world, human behaviour, and so on. These areas of knowledge, and others, are set out in diagrammatic form in Figure 1.1.

Figure 1.1 is not intended to represent every aspect of comprehension, indeed it omits a number of elements which other analysts with other purposes might wish to include. Furthermore it does not aim to represent the step-by-step process of comprehension, unlike process models of reading and listening (for example, those in Khalifa and Weir, 2009, for reading; Buck, 2001, for listening). Its purpose is simply to set out in diagrammatic form some of the areas to be addressed in this book as a whole, in relation to other areas of linguistic study such as lexis and syntax which will not be the main focus of the book.

Nonetheless, the areas of knowledge represented in Figure 1.1 do mesh with research findings over several decades concerning the types of knowledge we use as we read and listen. This research has led to the development of quite detailed and technical models of these comprehension processes which, while also attempting more ambitiously to set out the sequential processes involved in reading and listening, typically also include each of the elements identified in Figure 1.1. Khalifa and Weir's (2009) socio-cognitive model of the reading process, to take one recent example, has specific levels in it to represent each of the areas in our diagram, namely knowledge of lexis and syntax, and then, higher up the diagram, knowledge of genres and their structure, socio-cultural knowledge, world knowledge and so on, showing

When we understand spoken and written language we draw on our knowledge of these areas:

Top-down

Level	Type of knowledge
WORLD	Shared general knowledge of the world (people, places, etc.)
SOCIETY and CULTURE	Socio-cultural knowledge: understanding of social relations and social roles
CONTEXT	Pragmatic knowledge: speech acts, etc. Physical factors and other contextual information
TEXT and GENRE	Intertextual relations Genres, including
	Function of genres
	Structure of genres
	Discourse modes
CONCEPTUAL STRUCTURES	Mental models Schematic knowledge (schemas, frames and scripts)

MACRO level aspects (higher-order features)

MICRO level aspects (lower-order features)

COHESION	Cohesion and cohesive devices
SENTENCE	Syntax
WORD, CONCEPT	Lexis, Concepts
ELEMENT	Sounds / Letters or Script

Bottom-up

Figure 1.1 Types of knowledge used in language comprehension

their importance as part of the reading process. Similar areas of knowledge are also involved in listening, as can be seen for example in Buck's detailed framework for describing listening ability (Buck, 2001:104).

This diagram then, although deliberately modest in its ambition, does broadly concur with research findings as to the kinds of knowledge we draw on when we comprehend language. In addition, it follows the convention of setting out these areas of knowledge as a series of levels, from lower order elements to higher order elements, reflecting an increase in size from the smallest units, for example sounds and letters at the bottom of the diagram, to the larger units, for example texts, towards the top (Jeffries, 2006:5).

So the bottom of the diagram includes knowledge of more basic aspects of language, such as *knowledge of sounds* (in the case of spoken language) and *knowledge of letters or script* (in the case of written language). Above that is placed *knowledge of lexis and syntax* and *knowledge of cohesion*, i.e. the ways in which sentences link together. Together these can be termed the 'lower order' elements of the knowledge involved in linguistic and textual communication and have been extensively discussed in previous contributions to this series (see, for example, Jeffries, 2006; Clark, 2007).

At the top of the diagram are 'higher order' elements of knowledge which are also important in interpreting oral and written texts, for example *world knowledge* in general. To return to the 'Window' dialogue from the start of this chapter, it was important in that passage to know what a window is, as well as the fact that it can open and close, which is part of our general world knowledge. When we saw that Brian was reading 'a paper' we also drew on our world knowledge to guess that the 'paper' might be a newspaper. Similarly, in the 'Washing clothes' text our general world knowledge was activated to allow understanding of what a washing machine is and does. In similar ways many aspects of world knowledge enter significantly into text comprehension.

However, the concept of 'window' could equally have been treated as coming at the bottom of the diagram, under *lexical knowledge*. This highlights an important point about the diagram, namely that although it presents each element as a separate entity, each dimension interacts and overlaps with all the other elements in the actual process of comprehension in far more complex ways than the diagram implies. So it is strictly impossible to separate our lexical knowledge of the word 'window' from our knowledge of the concept 'window', or from our world knowledge of how windows operate. This means that although we can set out this diagram as a kind of hierarchy, as a useful way of demonstrating the different kinds of knowledge which we use when understanding texts, in actual comprehension and production we do not draw on them in any linear and ordered way. We should not make the mistake, in other words, of seeing this diagram as a literal model about how discourse comprehension and production operate in practice. As Jeffries has noted;

> [t]he levels model of language is a metaphorical device that enables us to visualise the relationship between different sizes of unit as though they were physically separate, when in fact they all occur in the same stream of speech. (Jeffries, 2006:3)

The importance of 'higher-order' knowledge

At the top of the diagram, just below the level of *world knowledge,* is the level of *society and culture,* in which are included aspects of social knowledge such as knowledge about human behaviour and relationships. In the 'Window' text, for instance, we guessed that the first speaker might be a woman, and the second speaker might be a man and that they might be married. Why was this? Perhaps we brought to the text a previous idea about how married couples speak to each other, which may be drawn from our own cultural experience, from social stereotypes or from books and films.

One of my students offered a different view, insisting that speaker A must be a mother and speaker B must be an older teenage boy. She then explained (with feeling) that she herself had a teenage son and had experienced such difficult exchanges with him. Clearly, along with our broad knowledge of the world, we also bring personal experiences of language in use, and personal experiences of human and social relations to every text as we try to interpret it.

The fact that this second level in the diagram includes both *society* and *culture* raises a question about culture: are interpretations of texts the same across all cultures? Some readers from Yemen once insisted to me that the characters in the 'Window' dialogue could not possibly be in the kitchen, since firstly the man would not normally be in the kitchen in their construction of the text, and secondly he would never read a newspaper there. For those readers the text made perfect sense as a dialogue, but not in the kitchen. Evidently then, much of the knowledge we bring to texts may either be personal to us or be culturally specific. In other words, we each construct meaning in subtly different ways, precisely because our own individual knowledge and cultural experiences play such a large part in the process. However, all readers/hearers will share some consensus about the core meaning of a text, otherwise communication would be impossible.

Moving down to the next level in the diagram, why do readers of the 'Window' dialogue usually understand that when Ann says 'It's cold with that window open', this is probably best interpreted as a request to close the window rather than, say, a promise? In the diagram, still at the level of *society and culture,* is an entry entitled *pragmatic knowledge.* When we hear people speak we bring to the process a store of knowledge related to what the speaker is *doing* with language, as was pointed out in the famous work by the philosopher Austin entitled *How to do things with words* (Austin, 1962; see the discussion in Chapman, 2006:118–22). This 'pragmatic' knowledge allows us to say that Ann was offering a 'speech act' which we would interpret as a request rather than, say, a descriptive comment on the weather. We know this not from anything we find in the text itself, but from extensive experience of other texts previously encountered, and also from aspects of the *context* as we have constructed it mentally. As with the other levels of the diagram, this highlights the fact that we also bring this *pragmatic knowledge* with us when we encounter texts, written and spoken.

Top-down and bottom-up

To the left of the diagram in Figure 1.1 are arrows going down and up, and labels indicating that one direction is termed *bottom-up* and the other *top-down*. These are useful terms to describe general ways of viewing comprehension: from a 'top-down' perspective, comprehension of a text is supposed to start at the top with general world knowledge and move downwards. By contrast, a 'bottom-up' perspective sees comprehension as focussing firstly on the lower levels, then moving up gradually towards the higher elements. Field explains the terms as follows:

> Underlying the metaphors 'top' and 'bottom' is the idea that listening and reading proceed through levels of processing, with bottom-up information from the signal assembled into units of ever-increasing size. In listening, the lowest level (i.e. the smallest unit) is the phonetic feature. The listener's task might be portrayed as combining groups of features into phonemes, phonemes into syllables, syllables into words, words into clauses and clauses into propositions. At the 'top' is the global meaning of the utterance, into which new information is integrated as it emerges. (Field, 2003:40–1)

Of course the reality of comprehension is more complex, as Field explains in terms of listening:

> First, it is not certain that bottom-up processing involves all the levels described. Some researchers have argued that we process speech into syllables without passing through a phonemic level; others that we construct words directly from phonetic features. Nor does bottom-up processing deal with one level at a time. There is evidence that in listening it takes place at a delay of only a quarter of a second behind the speaker – which implies that the tasks of analysing the phonetic signal, identifying words and assembling sentences must all be going on in parallel. (Field, 2003:40–2)

For these and other reasons few researchers in psycholinguistics nowadays would say that comprehension does in practice operate either in a completely top-down or a bottom-up direction. However, once researchers did model comprehension in these ways. In the early 1970s, for example, researchers into reading such as Gough (1972) suggested that we understand language in a rigidly 'bottom-up' way (*bottom-up processing*), by starting directly with 'lower order' areas of our language knowledge, mainly words. Indeed he produced diagrams of the comprehension process which were strongly linear, implying that we could not understand 'higher' levels unless we had first fully processed lower ones (Rumelhart, 1985). Gough claimed quite explicitly that reading takes place letter by letter, serially, from left to right (Gough, 1972; Barnet, 1989). By contrast, other researchers (for example, Goodman, 1967; 1973) attempted to suggest that when we read we work quite strictly in the opposite direction, top-down, starting with world knowledge then proceeding by 'guessing', not necessarily even reading every word of the text.

Nowadays, however, most researchers agree that neither rigid view is accurate, but that when we read (or listen) we understand language in a more *interactive* way, drawing on the different areas of our knowledge set out in Figure 1.1, be they from the top or the bottom, in a rapid, dynamic process which probably differs from person to person, from genre to genre and from situation to situation (see for example Grabe and Stoller, 2002). Nonetheless, the terms 'top-down' and 'bottom-up' are still widely used, and still useful, as metaphors to indicate one or other broad approach to explaining how comprehension works.

1.2 The focus and structure of this book

The discussion so far makes the point that comprehension of language depends on a wide range of types of knowledge, all of which come into the comprehension process in complex ways. As a result it is now possible to delimit with greater clarity the areas with which this book will specifically deal, namely discourse and genre, and to show how they relate to those other areas shown in Figure 1.1 which will not feature so prominently in this book.

The central, shaded part of the diagram, the part which has not yet been discussed in detail, relates broadly to the areas of *discourse*, *text* and *genre* with which this book is mainly concerned. In the course of the next three chapters the terms themselves will be discussed and defined in detail. Chapter 2 will discuss and define discourse and discourse analysis in general, including intertextuality; Chapter 3 will discuss and define genre; Chapter 4 will discuss and define discourse modes, and their place in analysis.

This will then form the basis of the discussion, in Chapter 5, of how we can carry out a discourse analysis in practice. In that chapter I set out an approach for analysing a piece of discourse systematically. This approach will then be used for the close analysis, in the second half of the book, of a wide variety of text types, including conversation, text messaging and political speeches, so as to offer readers a varied and extensive toolkit of approaches and techniques for use in their own analysis of discourse. The final chapter will then revisit the procedure, and will discuss two examples of discourse analysis research studies in order to illustrate how such analyses can be carried out in practice.

Returning to the diagram in Figure 1.1, then, it is the central shaded area which will be the main focus of the book, broadly speaking the area of text and genre. However, there is a danger in defining my focus of study in this way, as it can give the impression that discourse, text and genre could somehow be considered in isolation. This would be a mistake, since the contextual, socio-cultural and pragmatic elements above the shaded area on the diagram will certainly enter our discussion at various points; we can never fully separate them from the analysis of discourse. Likewise the 'lower order' elements of cohesion, grammar, phonology and lexis are essential elements of any discourse analysis, and will also come into our discussion in significant ways throughout the book, though it will not be possible within the scope of this book to consider them all individually in detail.

Nor is this necessary, since the two areas above and below the shaded part of the diagram have received extensive treatment in other books, and the reader is encouraged to address that wider literature (for example, in this series, Clark, 2007 and Jeffries, 2006) for a fuller understanding of how those areas impact on discourse.

Example text: a game

The two texts considered so far were both invented so as to make particular points about language and comprehension. However, the challenge for discourse analysis is to analyse genuine texts created and used in real communicative situations. To prepare for the fuller discussion of the nature of discourse and the aims of discourse analysis to come in Chapter 2, this chapter therefore concludes by considering two authentic texts.

It will quickly become clear that several elements of the first text are difficult to understand and explain, so it might be helpful to reflect on the areas of knowledge discussed above from the diagram in Figure 1.1. Which types of knowledge of those listed in Figure 1.1 – including knowledge of types of text, knowledge of the world, knowledge of social relations and of course knowledge of lexis and syntax – do we draw on as we struggle to make sense of this text (Illustration 1.1)?

In our attempt at interpretation, we inevitably draw on our 'lower order' knowledge at the bottom of Figure 1.1. For example we note the irregular and

Illustration 1.1 'Squirrel' text

uncontrolled handwriting and some of the spelling (e.g. 'bithday' instead of 'birthday') as well as the unusual use of capital letters and lack of punctuation. We would probably link this with our 'higher order' world knowledge about how people write, and guess (correctly) that the text is written by a child. However, what kind of text is it and what is its function?

We also draw on our *knowledge of genres*, and deduce that it is probably some kind of letter. The obvious reason for this is that it uses a standard letter opening, 'Dear + addressee', and a standard closing formula, 'From + sender'. This suggests that the text must be a letter sent to someone called 'king' from two writers named 'Bushy' and 'Chestnut'. We may also use our knowledge of *social relations* to infer something about the relative power of these writers and the king, namely that the writers are inferior in social status to him.

In addition, there is another formula in the letter which is familiar, namely 'Happy 50th Bi[r]thday' and this allows us to be even more specific. We can now use our prior knowledge of *texts and genres* to infer that this is a sort of *birthday greeting letter*. In terms of function, we can be reasonably sure that it aims to send good wishes to someone, and this is reinforced by the word 'hope' in line 2.

All of this demonstrates that readers use numerous elements of prior knowledge to start to unlock the text. Even so, there are still elements which are odd. Why does it say 'I' when there are two writers? Is that a child's mistake?

Why does the note say 'I hope your wife is good'? Is that meant to mean 'well' referring to the wife's health? Who exactly is 'king' and who exactly are the writers? This is where, as with the 'Washing clothes' text, more *contextual information or knowledge* is needed. Some readers who look at this text guess correctly that the names *Bushy* and *Chestnut* suggest animals, and a few even guess correctly from the colour chestnut and the link with a 'bushy tail' that they are meant to be squirrels.

This is in fact a note written by two 7-year-old girls playing a game. The girls explained afterwards that in this game they were following a book they both knew about an elephant, but that they were acting as squirrels instead of elephants because one of the girls happened to have a toy squirrel. In their story (borrowed partly from the book they knew) the queen of the squirrels had just died and the king was about to marry again. In many stories, as the girls explained, the second wife is often unpleasant (we recall the wicked step-mother stereotype from canonical fairy stories). They were therefore wishing the king a happy birthday and also hoping that this second wife would be a good person rather than hoping that she was well! This example therefore, as well as illustrating the intricacies of real discourse and how it is created, also serves to remind us of the dynamic creativity of discourse users, especially of children at play.

Now that we have the relevant background information, and have drawn on our lower order knowledge, as well as our knowledge of society, of the world and of genres, we have perhaps arrived at a sense that we understand this 'Squirrel' text quite fully. In general and simple terms, we have made use of our world knowledge (at the top of the diagram), together with knowledge of social relations (below it), knowledge of texts and genres (below that), and knowledge of grammar and lexis (at the bottom), in different ways and in different combinations and then put them together with the text to come to what has been called 'the click of comprehension' (Samuels and Kamil, 1984:206) – essentially the stage in the comprehension process where all the relevant parts of our knowledge work together with the textual information to give us the feeling that we 'understand a text'. The central point for our purposes in this book is that part of the knowledge base on which we draw is extensive knowledge about texts, text structure and genres, to which the next chapters will turn.

Context: Barbecue Sign

Since this book will focus on our knowledge of texts and genres, it is useful to consider one final example in this chapter to illustrate how that area of our knowledge can be influenced in crucial ways by the *context* in which a text is

Illustration 1.2   Barbecue sign

found. This was obscured in the previous three examples by the fact that they were relatively context-free.

Consider the photograph in Illustration 1.2. Which aspects of language knowledge, as identified in the diagram in Figure 1.1, might be needed in order to decode it and interpret it satisfactorily?

This is clearly a public sign or notice – our *genre knowledge* tells us that. Drawing on our previous experience of such signs we make use of a mental *genre schema* (to be discussed in Chapter 3) so that when we see a text such as this one which has the features we recognise, in the expected kind of context, we use these expectations so as to start to interpret the text. Our *genre knowledge* acts as a key which opens our minds to the possible language, function and structure which we associate with such texts.

The context is also crucial. Texts always occur in contexts of some kind, and it is important to take account of those contexts in any interpretation. In this case, the sign was encountered when I was walking by the sea, which allowed me to draw on the *contextual* information of my location to assist in my interpretation. In this case, the *contextual knowledge* about where the sign was, together with my *genre knowledge* drawn from seeing previous such signs, linked with my *lexical knowledge* (for example, in interpreting the word ATTENTION) all helped me to interpret the text. The main part of the interpretation for my purposes and for the purposes of those who put the sign there, revolved around the *function* of the text, namely what it is trying to achieve. In this case the function of the notice is obvious – it is an *instruction notice* telling me what I may and may not do.

In other words, *genre knowledge* alone was not enough for me to understand the text fully. I needed to draw on other sorts of knowledge, as set out in other parts of the diagram in Figure 1.1, to interpret different parts of the sign. For instance, my *lexical knowledge* together with my *contextual knowledge* drawn from looking around me allowed me to guess that the rather odd *BAR.B.Qs* (not even a word in my dictionary) means 'barbecues', and I could then guess from looking at the position of the sign (*contextual knowledge* again) that it must be referring to the beach behind. So I am not, I understand, permitted to have a barbecue on the beach itself, and fortunately I was not planning one.

The reference of the word 'promenade' in the notice is at first unclear to me, but using my *general lexical knowledge*, I look around me at the concrete walkway where I am standing as I read the sign, and so I can decode the reference of this particular word. The weather is freezing cold and I am alone, but I suppose (drawing on my *world knowledge*) that in the summer when people open up their beach huts they might put chairs and tables out and block this promenade – hence, I suppose, the need for this second prohibition on the notice.

This exemplifies the ways in which we constantly and efficiently make use of a range of knowledge – genre knowledge, lexical knowledge, knowledge of grammar, contextual knowledge and so on, to interpret the function and meaning of texts which confront us, and then of course – an important part of the process – having worked out the important *function* of the text, we decide how to act in a kind of dialogue with the text we have read.

1.3 Summary

This chapter has explored the nature of discourse from a reader's or listener's point of view, so as to bring out, through discussion of a series of short texts, the various kinds of knowledge we use in text comprehension. These were then set out in diagrammatic form not only to illustrate the extent of prior knowledge we draw on when using language, but also to identify the areas on which this book, in its discussion of discourse and genre, will primarily focus. The same diagram was used also to demonstrate the ways in which these areas of *text knowledge* and *genre knowledge* link up and relate to other aspects of knowledge addressed, for example, in sociolinguistics, pragmatics, the study of lexis and syntax and so on.

In essence, then, the focus of this book will be on the shaded area of Figure 1.1, relating broadly to text and genre. However, these terms themselves, as well as the term 'discourse', require more discussion and definition. Chapter 2 will therefore turn to the consideration of what exactly we mean by 'discourse', in the light of the comprehension processes which this chapter has examined, and also what is meant by 'text' and 'intertextuality'.

In order to understand the Barbecue Sign I needed to have a *concept* of 'barbecues' and also an understanding of the function and content of signs in general. The first of these kinds of knowledge, concerning *concepts* and *schemas*, will be discussed in Chapter 3. The reason for discussing these conceptual and 'mental knowledge structures' is that our knowledge of genres appears to have similar characteristics, in that my prior *genre knowledge* of how signs work in general, for example, assists me in interpreting any particular sign I encounter. The discussion of concepts and schemas therefore leads into the larger discussion of genres and genre knowledge in the same chapter.

Numerous writers have also identified a further, more abstract, level of analysis, above the level of genre, which has been labelled 'modes of discourse' (Smith, 2003), to include such modes as narrating, describing, reporting and arguing. The value of adopting this level of analysis will be considered alongside the discussion of genre in Chapter 3. The main discourse modes will then be discussed in greater detail in Chapter 4.

As I noted above, this will then lay the groundwork for the description and discussion, in Chapter 5, of a practical method of approaching discourse analysis, which will then be used in the second half of the book in the actual analysis of a wide range of texts from a variety of domains.

2 Discourse and Discourse Analysis

2.1 Definitions of discourse

The diagram in Figure 1.1 set out in general terms how discourse and genre, as the main focus of this book, fit with other areas of linguistic study such as sociolinguistics, pragmatics, psycholinguistics and grammar. This chapter can now discuss the central terms, starting with 'discourse' itself, and then 'text' and 'intertextuality'. It will also set out a working definition of discourse.

A good starting point is the definition of discourse analysis offered by Stubbs (1993). He starts by noting that definitions of discourse are varied and contentious, and then identifies three key elements of the area of study as he sees it. These features of discourse have been questioned in recent years to some extent, but they are nonetheless useful starting points for discussion. It is important to bear in mind from the outset that Stubbs was describing them rather than endorsing them completely.

One of these key elements of discourse, in Stubbs' characterisation, is its focus on the study of *authentic* language, rather than invented language. A second element is that discourse focuses on units of language 'above the level of the sentence', by which is meant units of language which are larger in size and scope than a sentence. A third is the focus on language *in context*, which implies that discourse is not to be seen as a set of linguistic tokens with meaning in themselves, like invented grammatical examples out of context, since meaning is to some extent governed by the contexts in which texts occur.

The views about discourse which Stubbs was outlining arose in the 1970s and 1980s, and need to be understood in their historical context. It is significant that each of the defining features which Stubbs identifies seems to have been a reaction to the kind of theoretical linguistics which was dominant at that time, usually associated with Noam Chomsky. Classic Chomskyan linguistics (see, for example, Chomsky, 1965) typically contravened all the three precepts delineated above – broadly speaking it did not use authentic language but *invented* sentences to illustrate grammar points, it took no interest in the *context* of an utterance, and it worked exclusively on the grammar of sentences and clauses, and had no interest in larger texts.

Given that Chomskyan linguistics was a powerful academic force for many years, it is perhaps no surprise that those engaged in the emerging study of discourse in the 1970s and 1980s should define their discipline against that prevailing set of ideas, to mark out their territory and to show in which ways their endeavour was distinctive. However, defining one area of study by contrasting it with another does not mean that the resulting definition is necessarily complete or appropriate, or that it will stand the test of time. For this reason, and also in the light of advances in our understanding of discourse, each of the elements of the definition of discourse and discourse analysis which Stubbs set out have come to be reconsidered in the intervening years, especially now that discourse analysis is no longer under pressure to react to the dominance of Chomskyan linguistics.

This chapter will examine the three features identified by Stubbs as a starting point and will proceed by accepting two of them, revising the third and identifying three further areas where that view of discourse and how to approach it has been amended and supplemented in recent thinking. The aim is to elaborate and explain, through the six features which will result from the discussion, a more satisfactory working definition of discourse and discourse analysis which can serve as the basis for our discussion in the rest of the book.

Of Stubbs' three defining features, the two which are still broadly retained in current views of the discipline are the view that the subject matter of discourse analysis typically consists of *authentic* texts, by which are meant texts which are not invented by the analyst but are naturally occurring, and secondly that these texts are to be studied and understood with reference to *context*. The first of these is relatively uncontroversial (although as Chapman (2006) argues, even non-authentic texts have their place in linguistic study). However, the issue of context, the second of Stubbs' features, needs closer examination.

Context in the study of discourse

The importance of taking account of context can be illustrated by the example of the Barbecue Sign text at the end of Chapter 1, from which it was amply clear that the context of the sign played a crucial part in my understanding of its function, as well as my understanding of its lexis and other features.

However, this arguably depends on a rather simplistic view of context, assuming that it is an objective, unchanging dimension of the text which all readers of that sign would be able to access in an identical way.

It has been suggested, most pointedly by Blommaert (2005), that the concept of 'context' has at times been treated too uncritically in the analysis of discourse. Blommaert accuses some analysts, for example in the Critical Discourse Analysis (CDA) tradition, of recognising the theoretical centrality of the concept in principle, but in practice of treating 'context [as] often a mere background to rather orthodox (linguistic or interactional) discourse analysis' (Blommaert, 2005:53). The point of this critique is that not only should we include in our analyses all aspects of context, so far as we can see them, including 'everything in the material, mental, personal, interactional, social, institutional, cultural and historical situation in which the utterance was made' (Gee, 2005:54), but that our approach to the analysis of discourse should incorporate these contextual elements far more systematically than it did previously.

One step towards this is to see context in terms of the concept of *contextualisation* (Gumperz, 1982; 1992) which

> comprises all activities by participants which make relevant, maintain, revise, cancel...any aspect of context which, in turn, is responsible for the interpretation of an utterance in its particular locus of occurrence. (Auer, 1992:4, in Blommaert, 2005:41)

To put it another way, 'context is not an external set of circumstances but a selection of them internally represented in the mind' (Widdowson, 2007:20). For this reason, the relevant context in a piece of discourse might include factors which are not even physically present at all – say in the case of a letter which mentions something known to the writer and recipient but which neither can actually see. However, it perhaps goes without saying that

> [a]lthough there can be no appeal to a common situation, however, there must be an appeal to a common context of shared knowledge or otherwise no communication can take place at all. (Widdowson, 2007:21, emphasis added)

How, then, can context be 'retrieved' by the discourse analyst if it is in the minds of the users? In conversational discourse, instances of hesitation or other linguistic and non-linguistic features could potentially be interpreted as clues to the response of the interactants to aspects of the context, and can therefore potentially provide clues about aspects of the context which are of relevance to them. For example, in a setting where there is a power differential between speakers it might be possible to identify elements of that power differential, as perceived by participants, in their actual linguistic and other choices.

However, the situation is more problematic with written discourse. In the case of the Barbecue Sign, for instance, the analyst would appear to have recourse only to the text itself. One answer is that even in this case the text does offer certain clues which allow deductions about the context – the use of imperatives for example carries implications about power relations. These could be complemented by research, perhaps ethnographic, into the responses of those in the community and the ways in which they construct the socio-political and other contextual factors affecting their interpretation. However, the issue is not a straightforward one.

Further discussion and examples of how context can be taken into account in the analytical process will be considered in Chapter 5, and also in several of the analyses of texts in the second half of the book. In addition, Chapter 10 discusses a discourse analysis project which uses ethnography to attempt to take account of context in the analytical process, which will serve as an illustration of how it can perhaps be done in practice.

Beyond the sentence?

The third plank of Stubbs' characterisation of discourse, that it concerns texts 'beyond the sentence level', is still mentioned in recent discussions, for example by Paltridge (2006:2): 'Discourse analysis focuses on knowledge about language beyond the word, clause, phrase and sentence' (Paltridge 2006:2). Thornbury even uses it in the title of his book about discourse analysis for teachers: *Beyond the Sentence: Introducing Discourse Analysis.* However, it has been pointed out (for example by Widdowson, 1995; 2004; and Cameron, 2001) that there are many examples of discourse which are authentic, and found in real contexts, but which cannot convincingly be described as being 'beyond the level of the sentence'. Widdowson gives numerous examples, such as a sign on a door which reads LADIES, and a sign consisting of the letter P to indicate a place to park (Widdowson, 1995; see also 2004). Here is a similar example (Illustration 2.1). What can we make of the picture? Where might we encounter it? Is it a sentence?

This photograph was taken in an airport – but is it a sentence or 'beyond a sentence'? Clearly it is neither, as it consists of no more than a question mark and the letter 'i', but the key point is that it is nonetheless perfectly comprehensible *discourse*, no matter how brief. When I saw it I understood at once that it was a sign indicating an airport information desk, a fact which was clear to me because of my previous experience of such signs, its location,

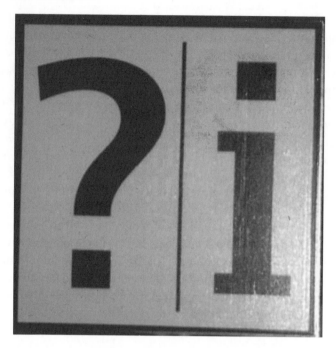

Illustration 2.1 Information sign

and my prior knowledge of airports, all of which led me to understand that the letter '*i*' indicated *information* of some sort.

The important point here is that such a sign is no less an example of discourse than a longer text, and we use the same processes to understand it. It therefore seems irrational for discourse analysts to exclude such short texts from their field of study simply for the apparently arbitrary reason that they are not 'beyond the sentence'. If we seek to understand discourse in the real world such arbitrary exclusions seem pointless. It is true that discourse analysts tend to *prefer* to study longer texts and to look at the relations between the parts of those texts, the ways they link together and so on, but why exclude shorter texts? In addition, Widdowson (2004) points out a further problem with the word 'sentence' in such classical definitions, because when we speak we do not always make use of complete sentences. For these and other reasons the definition of discourse in this book will dispense with any reference to sentences, or even clauses, or of discourse restricting itself to any domain 'beyond' them. That element of the definition described by Stubbs would seem, in the light of examples such as the one above, to be untenable and unhelpful. The definition of discourse study characterised by Stubbs can therefore be amended to say instead that discourse studies can include texts of any size, written or spoken, so long as they are authentic and considered in context.

2.2 What is a text?

It can be accepted, then, that discourse concerns itself with *authentic* texts, by which is meant texts which are not constructed artificially. Secondly, discourse relates to texts in *context,* broadly conceived, for reasons noted above. Stubbs' third point is now revised to say that the study of discourse concerns itself with texts of any size, written or spoken. But at this point it is important to ask: what is meant by texts exactly? As Widdowson (2004) points out, many writers on discourse seem to use the terms 'text' and 'discourse' interchangeably, and this can be confusing, so it will be useful at this point to try to distinguish them more clearly.

In the first place, of course, the word 'text' is meant – as in other books in this series (see Jeffries, 2006:2) – to cover both spoken and written language. However, can we distinguish between language which constitutes a text and language which does not? For instance, we might ask whether this list of words is 'a text' or not:

bank great age installation total amazing whiteboard classics

In some extreme circumstances (in modem poetry, for example) we might find language similar to this which someone might call a 'text', but usually we would not do so. (In fact it is a list of scattered words I happen to see when I look around the room as I type.) We might say in a commonsense way that it is not a text because it is 'not meaningful', but linguists have attempted rather more formal definitions of what distinguishes a text from a non-text. In a famous early account in the 1970s Halliday and Hasan proposed that what distinguishes a text from a non-text could be called 'texture', and they explained this as follows:

A text has texture, and this is what distinguishes it from something that is not a text. It derives this texture from the fact that it functions as a unity with respect to its environment. (Halliday and Hasan, 1976:2)

This may seem rather circular at first sight, but it helps us to understand why the string of random words listed above could not typically be called a 'text', because it does not in any way 'function as a unity'. Halliday and Hasan went on to argue that 'texture' is largely the result of cohesive ties within the text which link the parts together. Again this appears convincing because my random string of words does not have any ties of this sort, including any grammatical ties or relationships between the words. In short, Halliday and Hasan offer a useful starting point: texts are distinguished from non-texts because they seem to function as a unity, and also because they seem to have 'cohesive ties' of various kinds serving to link the parts together (in ways discussed further by Jeffries, 2006:183–7)

However, when we look more closely at this, it becomes rather problematic. In the short texts we mentioned above, namely the *P* on a sign for parking, or the *?i* on a sign for an information desk, it is difficult to see anything in those texts themselves which is 'cohesive'. It is true that each of them 'functions as a unity with respect to its environment' as Halliday and Hasan put it, but this is not owing to anything exactly 'cohesive' within the texts themselves, so much as to the prior knowledge which we ourselves supply. For this reason it is difficult to offer a definition of text which relies on an idea of 'texture' if that in turn relies on some 'cohesion' which may not be at all evident. Indeed Halliday himself later revised his definition of a text, making it far broader:

> We can define text, in the simplest way perhaps, by saying that it is language that is functional. By functional, we simply mean language that is doing some job in some context. (Halliday, 1989:10)

This is broader and more inclusive, and would now embrace the basic sign at the airport which we saw above, but it may at the same time be too general for our purposes. For example if function were the only criterion, how could we distinguish a 'text' from a 'genre' since both are 'functional'? Something more than this is needed in order to make such distinctions clear.

This book will therefore adopt a broad definition of 'text' as being, as Halliday says, an instance of 'language that is doing some job in some context', to include both written and spoken language. A text in this definition could be 'any tissue of meaning which is symbolically significant for a reader' (Parker and the Bolton Discourse Network, 1999:4), perhaps even to include 'objects like trainers, or events like football matches, or other things like food, or walking styles' (Rapley, 2007:133). However, unlike those authors who use the word 'text' very broadly to encompass also *non*-linguistic creations, I will use the word 'text' in this book to refer only to those artefacts which include a language element.

Genres are not texts

Furthermore, *texts* in this book will refer to *actual* instances of language. This will be important as the discussion proceeds, since they will be distinguished in this way from *genres*. In the definition to be elaborated below, genres will be viewed as 'prototypes' which we draw on as language users while we create or interpret actual texts. As such, genres will be understood as mental constructs similar to schemas, frames and scripts, also to be discussed below. Texts, by contrast, are defined as the actual manifestations of language in the world; they draw on our mental ideas of genres, but may differ from those genres in various creative ways, or may mix genres creatively for particular functional and communicative purposes.

2.3 Intertextuality

To summarise: the definition of discourse to be followed here subscribes to the standard view, expressed by Stubbs, that discourse deals with *authentic* language (not invented), with language in *context* (not decontextualised), and that discourse includes texts of all kinds and all sizes, texts being actual instances of language, written or spoken. The fourth dimension, to be considered next, relates to *intertextuality*, and can be explained through the following example, this time taken from a political speech.

Barack Obama, when he was fighting for the Democrat nomination for US President in 2008, had just been defeated in one of the primary elections when he delivered an inspirational speech to rally his supporters. Here is a small part of the speech (which will be analysed in greater detail in Chapter 9):

> It was the call of workers who organized, women who reached for the ballot, a president who chose the moon as our new frontier, and a king who took us to the mountaintop and pointed the way to the promised land: Yes, we can, to justice and equality.

As has already been noted, when attempting to understand this or any other discourse it is important from the outset to take account of the context in which it is encountered and produced, and this will be part of the fuller analysis of Obama's speech in Chapter 9. Here, however, it is sufficient to note that Obama had just lost a crucial vote and was aiming to rally his dejected supporters, and he did so by including several echoes of other events, references to other people and allusions to other texts.

This serves as an illustration, then, of the fourth feature of discourse which I consider important, and which was not part of Stubbs' classic account of the defining features of discourse, namely the fact that texts do not occur in isolation from each other. When Obama mentions 'a president who chose the moon as our new frontier', he is referring specifically to President John F. Kennedy, and in particular to his 1961 speech when Kennedy memorably set the aim of 'landing a man on the moon and returning him safely to the earth'.

Furthermore, Obama's naming of 'a king' who 'took us to the mountaintop and pointed the way to the promised land' is a deliberate reference to Martin Luther King and his 1968 speech, a speech which itself in turn used and borrowed the ideas of 'mountaintop' and 'promised land' from the Bible.

This brief example shows that for the analyst it is important to recognise that without knowledge of other relevant texts, the listener would miss the full impact of Obama's message. This relationship between one text and others is part of what is usually called *intertextuality* (see, for example, Allen, 2000). This aspect, which will be discussed more fully in Chapter 9, has long been recognised as important in discourse, but is usually treated as an interesting aside. To my mind, however, intertextuality is of such importance in the understanding of how texts work and are interpreted that it will be included in the main definition of discourse in this book as the fourth defining feature along with the other defining characteristics already cited.

It might be thought that intertextuality simply means textual references from one text to another, as for example when Obama in his speech refers to Martin Luther King's speech, and King in his speech referred to the Bible. Indeed some writers do present intertextuality in this rather restricted sense, as in this account:

> Intertextuality involves both the intrusion (or adoption by the speaker/ author) of aspects of previous texts into a new text either through citation, attribution or reference, and also the hybridization of one genre or text type with another. (Bloor and Bloor, 2007:51–2)

Here, Bloor and Bloor present intertextuality as having essentially two aspects, the first of which we can call the *referencing* aspect in which one text cites or refers to another (which is perhaps the type we have seen in Obama's speech) and the second being the *genre-mixing* aspect, or the way in which one genre or text type 'hybridizes' or mixes and merges with another (Fairclough, 2003:34). These are certainly important aspects of intertextuality, and will be considered further in later chapters, but in my view this represents a rather limited perspective on intertextuality because it focuses attention exclusively on the *product* or the artefact which is the text itself, and tends to ignore the *process*. It is crucial, I suggest, to realise that intertextuality is something even more fundamental to text production and comprehension than this characterisation implies.

Intertextuality in the 'Squirrel' text

This can be illustrated with reference to some of the texts examined in Chapter 1, particularly the 'Squirrel' text. Two key aspects of the girls' written note in their squirrel game are, firstly, the fact that they were copying *their whole game* from a text they knew (a story book about an elephant), and secondly, the fact that the concept of second wives, which entered in an important way into their writing of the text, was directly drawn from stories they know about wicked stepmothers. (Neither of the girls had a wicked stepmother themselves, incidentally).

This is therefore an example of the way in which behaviour, and also texts and text creation, derive from and in other important ways relate to a variety of texts *intertextually* in an interwoven net of allusions. The girls in their game were drawing on a range of intertextual links throughout the process of text construction. Intertextuality here was far more than the type of simple referencing which Bloor and Bloor mentioned, but was instead at the heart of the process. Indeed it arguably played even more of a role, since besides the allusions to actual stories they knew, the girls were also drawing on their intertextual knowledge of wider conventional genres as a whole, namely their knowledge of the letter genre, and their knowledge of the birthday card genre, to produce a sort of hybrid which is not quite a letter and not quite a card. As readers, we too needed to follow similar processes in order to comprehend the text. Intertextuality, in other words, came into the creation and interpretation of the text in a number of fundamental ways and from a number of sources.

In the light of this example intertextuality can therefore be seen to be not only an intrinsic feature of texts themselves but a crucial and integral part of the *process* of a text's creation, and also the process of its interpretation. Without the girls' knowledge of those other genres and particular texts they could not have created that letter; without our knowledge of those same other texts, or at least of some of them, we could not as readers have understood it.

This demonstrates the fact that *intertextual knowledge*, far more than simply a matter of identifying references in a text, or noticing genre-mixing, is closely related to our *genre knowledge* and therefore enters into the whole process of text creation and of text comprehension in fundamental ways. For this reason intertextuality will be treated here as a fundamental part of the revised definition of discourse; our fourth defining feature.

2.4 The relation between language and the world: discourse and social constructionism

The second feature of Stubbs' original description of discourse has already been discussed and accepted; namely that context is an important aspect of discourse and of how we understand it. However, it is useful to expand on this to address the question of precisely how the relationship between language and context operates. Answering the related questions of how the world impacts on discourse and vice versa will provide the fifth essential feature of discourse, namely the way in which discourse operates in part to *construct* viewpoints and ideologies.

Clearly the world has an impact on the language we use and choose. An elementary example is that when we write about a woman as opposed to a man we must in many languages choose a feminine pronoun instead of a masculine one (in English 'she' instead of 'he'). Real world gender therefore impacts in an obvious way on the language we use. At a more complex level we can find within the 'Squirrel' text several elements which reflect the real world of its production. For example the graphical aspects of the writing, as well as the spelling and some of the punctuation, reflect the fact that it is written by a child. Similarly, whenever we read or listen to language, we can see elements reflected from the world outside the text. So language use is obviously affected by aspects of the world around us, and reflects that world.

How language affects the world: social constructionism

However, this does not mean that language is merely a passive mirror reflecting the world around us. The relationship cuts both ways, because language both *reflects* the world and *affects* it. In fact it is fundamental to discourse analysis that we see language from a broadly *constructionist perspective* (Rapley, 2007). Social constructionism is in essence a philosophical approach which considers that the world around us, particularly the social world, is not merely given to us fully formed, but is in some sense 'constructed' by us. This broad world view was in part spearheaded by the publication in 1966 of Berger and Luckmann's *The Social Construction of Reality: A Treatise in the Sociology of Knowledge*. That treatise argued that our sense of reality is not simply 'there', but is to some extent constructed and learned socially as we grow up.

Discourse analysis takes this a step further by assuming that language plays a crucial part in that process of *constructing* reality. When we hear an adult telling a child that 'schooldays are the best days of your life', this is not simply a statement of fact. It is part of a particular *construction* of schooling projected by adult discourse, probably to make the child go to school and study harder. Fundamental to the study of discourse, therefore, is the sense that the world around us is *constructed by the discourse* we use: discourse analysts implicitly assume a constructionist position from the start. 'The basic premise for the discourse analyst is that the "social" world does not exist independently of our constructions of it' (Wood and Kroger, 2000:167). We can illustrate this constructive dimension through some short examples. The first exemplifies the way in which discourse can construct our sense of place, and the second shows how discourse can construct a person and gender.

Constructing places

The first example of discourse construction, then, comes from a tourist website promoting sights in Sydney, Australia. Its intention is clearly to persuade us to visit the places in question. Here is one part of the text of that webpage.

> *Skywalk Sydney Tower for an exhilarating 60 minute outdoor experience! Feel perfectly safe, yet perfectly exhilarated, taking in views 260 metres above the harbour city. Dare to step out over the edge and face Sydney like never before, feel the high-altitude breeze and touch the clouds! Skywalk will literally send you over the edge! Suspended from Sydney Tower's limits, you will get sensational 360-degree views of Sydney from 260metres above street level!* (http://www.redballoon.com.au)

Every text, even a small one like this, can be seen in terms of how it constructs the world around us. In this case, how did the text construct the Sydney Skywalk? The photograph which accompanied the original text played its part, as it viewed the skywalk from high above, capturing both the distance to the ground and the apparently slender support holding up the platform, to give a sense of danger and excitement. This is reinforced by the linguistic elements, for example the imperative verb 'dare' and the many exclamation marks in the text, the focus on the height and the panorama with the repeated figure '260', the frequent use of words like 'sensational', touch the clouds!' 'exhilarating'. In summary, the text aims to construct the Skywalk as thrilling and adventurous, fulfilling the first part of any advertisement's function, namely to attract the reader. Other elements of the webpage text, such as the booking and transport information, then enable tourists to reach the location straightforwardly, thereby fulfilling the second part of the text's function, namely to give enough information so that the consumer can actually 'buy the product' in practice.

Constructing gender

A second example of how discourse can construct our viewpoint relates to gender. In September 2007, Harriet Harman was an important Labour Party politician in Britain. At the time she was campaigning on an important issue, namely equal pay for women. This could have been presented in the media as an important intervention by a significant national figure. However, this is how one national newspaper chose to present her:

> Long-legged lovely Harriet Harman stomped around town yesterday angrily demanding pay increases for women in the public sector to put an end to the 'equality gap' with men's salaries. (*Daily Mail*, 22 September 2007, p. 24)

Instead of presenting her as significant and serious-minded, as they could have done, the newspaper (which supports the opposing political party) has chosen to present her as 'long-legged' and 'lovely'. At first glance this might seem to be a compliment, but of course by emphasising her appearance the newspaper succeeds in drawing attention away from her ideas. To put it another way, in *constructing* her in terms of a female body, emphasising her physique, and then later in the text *constructing* her as a temperamental child 'stomping...angrily' the writer succeeds in distracting us and therefore sidelining and belittling her ideas. What is more, it reinforces existing stereotypical views of the value of women as being largely decorative, and nothing more. This shows how the choices we make in language, of what to focus on, of which verb to choose for an action, of which adjective to choose when describing someone, all *construct* for readers important impressions about the world. Discourse should not be seen merely as a neutral vehicle for conveying facts, but as a *constructionist* device, playing its part in constructing the world around us.

George Orwell knew about this. At the beginning of his political novel *1984* the country of Oceania is at war with Eurasia. However, during the course of the novel allegiances suddenly switch without explanation and the enemy now becomes Eastasia, the former ally, with Eurasia now a friend and ally. Winston, the main character of the novel, finds this out at a demonstration, and has to rush to the Ministry of Truth where he works.

> The instant that the demonstration was over he went straight to the Ministry of Truth, though the time was now nearly twenty-three hours. The entire staff of the Ministry had done likewise. The orders already issuing from the telescreen, recalling them to their posts, were hardly necessary. Oceania was at war with Eastasia: Oceania had always been at war with Eastasia. A large part of the political literature of five years was now completely obsolete. Reports and records of all kinds, newspapers, books, pamphlets, films, sound-tracks, photographs – all had to be rectified at lightning speed. Although no directive was ever issued, it was known that the chiefs of the Department intended that within one

week no reference to the war with Eurasia, or the alliance with Eastasia, should remain in existence anywhere. (Orwell, [1948] 1981: ch. 17)

In Orwell's depiction, the government had deliberately over many years *constructed*, through extensive propaganda texts and images, a negative impression of Eurasia and a positive one of Eastasia, and this manipulation of the discourse through large-scale propaganda had apparently been largely effective. Now that the situation had changed, the entire discourse apparatus also had to be changed to create a new impression and wash away the old one.

Of course, not all texts and discourses attempt deliberately to create falsehoods in this way, but society is always to some extent involved in a struggle between competing influences, and discourse is created within that 'site of struggle'. As they did in the world of *1984*, so texts in our world play their part in the struggle between competing ideologies and points of view. This means that as discourse analysts we must be aware of how texts might be constructing biased or one-sided pictures, projecting and constructing through linguistic choices one particular viewpoint and privileging it over another.

Our fifth point of definition, then, is the fact that when analysing discourse we need to be constantly aware of how language can be used in the construction of *viewpoint* and *ideology*, sets of ideas which if they are prevalent and widespread might be treated as commonsense, but which in fact could hide aspects of power and injustice. (Ideology will be discussed further in Chapter 7.)

Socio-political dimensions

A number of researchers in recent years have been operating within what they call a Critical Discourse Analysis (CDA) perspective (see Chapter 10). In the present series, for example, Jeffries (2010) takes a textual analysis (stylistic) approach to CDA. One impact of CDA is an enhanced awareness of the ways in which discourse is used to gain and maintain power, and is not necessarily as neutral as it might appear. To return to our earlier examples, the sign LADIES on a door, or a road sign which tells us to STOP, are placed there by some agency with power, to the extent that if a man enters the ladies' toilets, or if we fail to stop at a STOP sign, we can expect some sort of punishment or other social sanction!

This illustrates the point that not only is it important to consider the full context in which any text is interpreted (the third defining feature of discourse, as noted above) but that this must be taken to include the socio-political implications of the discourse we are studying (as Blommaert (2005) in particular has argued). Many of the language choices we make will *construct* someone or something to advantage or disadvantage, since – to borrow from the title of Dwight Bolinger's (1980) book – language is truly a 'loaded weapon'. This means that even in relatively uncontroversial areas of discourse study, there will probably be socio-political implications of one sort or another. For this reason the socio-political dimension of discourse is included as the sixth part of my definition.

2.5 A working definition of discourse

The field of discourse analysis can, in summary, be seen in terms of six defining features. To start with it considers its material or data to be:

1. Texts which are *authentic*;
2. *Texts* of any size, spoken or written.

In addition discourse analysis as I define it takes it as essential that the texts which form its subject matter be analysed in the following terms:

3. Texts are to be studied in terms of the *contexts* in which they are found, broadly conceived, as an essential dimension in their interpretation.
4. Texts are to be studied not in isolation, but in terms of their *intertextual* relations with other texts.
5. Texts are to be analysed with reference to the *ideologies and viewpoints* which underpin them.
6. Texts are to be analysed with reference to their *socio-political implications and consequences*.

2.6 Summary

This chapter used as its starting point an established definition of discourse, which was then discussed, modified, revised and augmented in the light of more recent thinking so as to offer a working idea of the scope of the discipline. The result was the six defining features of discourse set out above.

Two of these defining features were retained from the standard view, namely that discourse concerns authentic texts, considered in their contexts. Where my definition of discourse began to depart from that older view was in the third defining feature, which discarded any sense that discourse is concerned with language 'above or beyond the level of the sentence'. This was revised so as to include within our scope a wider range of texts, of all sizes. The fourth defining feature noted that intertextuality is more than simply referencing from one text to another but is an integral part of a text's creation and interpretation, and therefore should enter into a definition of discourse in a fundamental way. One reason for including intertextuality as a defining feature is in order to ensure its inclusion in any approach to analysis, so that texts are not treated as isolated separate units.

It was also noted, as the fifth defining feature, that discourse is not neutral, but serves to construct impressions of the world. This then links with the sixth feature, namely that discourse has an unavoidable socio-political dimension which must therefore equally be taken into account in any analysis. This is the corollary not only of the fifth feature, that discourse serves partly to construct the world around us ideologically, but also reflects the third feature, that discourse cannot be abstracted and extracted from its context, which includes the socio-political dimension.

These dimensions will be integrated into the method for analysing discourse to be presented in Chapter 5, but before that it is important to consider and define genre and discourse modes, to which the next chapters turn.

3 Genre

Bransford and Johnson's 'Washing clothes' text, which was discussed in Chapter 1, was part of a wider research effort in the 1970s investigating the ways in which topic knowledge and mental constructs of various kinds appear to be essential to text interpretation. On the basis of that research it was argued that as part of our efforts at comprehension we access various 'mental structures', which contribute to the comprehension process. Some of these were included in the diagram in Figure 1.1 above.

To begin this chapter, the nature and role of some of these mental structures will be considered in more detail. It will then be suggested later in the chapter that as well as drawing on mental representations of concepts, situations and procedures, we also make use of mental representations of genres, and that these are also important factors in our comprehension and production of texts. When we see a sign on the beach we do not act as if we have never seen such a thing before; on the contrary, we draw quickly and efficiently on a host of *genre knowledge*, organised in a *genre schema*, to help us in our interpretation of what the sign tells us.

3.1 Mental representations in text comprehension

One aim of the research effort in the 1970s into these mental structures and their role in reading and listening, was eventually to devise artificially intelligent computer programmes which might imitate this complex human behaviour. Despite these efforts, and many efforts since, computers still cannot fully imitate human text comprehension (which shows incidentally how complex and intricate the processes are) but in the process, researchers in this field proposed a number of terms such as 'schema', 'scripts', 'frames' and 'mental models', terms either adapted from earlier research (for example, Bartlett's research on schemas in the 1930s; see Bartlett, 1932), or else introduced into cognitive psychology and linguistics from computing or other areas of cognitive science (see Schank and Abelson, 1977; Jeffries and McIntyre, 2010: Chapter 5).

The research into mental models demonstrated that comprehension cannot be described simply as a matter of decoding words and grammar from the page in some sort of direct and automatic way, as was once assumed in early more linear models of communication (for example, Cherry, 1957). It was now clear that some sort of 'mental structures' must exist in order for us to understand texts as we do, but research continues into the exact nature of these cognitive structures.

The first part of this chapter will sketch out a broadly accepted position concerning the importance of such mental constructs in our process of text comprehension, as well as outlining the meaning of *concept, script, schema, frame* and *mental model*, and their general role in the comprehension process. The aim here is not theoretical completeness but rather to set the scene for the more substantial focus on our understanding of genres in the rest of the chapter, since it will be argued that genres can be seen as mental constructs somewhat akin to schemas.

Concepts and mental models

Let us start with the most basic of these mental entities, namely the *concept*. If I asked twenty people to draw a cat, or a chair, I would get twenty subtly different representations, and part of the reason for this is that we all have slightly different mental *concepts* of each object. But where do we derive our concepts from? Concepts have been debated in philosophy for thousands of years (and the debate still continues in philosophy, in cognitive psychology and in artificial intelligence) but of course concepts are important in linguistics too, since when someone tells us 'It is cold with that window open', as Ann did in Chapter 1, we must have in our mind some 'concept' of a window which tells us what it is physically, and also tells us what it does or what it can do, that is, it can open and close. Without such mental concepts we could not understand language and texts, which is why concepts were included in the diagram in Figure 1.1 in Chapter 1.

An early, relatively clear and helpful discussion of the nature of concepts and how they relate to other conceptual structures was offered by Skemp (1979:24–6,113), who suggested that concepts group together in our minds to form 'mental models', which are similar in some ways to maps, diagrams and anatomical drawings. In Skemp's account 'mental models' are similar to such real physical maps, except that mental models are not physical, but internalized into our psychology. For Skemp, an important point about both concepts and mental models is that 'their elements nearly always represent not just one actual object or event, but what is common to a number of these' (Skemp, 1979:24). So as we encounter real-world examples of, say, ticket offices, we gradually 'abstract' what is common about all of them and that gives us the abstract *concept* of 'ticket office' which allows us to recognise them in future and also to buy tickets from them. (This process of abstraction, as I shall argue, is also part of how we come to have a mental sense of *genres*.)

Skemp explains the process, and the relation between concepts and mental models, as follows:

> when I get to London and go to the ticket office on the underground station, the mental representation which I use for directing my actions is not of just that particular ticket office, but of a class of places where, by giving money to the person behind the counter, I get in exchange a piece of paper or card which entitles me to ride on a train, or bus, or boat. (Skemp 1979:24)

From this discussion we can derive a simple but useful definition of a *concept*, and also of larger mental models, which is conveniently set out as three points:

> A mental entity of this kind [e.g. a ticket office] is called a <u>concept</u>...
>
> A <u>mental model</u>, which is made up of a number of interconnected concepts, is a conceptual structure.
>
> The process by which certain qualities of actual objects and events are internalised as concepts, while other qualities are ignored, is called <u>abstraction</u>.
>
> (Skemp, 1979:24, spacing and emphasis added)

This definition still raises questions – for example, when does a *concept* become complex enough to be called a *mental model*? How can we produce any empirical evidence of such structures? Do they help to explain understanding of language? Some such questions have been considered in the specialist literature (see, for example, Halford, 1993), but for our purposes this definition offers a sufficient starting point in our attempt to understand larger mental organizing elements such as schemas, scripts and genres.

Concepts are fuzzy

Birds can fly. Flying is a central characteristic of birds, as even a child knows. But penguins and ostriches cannot fly, so does this mean that penguins and ostriches are not birds? In the 1970s Rosch and others, in an area of research which is now known as Prototype Theory research, sought to explain this kind of apparent anomaly in human cognition. Put simply, Rosch showed that when we think of a concept such as 'bird' we have in mind certain core characteristics of birds which are central to our concept, such as flying and beaks. She demonstrated this by showing that when we are presented in an experiment with examples of birds such as robins and eagles which have these central characteristics we quickly agree that they are birds, but when presented with examples which do not have all of the central prototypical characteristics (such as penguins) we tend to be slower to agree (Rosch, 1978).

Her conclusion, in very rough outline, was that our mental concepts are 'fuzzy', and not fixed and clear, and that when we think and speak about such concepts we tend to operate with *prototypes* of each class, clear examples which fit all features, and we then decide on a case by case basis whether less clear examples fit the category or not. In short, concepts are not clearly defined, but 'fuzzy', and revolve around a few clear-cut examples which are the *prototypes*. So in terms of the question posed above, eagles are *prototypical* birds, because they do all the 'birdy' things and possess all of the 'birdy' features which are prototypical. When it comes to ostriches, however, we recognise them as being in the same class of 'birds', even though they are not prototypical because they lack one central defining feature, namely the ability to fly.

The importance of this for texts and discourse is that when we are confronted with a particular text it is probable that a similar mental operation occurs, in other words we probably evaluate that text with reference to our *prototypical* concept of one genre or another, and we then categorise that text as being either close to that mental idea of the genre, or perhaps less close but still a member of that broad class. In other words we probably operate with texts as we do with other concepts, by drawing on a set of mental prototypes, but also allowing a certain degree of 'fuzziness'. Indeed it is likely that this 'fuzziness' is a crucial part of the flexibility of various levels of discourse. At the level of lexis, when a politician in a speech talks about 'democracy', for instance, we perhaps have central core examples or prototypes of democracy in our minds and we use these, rightly or wrongly, to respond to what he or she is saying. Likewise with genre labels such as 'greetings card' – recalling the 'Squirrel' text – it is probable that we draw on certain *genre prototypes* as a means of assisting our interpretation of the class and function of texts, as a key part of our interpretative process.

Combining concepts

Concepts then, according to Skemp's account above, can combine in our minds to give larger conceptual structures which Skemp calls 'mental models'. These can be models of physical entities, such as railway stations (since we all have a mental model of railway stations, for example, which includes concepts such as ticket offices, platforms, trains, public toilets, and so on). Mental models can also be representations in our minds of more abstract things, for example about how a management structure works in a company. These concepts and mental models then operate in intricate ways as we use them in our everyday behaviour and discourse, but nonetheless we seem to be surprisingly efficient at using our mental models and concepts first to understand and negotiate our way around the real world, and then to understand and to produce texts about them.

3.2 Schemas

It seems from research evidence that as we grow up and experience the world around us, including texts, we develop certain patterned ideas about the world around us, through the important process of *abstraction* which Skemp mentioned, and we then use these ideas to interpret other things we experience. In order to explain this numerous researchers have posited the notion of 'schemas' (sometimes called 'schemata' from the original Greek plural), to refer to clusters of mental concepts which we draw on in order to interpret the world around us and also to interpret language. A schema can be defined as 'a set of interrelated features which we associate with an entity or a concept' (Field, 2003:39) and which helps us quickly and efficiently to understand language and to produce it so others can understand it.

It has been pointed out that the term needs to be used cautiously, and that since 'there is relatively little empirical theory attached to schema theory' (Grabe, 1999:24) the notion of schema might best be seen as no more than 'a useful metaphor for the role of background knowledge in reading' (ibid). Others have also argued that the term is too general and poorly defined to be of use in understanding, for example, the reading process (Urquhart and Weir, 1998:68–72). These caveats need to be borne in mind, but it is nonetheless generally accepted that schemata seem to be broadly helpful ways, if only metaphorical, for explaining some of the types of knowledge we appear to draw on when we come to interpret reading and listening texts.

According to schema theory, schemata are, like mental models, groups of concepts related in various ways. If we see a series of concepts like this:

classroom, book, desk, board, teacher, bell, learning

we would probably all agree that they relate to a socially shared schema ⸜ 'school'. To put it more formally, *schemas* or *schemata* are 'well integrated chunks of knowledge about the world, events, people and actions' (Eysenck and Keane, 2000:352) which we all possess and use to interpret events and texts. Like mental models they are conceptual or mental structures which we develop through experience, and which allow us to interpret the world and also to share that interpretation with others. However, where schemas differ from mental models is in the ways in which the concepts in each relate to each other. For example, I have a *concept* of teachers and desks, a general *schema* about schools, and a more complex *mental model* about how exactly a school is structured, organised and operated, and how I can behave within it. Mental models therefore include a more complex relationship between the various concepts, the parts of the model, whereas a schema is a more general association of ideas.

All of these mental structures – concepts, schemas and mental models – are important as we interpret texts. If I read a story and come across the word 'teacher' my *concept* of teachers is activated, which leads me towards certain ideas (sometimes stereotypes) of what the teacher in the story will do. When I read the word 'school' my general *schema* about schools is activated, which includes several concepts and leads me to have further expectations about the story. As I then read further so I may also draw on my particular *mental model* of my own former schools to help me further interpret what is going on in the story.

Frames and scripts

This story has something strange about it:

> When I entered the restaurant the waiter said goodbye, gave me the bill and then handed me my coat. I sat down at the table. Then I paid the bill and ordered ice cream. He brought me some soup.

Here the elements of the *schema* are all in place, since everything that happens here fits into a typical restaurant schema in terms of content. The social roles are as expected (waiter, customer) as are other important elements (food, bill). However, what is unexpected and peculiar here is the *order* of the events, since in most restaurants we receive the bill after and not before the meal, and in many societies we eat the sweet ice cream after the savoury soup. The reason, in other words, for the oddity of the story lies in what we perceive as the wrong or muddled ordering of events. This has led researchers

y to suggest that we use several different kinds of schema, as
Gregoriou:

> ....ists make a useful distinction between two types of infor-
> mation stored, that which is ordered sequentially (in a sort of narrative)
> and that which is not. Non-sequentially ordered information is said to
> be stored as a 'frame', and sequentially ordered information as a 'script'.
> (Gregoriou, 2009:87)

The term *frame* can therefore be reserved for non-sequential sets of concepts,
while the term *script* refers to a conventional sequence of activities (Eysenck
and Keane, 2000:352; Schank and Abelson, 1977), a 'socioculturally defined
mental protocol for negotiating [or understanding] a situation' (Stockwell,
2002:77). An important feature of scripts is that typically with the people
around us we share an understanding of how that sequence will unfold,
which enables us all to cooperate in such things as restaurant meals, and
also of course, in texts which we hear and read. Like all schemas, the precise
makeup of scripts will inevitably differ slightly from person to person and
from culture to culture, both in terms of their elements and in terms of their
sequence, but there is nonetheless enough consensus to allow us to cooperate in most sequential events, and also to interpret texts which draw on our
script knowledge.

Schemas in the comprehension process

Our mental schemas therefore set up expectations which help us to predict
what we will find in any new situation, and scripts help us to predict what
will happen next. Both types of conceptual structure help us to function and
cooperate effectively in the real world, and both also impact on our understanding and construction of texts. A reader or listener combines her or his
knowledge of the world, partly structured in the form of schemas and scripts,
together with knowledge of lexis and grammar, in order to build up interpretations. Drawing on an example text about assassination and invasion,
van Dijk, in his discussion of news reports and how we understand them,
describes the process as follows:

> generally, socially shared script information is combined with actual
> personal ('remembered') model information, and with the new infor-
> mation in the news text, to form a new model, namely about the
> actual events of the assassination and the invasion. (van Dijk, 1985:81,
> emphasis added)

This neatly captures several key elements of the process – we draw on 'socially shared script information' (a specific type of 'schema information') then we also add elements derived from personal experience, and combine them with what the text itself tells us, so as to construct a new model of the situation. The process is rapid, complex, dynamic and constructive.

Text schemas and genre schemas

Field distinguishes further between types of schema as follows:

> When considering how listeners and readers process language information, it is useful to think in terms of three types of schema:
>
> a 'World knowledge': including encyclopedic knowledge and previous knowledge of the speaker or writer. This helps us to construct a content schema for a text.
> b Knowledge built up from the text so far: a current meaning representation.
> c Previous experience of this type of text (a <u>text schema</u>). (Field, 2003:40, emphasis added)

The general schemata discussed in the previous section, including frames and scripts about the world in general, would come under Field's first category. His second category would include the ongoing representation about meaning which a listener or reader uses while reading or listening, so as to move towards a full interpretation, in ways described in process models of listening and reading (such as Emmott, 1997; Khalifa and Weir, 2009; Buck, 2001). However, it is the third category in Field's summary which is of particular importance to our discussion of genre, since it brings out the point that in comprehension we draw specifically on prior knowledge of various aspects of *texts*. This insight derives in turn from Carrell who distinguished between two types of schema, the first concerning the form of the text (*formal schema*) and the second the content (*content schema*) (Carrell, 1983; Carrell, Devine and Eskey, 1988).

In some accounts this concept of *text schema* appears to be restricted to our knowledge of the *structure* of texts, as indeed is suggested by the idea of 'form' in Carrell's original discussion of it. However, given that we appear to store and make use of far more information about texts than simply their structure or form, this interpretation of text schema may be too limited a way of explaining this part of the comprehension process. The point can be illustrated by reference once again to the Barbecue Sign text which was discussed in chapter 1. When we see such a public notice we interpret it on the basis not only of our knowledge of the structure and form of similar texts we have seen previously, but also on our knowledge of the *function* of such texts, our prior knowledge of their *layout*, of their typical *lexis* and *grammar* – in short we bring to the text the full range of our prior *genre knowledge* built up over experience of many similar public signs, and not only knowledge of the structure or form of such texts.

For this reason – and to emphasise specifically the fact that that we bring to comprehension more than knowledge of textual structure and form alone – the term *genre schema* (following Frow, 2006; Harris, 2005) will in this book be used to complement the term *text schema*, to refer to the ways in which we draw on and make use of the prior knowledge of all aspects of genres, including their typical contexts, forms, functions, lexis, grammar and so on, which we bring to bear as we interpret written and spoken texts.

3.3 Genre expectations

A video on the website YouTube is simply called *Car Advert* and this title sets up an expectation about what kind of video it will be, deliberately evoking our *genre expectation* or *genre schema* of car advertisements. The video starts by meeting our expectations perfectly. We are shown a distant shot of an expensive new car driven along a calm winding road accompanied by relaxing music, beautiful countryside and a sense of luxury, just as in typical television advertisements for luxury cars. But suddenly a huge hideous zombie figure jumps up screaming in front of the camera and scares the viewer, the music cuts out, and the video ends. It is not a real advertisement at all, but a spoof or parody, whose effect comes from activating our genre expectations, and then disrupting them suddenly for humour and shock purposes.

This example helps to highlight the difference, noted above, between *text* and *genre*, and also to illustrate once again the concept and role of *genre schemata* in comprehension. Texts, as defined above, are the actual manifestations, visible or audible, such as the YouTube zombie video described above. Frequently texts draw on our genre knowledge, for example by following a genre prototype closely, but they may also – as in this case – deliberately undermine our genre expectations for humour or other effects. In that particular text, the director of the video was drawing on our genre schema to trick us, subverting our expectations to make us jump.

It will be appreciated from this that genre, or rather our knowledge of genres, acts on our comprehension like mental structures such as schemas and scripts. This view of genre sees it not as a grouping of texts in a sort of library, but rather as a mental construct which we draw on as we create and interpret actual texts. As Johns puts it, genres in this view are 'socio-cognitive schemas' which 'often have to be reformulated as [the] writer produces texts for the demands of specific contexts' (Johns, 2008:239). Johns then offers a clear example of how this works for a writer, using as an example the situation of preparing a paper for a conference:

> an expert writer might have a genre schema for the academic abstract, but as she prepares the actual abstract for an identified conference, she must adapt her schema, and the resultant text, to the conference requirements. (Johns, 2008:239)

Genres in this view, then, are ideal, whereas texts are actual. To give another example, we have a notion in our minds, a genre schema, of what a recipe consists of, first of all in terms of its function, and of its structure, content, lexis, grammar, layout, illustrations and so on, including the possible contexts of occurrence. We use this idealisation both to identify recipes and to write recipes. However, each actual instance of a recipe – a *text* – might differ slightly from the prototype in our minds and from other actual recipe texts. This is because texts are free – they can borrow in a highly flexible and creative way from one or more genres, or from none, and of course in the practice of comprehension this is not a problem, precisely because users of the language implicitly know this and expect it.

Just as we develop our concepts, mental models, schema knowledge and script knowledge from our experience of the world and from what we read, see and hear, so we probably develop our genre knowledge largely through our experience of texts in the world around us and also more explicitly in educational contexts, which means that our knowledge of genres is part of our broad *intertextual knowledge*. Genre knowledge is therefore related to intertextuality because it concerns the relation between one text and other texts. For this reason, as intertextual knowledge was included as a fundamental part of the definition of discourse, in the previous chapter, it can now be seen to relate to genre knowledge also.

3.4 Classifying and sorting genres

The characterisation of genres here differs, then, from more traditional accounts which tend to see them as somehow more physical, as sets of text which could literally be sorted into piles, or found in distinct sections in a bookshop or library. This view, that texts can be sorted into clearly defined groups such as fiction, poetry, drama and so on, and then perhaps into subgroups such as romantic fiction, cowboy fiction and so on, in what we could call the 'classifying' approach to genre, has been common and valuable in literary analysis and in practical contexts, such as libraries and bookshops, for many years. However, even in the seventeenth century Shakespeare saw the problems of trying to sort texts in this way and then give names to the groupings, referring ironically to 'tragedy, comedy, history, pastoral, pastoral-comical, historical-pastoral, tragical-historical, tragical-comical-historical-pastoral' (Hamlet II ii).

As Hamlet implies with this mild mockery, even in literature it is difficult to make classifications account for all texts. So when we try to enlarge the scope of our analysis to encompass everyday texts as well, the attempt at classification becomes even more complex and unwieldy.

Unger discusses some of the different criteria used by researchers in their attempts to classify genres. These have included aspects of the situation in which the genre occurs (such as the number of speakers, or their social rank) or their mode (whether they are written or spoken) or the purpose of the genre (Unger, 2006, following Renkema, 1993). However, faced with the natural complexity and 'hybridity' of real texts, these attempts have generally been unable to cover all occurring examples, and often resort to a host of complex and unconvincing groupings, rather like Hamlet's list of types of drama, with the result that we find terms such as 'pre-genres', 'primary genres', 'secondary genres' and 'super-genres', whose connection with each other is often unclear (see, for example, Bregman and Haythornthwaite, 2001).

It is not surprising, given the wide range of texts in the world and their perplexing hybridity, that this broad 'classifying' approach repeatedly runs into problems. Indeed if we accept that texts can draw on a wide range of genres creatively and flexibly, as was illustrated above, we might conclude that such attempts at classification are doomed to failure from the start, simply because most texts are naturally 'hybrids', drawing on genres as their starting point, but then developing in highly fluid and creative ways in response to their creators' particular aims and contextual conditions. So although we may try to set up ideal categories, we should not be surprised when actual texts stubbornly refuse to fit them; an element of 'fuzziness' is inevitable.

This causes obstacles for disciplines (such as librarianship) which see a need to establish clear categories and classifications of the texts they deal with, but fortunately discourse analysis does not in principle need to have any such fixed sets at all. Perhaps it is more important simply to acknowledge that a key fact about genre schemata is that language users operate with a very fluid and flexible set of categories – so that as we listen to or read a text and ask ourselves 'what genre is this?' we might frequently be unable to reply with any certainty. One reason for this, as has already been argued, is that real world *texts* do not neatly correspond to ideal mental *genres*. A second reason is that the genres we have in our minds are not clearly separate from each other, and may not even be clearly delineated in all their characteristics. They are – like concepts, schemas and scripts – useful general ideas which are 'fuzzy', and that fuzziness is an important reason for their usefulness. This means that just as users accept a degree of fuzziness in their acts of interpretation, so discourse analytical approaches and frameworks must allow for a similar degree of flexibility.

3.5 Genres: linguistic or social practices?

In moving towards a working definition of text and genre, then, it is important to accept the fact that any classification will be fuzzy and flexible. One reason for this inherent fuzziness and flexibility where texts and genres are concerned is that they are affected not only by linguistic considerations but by social factors – indeed they could be said to be at the interface between language system and society, as would appear from the place of discourse at the centre of the diagram in Figure 1.1 (see p. 9).

Since discourse and genre have this dual linguistic and sociological dimension, writers who seek to define the terms may emphasise one over the other (Widdowson, 2007: xv). If we look at the definition of genre in the quotation below, for example, we can see an emphasis on the linguistic – indeed Paltridge (contrary to the practice followed in this book) even treats genres and texts as roughly the same kind of thing:

> A genre is a kind of text. Academic lectures and casual conversations are examples of spoken genres. Newspaper reports and academic essays are examples of written genres. (Paltridge, 2006:84)

My preference in this book has been to distinguish more sharply between genres (as abstract) and texts (as actual) than Paltridge does here. That aside, Paltridge clearly adopts here a relatively linguistic approach to genre, since he places linguistic texts at the forefront of his definition. By contrast, other writers tend instead to emphasise the *social* or the *activity* dimensions, as in Martin's definition here:

> genre is a staged, goal-oriented, purposeful <u>activity</u> in which speakers engage as member of our culture. Examples of genres are <u>staged activities</u> such as making a dental appointment, <u>buying vegetables</u>, telling a story, writing an essay, applying for a job, writing a letter to the editor, inviting someone to dinner, and so on. (Martin, 2001: 155, emphasis added)

While all of the activities in Martin's list probably do typically involve some element of language use, his definition emphasises the activity rather than the linguistic dimension, thereby adopting a rather more social view of genres. Fairclough likewise, in his definition below, also stresses the activity aspect, subsuming language within a broader world of signification (the 'semiotic' mode):

> Genres are <u>diverse ways of acting, of producing social life,</u> in the semiotic mode. Examples are: everyday conversation, <u>meetings</u> in various types of organisation, political and other forms of <u>interview</u>, and <u>book reviews</u>. (Fairclough, 2003:206, emphasis added)

In describing genres as 'activities' and 'ways of acting' in these two definitions, Fairclough and Martin are in essence choosing to prioritise the social interaction over the linguistic. This of course is a matter of the analyst's particular emphasis and perspective, since all would probably agree that genres include both the linguistic and the social, but my preference in this book will be to confine the term 'genre' to behaviour or activity which has a clearly linguistic dimension to it.

To illustrate what this means in practice, and to show how the terminology will be used from now on, my analysis of a person buying vegetables – to take up Martin's example – would be to say that s/he is drawing first of all on a mental *schema* of shops and shopping, and on a *script* of how such interactions are sequenced. The participants would thereby be drawing on the first of Field's three categories cited above, namely 'world knowledge'. The concept of *genre* only becomes relevant, in my view, if and when the participants start to use language, at which point the activity might involve a linguistic *genre schema* of 'buying and selling', including an expectation of how such interactions typically proceed, to include typical lexical patterns and grammatical structures. All of these – schema, script and genre schema – would operate to shape the participants' language behaviour, and on this basis they would then jointly construct and participate in an actual *text*, namely the conversation between the two of them, which might in practice be close to the expected *genre prototype*, or might diverge from it.

The function of a genre

A further well-known view of genre is that of Swales, who defines genres as follows:

> A genre comprises a class of communicative events, the members of which share some set of communicative purposes. These purposes are

recognized by the expert members of the parent discourse community and thereby constitute the rationale for the genre. This rationale shapes the schematic structure of the discourse and influences and constrains choice of content and style. (Swales, 1990: 58)

Swales was mainly concerned with written language and with academic writing in particular, but his definition usefully makes the general point that genres are guided by *purposes*, in other words by the *functions* which they are intended to fulfil. Furthermore, 'the purposes expressed in genres are defined by the community which uses them, not by individuals: shared rules must be learned and used for genres to operate' (Bregman and Haythornthwaite, 2001). This means, among other things, that members of the community (which in my view should include non-experts, incidentally) will recognise and broadly agree on the key *function* of the genre. This *function* then to a large extent governs the other *features* of the genre, its structure, content and so on.

This is not only a valuable insight into genres, but it also allows us an important methodological starting point in any discourse analysis. Take as an example the Barbecue Sign on the beach discussed in chapter 1. It is clear that the main *function* of that text, typical of the genre of public notices on which it draws, is to instruct and inform the general public. Accordingly all of its *features* were designed to achieve that function – features such as its location secured to a post, its vertical orientation, the size of the lettering, the choice of grammar and lexis and so on. In other words, its *function* governs its *features*. Likewise, to take again the example of recipes, the function of a recipe is to inform us how to cook a particular dish, and to do so economically and quickly (as we might be preparing and even cooking as we read). This key *function* of the recipe then governs its length (usually quite short), its structure (title, picture, list of ingredients, instructions and so on), the layout, the style of language and so on. *Function*, in this approach, is taken frequently to govern the text's *features* to a large extent.

Features of a genre: lexis and jargon

When I was a student living away from home for the first time, and came across the instruction 'fold the flour into the cake mixture', it was not clear to me how to 'fold' flour. On asking someone more experienced, I was told that the verb in cookery means to take a spoon with some flour in it to 'cut' the mixture lightly down the middle, then turn the flour into it bit by bit until it was all absorbed. If you put the phrase 'fold the flour' into an internet search engine it consistently appears in recipe contexts because it is part of cookery *jargon*, that is, language specific to a particular occupational or social group.

Table 3.1 The relation between text function and text features

FUNCTION	FEATURES	EXAMPLE: RECIPE GENRE
The function determines to a large extent the features	A recipe aims to inform us quickly and efficiently how to prepare a particular dish. Therefore the function determines these features:	
	Location	In a magazine or recipe book
	Topic focus	How to prepare food
	Visual aspects and layout Pictures, position of different parts, diagrams, colours	Frequently starts with a bold title and has pictures, perhaps with various colours to make it attractive
	Length	Typically no longer than one page
	Structure	Title, picture, ingredients, instructions, etc.
	Subjects / agents / focus Who is actually doing the actions? Subject of the verbs?	Imperatives. The ingredients are in *describing* discourse mode and the instructions in the *interacting* discourse mode
	Style and register Formal or informal? Related to any particular professional domain?	Typically relatively informal
	Grammar Tense (past, present future) Syntax (word order) Length of sentences	Imperatives, some conditionals (*if/when it is tender, then* ...) Standard, but simple Simple short sentences
	Lexis Any jargon or technical language?	Cooking terms, names of foods, weights and measures

From a functionalist perspective, we can explain this by saying that the *function* of the recipe genre – in particular the need for brevity and speed – leads recipe writers to use shorthand (jargon) terms when referring to common and familiar actions and objects. A genre's function, in other words, can govern or influence not only the structure and contents of the genre, but also the lexis and grammar.

This principle will play an important role in the approach to discourse analysis to be set out in Chapter 5. In the method which I set out there as a broad plan for analysing discourse, the function of the text will be of central importance, followed by analysis of how the features of the text help to achieve that function. This relationship between the two elements is set out in Table 3.1, which shows how the *function* of the genre (in the column on the left) can typically lead to particular combinations of *features* (in the middle column). The final column offers a fuller example, showing how the features of a recipe can be analysed as meeting the recipe's main function.

The point of this illustration is to exemplify ways in which the function of a text can act as the first point of departure in any analysis, so that the various features of a text can subsequently be explained by reference to that function. So the *style* and *lexis* of a text, for example, can be explained in terms of the role they play in the function of the text as a whole.

Classifying and organising genres

Having suggested that genres can usefully be seen as idealisations, and having also seen the way in which their perceived function typically determines or guides their features, the next step is to consider how genres are organised, and how one genre relates to another.

Over the last two decades substantial research into genre and the relations between genres has been carried out and this has naturally involved classification. To take one interesting example, the group of researchers known as the Sydney School identify a number of genre classes in ways exemplified in Martin and Rose's recent work, to include amongst others recounts, descriptions, reports, protocols, narratives and explanations (Martin and Rose 2008:1–8).

Martin and Rose acknowledge the generally educational bias in the genre theory which they present, and it is undoubtedly useful to approach genres in this way if the aim is to use them in education, since it allows for the development of school curricula where progression is linked to different genres. Nonetheless, when we try to deal with texts from other domains outside education we may need to look beyond such analytical frameworks, because many real-world texts cannot easily fit straightforwardly into such classificatory schemes. The central problem here is essentially textual hybridity, the fact that frequently 'a text may not be "in" a single genre, it may "mix" or hybridize genres' (Fairclough, 2003:34), and may draw on a mixture of genre schemata in order to achieve its effects. The 'Squirrel' text discussed previously illustrates this kind of hybridity or mixing, of the letter and greetings card.

This issue can be further illustrated through consideration of 'narrative' in particular, which can be characterised as the reporting of a sequence of events, usually in the past. Narrative has sometimes been treated as a genre in its own right, and in some domains such as education, or others in which narrative may be used in fairly 'pure' ways, this may be sufficient as a category. However, any scheme which wants to explain all texts we encounter must face the problem that narrative enters in fundamental ways into a wide variety of texts which seem best associated with other genres, such as news reports, jokes, histories, biographies, films and so on. Since it seems problematic to say at the same time that narrative is a genre in itself, and also that it enters in fundamental ways into other genres, it seems more satisfactory in any classificatory scheme to consider narrative at a more general abstract level, somewhere 'above' particular genres, and entering into many genres in flexible ways, rather than being a genre in itself. As these authors put it:

> [b]ecause narratives are used in many different kinds of texts and social contexts, they cannot properly be labelled a genre. Narration is just as much a feature of non-fictional genres...as it is of fictional genres... It is also used in different kinds of media...We can think of it as a textual mode rather than a genre. (Thwaites, Davis and Mules, 1994:112, emphasis added)

Other writers note the same phenomenon and move towards a similar solution. Fairclough, for example, makes the same point that the narrative would seem to be best considered as being at a different 'level' of abstraction than, say, the news story, and he considers the same to be true of other categories, noting that: 'If Narrative, Argument, Description, and Conversation are genres, they are genres on a high level of abstraction. They are categories which transcend particular networks of social practices...' (Fairclough. 2003:68). For this reason Fairclough terms them 'pre-genres' (following Swales, 1990) to take account of the fact that they seem in some sense to be 'prior' to actual genres, and that they enter into several different genres in flexible ways, transcending the particular.

In essence, these proposals turn on the view that any fully operational framework of texts and their relationships requires some sort of analytical level 'above' genres and texts, this level to include narrative and a number of relatively abstract modes of discourse which seem to enter into many actual genres, and which might be termed 'pre-genres', 'textual modes' or similar. In fact, this idea of positing some more abstract general level above genres has a long history, with its roots in traditional categories of rhetoric such as description, exposition, argument and narrative (Smith, 2003; Brooks and Warren, 1972). Grabe refers to 'a long rhetorical tradition of modes of discourse going back to the eighteenth century, and taking on a preeminent status in the nineteenth century with Bain's (1877) formulation of expository, descriptive, narrative, and argumentative modes of discourse' (Grabe, 2002:252).

In more recent times this approach has been given a more linguistic basis. A relatively early example is Werlich's proposal for a Text Grammar (1976). Werlich identifies five categories, which he considers basic to human discourse, namely the four cited above, *narrative, descriptive, expository, argumentative*, along with a fifth, *instructional*, and his *Text Grammar* describes in detail the typical linguistic features of each. In his view these types of discourse are so central to communication in all languages that they are probably related to basic human cognitive processes, rather as Ricouer has argued for narrative (Ricouer, 1990).

Werlich's detailed treatment was followed by Smith's (2003) no less meticulous attempt to analyse the linguistic features of such modes (though curiously she does not refer to Werlich's work). Smith identifies in her analysis *narrative, description* and *argument* to parallel three of Werlich's categories, but her analysis discusses *reports* and *information* instead of Werlich's *expository* and *instructional*. The thrust of her work is in essence the same as Werlich's, namely to identify and analyse in depth certain modes – she calls them *discourse modes* rather than Werlich's *text types* – which she considers to be basic to human discourse and 'above' texts and genres in terms of abstraction. She takes as her unit of analysis the 'passage' which she defines as being as small as two sentences, and her analysis includes detailed discussion of each of the discourse modes in turn and how they enter into a range of texts in flexible ways.

Applied genre theory

A further extended proposal for such an approach, again involving a more abstract level of analysis 'at a superordinate level' above genres, is Grabe's argument for what he calls 'macro-genres' to include *narrative* and *exposition* (Grabe, 2002). Part of Grabe's reasoning is, again, that both narrative and exposition seem to be very general in nature and to enter into many genres rather than being genres themselves. In addition he alludes to the argument (citing Bruner, 1986; 1990) that these modes are as much 'modes of thought' as modes of discourse, and in fact represent clear ways of interpreting the world and 'of drawing meaning from interactions with the world' (Grabe, 2002:252).

Bhatia (2002), responding to Grabe's proposal, first outlined an approach which he later elaborated in greater detail as part of an 'applied genre theory' (Bhatia, 2004), and which attempts to set out in some detail the relation between texts, genres, and discourse modes (which he terms 'generic values'). Bhatia's approach to analysis consists of three levels, the first of which is termed *generic values*, such as narration, description, explanation and persuasion, which Bhatia says are 'independent of any grounded contextual constraints' (Bhatia, 2002:281), in other words they are not dependent on any particular context. This distinguishes them from the elements of the second level which he calls *genre colonies* (for example, promotional genres), which are 'constellations of genres...across genre boundaries' (Bhatia, 2004:xv), 'serving broadly similar communicative purposes' (Bhatia, 2004:59). The third is the *genres* themselves, for example advertisements. This gives us, in Bhatia's scheme, the following hierarchy:

Bhatia's levels	Example
Generic values	Persuasion
Genre colonies	Promotional genres
Genres	Advertisements

3.6 Discourse modes in the analysis of discourse

All of these approaches, although they use different terminology and offer varying analyses of the different modes, nonetheless share the conviction that it is theoretically valuable and analytically useful to identify and make reference to a relatively abstract level of operation, above genres and texts in order to explain how texts and genres operate in discourse.

It can be seen that the elements at this level have been given different names in different accounts, including the terms 'pre-genres', 'generic values' and 'discourse modes'. The last of these terms, *discourse modes*, will be adopted here, firstly because it is the term used by the majority of writers who discuss this area, secondly because this is the term adopted by Smith (2003) in her particularly detailed linguistic elaboration of these modes, and thirdly because the term captures the sense that these ways of using language are general 'modes of operating' with language, (rather than simply being 'values', as Bhatia sees them.)

To make it clear from now on when I am referring to discourse modes I will refer to them as *narrating, describing, reporting* and so on, in italics. It should be noted, incidentally, that these *discourse modes* are not to be confused with the Hallidayan term 'mode' (Halliday and Hasan, 1985:12; Martin and Rose 2003:243).

Table 3.2 summarises the ways in which some of the writers mentioned have envisioned the different discourse modes (or the equivalent in each discussion).

As is clear from the table, narrative, description and argumentation – or as I term them *narrating, describing* and *arguing* are generally taken to be typical at this level of abstraction, but writers vary in their inclusion or exclusion of other modes, partly owing to their different interests, approaches and terminology. In addition it will be noted that an important limitation in most studies (for example, those of Bhatia, Smith and Werlich) is the fact that they restrict themselves explicitly to written discourse, and exclude all discussion of speech. Since any broad analytical scheme for our purposes must include spoken discourse as well as written, this limitation needs to be addressed.

Consider the start of a simple joke: 'Have you heard the one about...?' Jokes frequently make use of *narrating mode* in the form of a short story with a punchline (in ways to be further discussed in Chapter 7). However, some have a different approach, starting with a question such as that above. Question forms cannot easily be incorporated into any of the modes identified in Table 3.2; this joke form, for example, is neither *narrating* nor *describing*, nor *arguing*. In fact, it is quite different from the modes already identified, since here the speaker is not using *narrating* or *describing* or *arguing* mode, but is using a question to elicit a conventional response before completing the joke with a punchline. Just as the listener can recognise *narrating mode* and respond appropriately, so s/he can recognise that this joke starter is part of an *interaction* which will require a certain response.

Table 3.2 Discourse modes

Bain (1877)	Werlich (1976)	Smith (2003)	Bhatia (2004)	Fairclough (2003)
Descriptive	Description	Description	Description	Description
Narrative	Narration	Narrative	Narrative	Narrative
Argumentative	Argumentation	Argument	Argument	Argument
	Instruction		Instructions	
Expository	Exposition		Explanations	
		Information		
		Report	Reporting	
			Evaluation	
			Persuasion	
				Conversation

This kind of interactional activity seems, like *narrating, describing* and *arguing*, also to be in some sense prior to or 'above' genres, partly because it enters into many genres and actual texts, both spoken and written. Although it is different from the other discourse modes in several ways, it appears plausible to suggest that it resembles them in that users can employ it flexibly in a wide range of genres, such as jokes, interviews, emails, text messages and so on, and it therefore operates as a sort of discourse mode.

Some analysts include spoken discourse at the same level of abstraction as the other modes. As noted above, Fairclough (2003) includes conversation with the other pre-genres, suggesting that it is at the same level of abstraction as narrative, description and so on. Renkema (1993) also includes what he terms 'interaction' at this level, considering it to be at the same level of abstraction as narration and argumentation. In both of these discussions the implication appears to be that spoken interaction (at a more general abstract level than conversation in fact) can be seen to be in some way 'basic', somehow more abstract than genres themselves, and entering into several. This will be revisited in the next chapter, but for these reasons *interacting discourse mode* will be provisionally included as a discourse mode alongside those itemised above, despite its differences.

3.7 The relation of discourse modes to genre

Having discussed and described discourse modes in a preliminary way, it is useful to sketch out in greater detail the relationship between these modes and genres. It has already been noted that discourse modes are at a more abstract level than genres, and can enter into several genres in flexible ways, but how does this happen?

To take an example, texts which draw on the broad genre of Advertisements can make use of the discourse mode of *interacting* (in an advertisement which uses a conversation) or the discourse mode of *narrating* (if it uses a story), or other discourse modes, in flexible ways according to how it seeks to achieve its main function of selling a product or service. Similarly, the broad genre of the Novel might include both the *narrating* and also *interacting* modes in reported form (in reported conversations). The same applies to jokes and to many other genres in ways which will be elucidated in the later chapters devoted to particular spoken and written genres.

Table 3.3 offers a characterisation of the way in which *discourse modes* can be seen to link up with *genres* and then with actual *texts*. It is intended to allow the analyst a vocabulary and a framework by which to describe and explain a wide variety of genres and texts. In this view, the discourse modes can be analysed as being at a more abstract level than genres, and so are

Table 3.3 Aspects of genre and text

Discourse modes				
Discourse modes do not have unique functions in themselves but enter into many genres				
Examples	**Interacting**	**Narrating**	**Describing**	**Instructing**	**Others**
Typical main features	Turn-taking, adjacency pairs	Sequencing of events, often in the past	Combining of descriptive elements, non-sequential	Listing or sequencing of actions or items, non-historical	

↓ *Discourse modes* enter into *genres* (*or genre schemas*) in flexible ways

Genres / genre schemas		
Our mental idea of groups or families of texts which share common functions and features		
Example of genres/ genres schemas	Genres typically perform particular **functions**	As we use genres, we can draw on any of the various **discourse modes** in flexible ways
Conversation	Social interaction – to make social bonds and relationships	The genre of **conversation** mainly draws on the **interacting discourse mode**, but it might also include **narrating** (when someone tells an anecdote), **describing** (when someone describes a person or place) and also **instructing** (when someone tells you how to do something or get somewhere)
Classroom lessons	Educational – to teach something	The genre of **classroom lessons** is typically a form of **interacting discourse mode** between pupils and teacher, but the turn-taking is different from a conversation. It might also include any of the other discourse modes such as **explaining, describing** and **narrating**
Novel	Entertainment, aesthetic	The genre of **novel**, which is often divided into sub-genres such as romantic novels and historical novels, predominantly draws on **narrating** discourse mode, but of course frequently includes **interacting and describing**
Weather forecast	Informative	The genre of **weather forecast** typically draw mostly on **describing discourse mode**, telling us what the weather is like, and will be like, but can also include **instructing**
Recipe	Informative, instructing	The genre of **recipe** typically draws on **instructing discourse mode.**

↓ *Genre schemas* are then used flexibly in *actual texts*

placed at the top of the table. Discourse modes are abstract ways of expressing relationships about the world. They can enter in highly flexible ways into various genres, as shown by the arrow leading downwards to the second level of genres, illustrating the point that one genre might draw on one or more modes. The recipe genre, for example, typically uses *describing* mode to set out the ingredients and then *instructing* mode to give the cooking sequence. At the bottom of the table are the actual texts, which may draw on the discourse modes, or on the genres, as they choose. So an actual recipe might follow the genre closely, if it is prototypical, or it might diverge from it.

While offering this representation as a general view of the way in which discourse modes can enter into genres and then be taken up in actual texts, it is worth repeating that many texts deliberately break our expectations for particular effect. A key aspect of the way we deal with texts in the real world, as producers and consumers, lies in our flexibility and our ability to shift and mix discourse modes and genre expectations in ever-changing ways, as has already been argued. For this reason the table, whilst it may be of use as a depiction of the general relationship between discourse modes, genres and texts, should not disguise the fact that texts often stubbornly resist the categories we set for them.

In Chapter 5 it will be suggested that it can be useful to take account of these discourse modes in discourse analysis, but it is important not to overstate their role in texts and genres. Noting that these discourse modes have been advocated before as a way of understanding texts and genres, Grabe (2002:252) warns that 'such a scheme has been conventionalized as a generic instructional format with unrealistic models that artificially highlight each mode.' Grabe is correct here to warn against setting too much store by the discourse modes in an analysis, and also against assuming that each mode has greater weight in particular genres than in fact it has. The lesson from this is that discourse modes might be identified and discussed as one of a genre's or text's strategic resources, but we should not expect to find these modes entering into every genre or every text in any systematic way, nor should we seek to set up an elaborate analytical scheme on that assumption.

3.8 Genre, style, register and jargon

Additional terms which are often mentioned in the literature, and which it is useful briefly to mention at the close of this chapter, are *style*, *register* and *jargon*. With regard to the term *style*, van Dijk offers a definition through this example:

> For instance, in order to describe the civil war in Bosnia, we may refer to the various groups of participants in terms of 'fighters', 'rebels',

'insurgents', 'terrorists', etc. The choice of a specific word in this case may depend on the type of discourse (for example news report, editorial or political propaganda), or on the group membership, position or opinion of the speaker or writer. That is, in order to refer to the same people, we may use different lexical items. <u>If such variation is a function of the context (speaker, perspective, audience, group, etc.) we usually call it a property of the style of the discourse.</u> (van Dijk, 1987a:11, emphasis added)

This broad definition of *style* will be followed here, to refer to the general way in which language is used in any written or spoken text, mainly in terms of its formality or informality. (Though note that in the field of stylistics the term *style* has a rather different sense, as discussed in Jeffries and McIntyre 2010). The main determinant, as van Dijk notes, is the context of use, and this does not mean only the physical location. A lawyer in a law court, for example, might use a relaxed informal style in court if speaking to a clerk before the judge enters, but when the case begins, s/he will use a more formal style. The reason for this style choice is the social occasion, and not merely the physical location.

Some writers would use the term *register* to describe this more formal legal style, defining it for example as: '[a] set of specialized vocabulary and preferred syntactic and rhetorical devices/structures, used by specific socioprofessional groups for special purposes' (Schiffman, 1996:41). These include, for example, a legal register, a medical register and so on. I will also make use of the term *jargon* to refer specifically to lexis which is used in particular, usually professional domains, such as *legal jargon, medical jargon* and *cooking jargon*.

How do styles relate to genre? A good way of understanding this relationship is through the example of conversation. If we speak of the *genre* of Conversation we mean something which is structured, in that it has a beginning, middle and an end, however informal, which users can recognise and respond to. Conversational *style*, by contrast, in my definition, means simply a general informal way of talking, probably influenced heavily by the location and the occasion. The Conversation *genre* will typically make use of the conversational *style*, of course, but other genres may also use a conversational style for particular effects. A politician working within an Interview *genre* might for example adopt a conversational *style* to make him/herself seem more friendly and personable (Fairclough, 2000:101).

As I use the terms here therefore, *genres* have structures, beginnings and ends, or structural layouts, which we can recognise, whereas *styles* indicate more general ways of talking or writing which vary according to the occasion and situation, usually along a continuum of formal-informal. In practice, it is not always easy to see the distinction. For example we may ask whether text messaging is a style or a genre. It does not seem to have any clear structure, any beginning or end, so in that sense it seems more like a style, but we could say that a finite *text message exchange* is more like a genre, and can be analysed as such. Despite these difficulties, the distinction is generally a useful one.

3.9 A summary definition of genre, style and discourse mode

The discussion in this chapter now allows us to present a working definition of genre as it relates to texts, drawing together the various threads of the preceding discussion. Our definition can be presented as a series of key defining features:

1. Genres are akin to mental structures such as *concepts* and *schemas*, in that we carry mental representations about genres around with us and make use of them to prepare for communicative events, and to interpret communicative events.
2. Genres are *ideals*, whereas texts are real.
   Texts can therefore draw on one or more genres in their realisation.
3. Genres may include language or they may not.
   For example, a mime show could be classed as a genre, with function, features, structure and so on. However in my discussion I will focus only on genres which do have a linguistic dimension.
4. Genres are *shared* as mental constructs by members of a particular community.
   For this reason, the features of any genre are in part socially endorsed. However, individually 'people participate in genre usage rather than control it' (Mulholland, 1999:59).
5. Genres often have particular names, but not always.
   Because genres are often shared amongst users in the same speech community, they sometimes have accepted names, as well as clearly identified function and features (in the case of prototypical genres). However, many genres do not have socially agreed names, but are genres nonetheless.
6. Genres are characterised first and foremost by the *function(s)* which they perform.
7. The function of a genre then guides the *features* of the genre.
   These features include the location, structure, layout, style, lexis, grammar, and other aspects.

8. Genres have *structure*, as one of their main features.

   One important feature of genres is the fact that they have structure, and we can identify and recognise that structure, perhaps subconsciously. This distinguishes them in my analysis from *styles*, which are simply *ways* of speaking or writing.

9. Genres are identified not only by *formal* criteria, but also by *social* and *contextual* factors.

   When we examine a genre we look not only at its grammar and lexis, say, but at where it is used, who makes use of it and so on.

10. Genres are highly *flexible*, and they can change, blend, evolve and die out.

This means that, for example, *legal language* or *courtroom discourse* are not in themselves genres in this definition, as they do not have a structure with a beginning and end. They are more like a style or register. However, a notional *Cross-Examination* in a courtroom is a genre in this definition, as it has a clear structure, with beginning and end, which lawyers and other participants can recognise. An actual cross-examination in a real court would be a *text* in this definition, which might conform to the expected genre but might diverge from it for various reasons. (Genres under this definition will be signalled by an initial capital letter.)

   Similarly when we talk about conversation, we might mean simply an informal *style*, or we might mean a *genre*, in which case it is a discourse with a clear structure, with an opening, middle and end. In other words, what distinguishes a genre from a style, in the definition to be followed here, is in essence a matter of *structure*.

Genres and text-types

Some writers (e.g. Paltridge, 2001) distinguish between *genre* and *text type*, largely on structural grounds, identifying as text types such categories as 'problem-solution...description, discussion, cause-and-effect, and compare-and-contrast texts' (Paltridge, 2001:24).

   This distinction between *genre* and *text type* will not enter into the discussion and analyses in this book, however. For one reason, some of these categories are already included as discourse modes, for example, 'description'. Furthermore, in the definition to be adopted here, the term *genre* is already taken to include structural features such as the problem-solution pattern, so any such features of texts will be examined as integral parts of a particular genre, and not separately.

3.10 Summary

This chapter has addressed the nature of the term *genre*, emphasising the ways in which readers and listeners draw on *genre schemas*, along with other types of *schemas* and *scripts*, in their efforts to interpret texts. It drew a distinction between notional 'genres' and actual *texts* in the world, and considered the ways in which a text can draw flexibly on one or more genres in its creation. Some texts, for example those in more formal settings, might follow a partic-ular genre closely (for example, an academic essay or business letter) whereas other texts (for example, those in the media) might draw more flexibly on a variety of genres to create more hybridity.

For readers and listeners it was argued that the *function* of any text and genre is central. For this reason it is useful for the analyst to start with the text's function and then examine ways in which the features of the text support that function in various ways. The features of a recipe, for example, might be analysed to see how far they support the main function of that genre. An actual recipe might then be analysed to see to what extent it fits with those expectations, in ways which will be considered in detail in the heuristic scheme for analysing discourse set out in Chapter 5.

The present chapter also discussed a more abstract level of analysis, in the form of *discourse modes* such as *narrating, describing* and *reporting*. It was sug-gested that these modes appear to be common to a number of genres and in some way 'above' them, as well as being identifiable in terms of common sets of features. It was suggested that for this reason it can be useful to examine the ways in which these modes operate in texts. However, although it was stressed that these modes are an additional useful way of approaching genres and texts, it would be a mistake to set too much store by them, for example by building an analytical framework upon them.

Having seen, then, what genres are in principle, how they operate with respect to texts, and how they can draw on various discourse modes, we can turn in the next chapter to look at a number of the discourse modes in detail, as this will allow us in the later chapters, when we look at a range of genres from a variety of situations, to understand and appreciate how these discourse modes and genres can be used by texts in various ways and for a variety of purposes. This will also prepare for discussion in Chapter 5 of how in practice to carry out a discourse analysis.

Discourse Modes 4

Chapter 3 examined the nature and role of genres and genre knowledge in discourse, and introduced the notion of discourse modes. These are important because they feature in many of the genres we know in daily life, and therefore occur in many actual texts, as will be illustrated in the analyses of jokes, conversations, advertisements and other texts in the chapters to come. As noted above, discourse modes differ from genres because they do not have a specific social function in themselves; instead they are building blocks which we can draw on in many different genres and then use in actual texts in flexible ways for a range of purposes.

4.1 Patterning in discourse modes

Smith offers some general insights into the way in which discourse modes relate to the real world:

> People intuitively recognize passages of the Discourse Modes, although they are probably unaware of the linguistic basis for the differences between them. Each mode – Narrative, Description, Report, Information, Argument – introduces certain entities into the universe of discourse, with a related principle of discourse progression. The features have linguistic correlates of a temporal nature. In fact temporality in the larger sense is the key to the discourse modes. Temporal factors are woven into the fabric of a language and are part of our tacit knowledge of language structure. (Smith 2003:22)

She later clarifies the way in which each mode relates to temporal and other aspects of the world, setting out her reasoning as follows:

The temporal modes are Narrative, Report, and Description. They introduce situations that are located in the world. In Narrative, events and states are related to each other in time; the text progresses with bounded events interpreted in sequence, and/or time adverbials. In Reports, events, states, and General Statives are related to Speech Time: texts progress back and forth. The mode of Description has events and states, and time is static. The text progresses spatially through a scene. Text progression in Description depends on lexical information, unlike the two other temporal modes.

The Information and Argument modes are atemporal. General Statives predominate in the Information mode, while Argument has both General Statives and abstract entities. Text progression in these modes proceeds by metaphorical motion through the domain of the text. (Smith 2003:243)

This illustrates the fact that the discourse modes can be characterised and distinguished in terms of their relation to the world, and also by their internal linguistic features, as Smith goes on to discuss in detail. Some of the modes relate to aspects 'located in the world', while others are more cognitive. They relate to time and space in different ways. For example, as Smith notes, *narrating* mode (as it is termed here) is characterised by the fact that the text typically progresses 'with bounded events interpreted in sequence, and/or time adverbials' whereas *describing* mode 'has events and states, and time is static. The text progresses spatially through a scene' (ibid).

Smith's concern is with written texts rather than spoken language, so her analysis does not include anything resembling the *interacting* mode to be included here. However, in the past few years technology has opened up the possibilities for synchronous written communication such as text messaging and online synchronous messaging, in which it is clear that the interaction between participants closely resembles spoken interaction in many ways. This again demonstrates the value of including some sort of interactive mode in our framework alongside *narrating*, *describing* and *reporting*.

Seen in this light, *interacting* is not a temporal mode like *narrating*, but progresses as a result of interaction between speakers or writers. One of its main linguistic realisations is the question. It is arguably not the only mode which sets up a two-way dialogue, since *instructing* (not included as a discourse mode by Smith, but included by others, as noted in chapter 3) also implies a dialogue, in this case with a silent partner whose role is to follow the sequence. These two discourse modes, *interacting* and *instructing*, could therefore be seen as 'dialogic', as they imply a dialogue, to stand alongside the temporal modes of *narrating*, *describing* and *reporting*, and the mental modes of *informing* and *arguing*.

The aim of this chapter is not to set out in full the characteristics of each mode, (since the reader can consult Smith, 2003, and Werlich, 1976 for closer discussion of linguistic features of each) but to describe them only to the extent that their contribution to my overall framework of analysis, the heuristic approach set out in Chapter 5, can be appreciated, and also so that their role in the many spoken and written texts to be analysed from Chapter 6 onwards can be understood.

4.2 Narrating

When we read or listen to a text we usually manage to 'place' it quite quickly in terms of its genre, even if we might not always have a name for the genre precisely. For instance, with which genre would this text typically be associated?

> There are these three men abandoned on a desert island. Suddenly one of them notices something shining in the sand and pulls out a magic lamp. Smiling hopefully he rubs it and a genie comes out. The genie greets them and says that it can grant them one wish each, so the first man jumps up and down and says, 'Great! I wish I could go back home to my wife and kids', so the genie snaps his fingers and the man disappears.
>
> The second man then jumps up and down with joy and says, 'My father is sick. I wish I could go back to see him', so the genie snaps his fingers and the man disappears.
>
> The third man looks around him and is depressed to find himself all alone, so he says, 'Hmmm, I feel so lonely. I really wish my two friends were still here with me.'

It is clear from the fact that 'the text progresses with bounded events interpreted in sequence, and/or time adverbials' as Smith expresses it (2003:243) that this text draws on the *narrating* mode. It also follows a familiar genre – most readers from most cultures would have no difficulty in identifying it as a joke. The genre of Jokes includes many types or *sub-genres,* as we will discuss in more detail below, but what links them all is their *function,* as they all aim at humour. This example is of a fairly standard type which involves a story, in this case about three people, and conforms to a type which is quite common internationally, namely a story in which a stupid character is contrasted with one or more 'normal' people.

Since Chapter 7 will discuss the Joke genre more directly, the focus here will be on one particular aspect of this joke only, namely the discourse mode of *narrating* which it employs. As already noted, a useful starting point for any analysis is the text's function, which is humour. In this light the *narrating* mode can be seen as one *feature* which helps to achieve that function. Narrating as a discourse mode is characterised by particular linguistic patterning, to which we can now turn, and also by particular structural organisational features, which will be considered below.

Narrating mode: linguistic features

Smith offers a general characterisation of this discourse mode: 'Narrative presents a sequence of events and states that have the same participants and/ or causal and other consequential relation... They occur in a certain order, which is crucial for understanding' (Smith 2003:26). These features – for example, the fact that the participants tend to recur through the story – distinguish this mode from others. However, as with all the discourse modes, *narrating* mode is also associated with particular lexical and syntactical patterns. An obvious one is the use of a high frequency of verbs typically in the past tense and in general the use of *finite* verb forms. Also common in this discourse mode is the use of adverbs with a time or sequencing element such as 'suddenly', 'then', or 'so' in the joke above. A third feature of *narrating* mode is that, as Almasi puts it, 'characters are introduced in the beginning and referred to using various referents (e.g. he, his, him) throughout the text. This process is known as "co-reference"' (Almasi, 2002:142). This use of co-reference will then give a relatively high number of pronouns. This is not to say that all texts in narrating mode will share the same features exactly, but only that a prototypical text which uses this mode is likely to make use of them.

Narrating mode: advancement

Smith makes a further point about the typical advancement in *narrating* mode, one which allows us to distinguish this mode from *reporting* mode, to be discussed below:

> Narratives advance dynamically. After the first sentence, the Events and States of a narrative are related to previous events and times in the text, rather than to Speech Time. (Smith 2003:93)

In Smith's terms 'Speech Time' is the time, as understood by the reader or listener, when the written or spoken text in question was created. As will be discussed in a later section, this is considered an important reference point in *reporting* discourse mode, as distinct from *narrating* mode, in which the central point of reference is a time or times in the narrative itself.

Narrating mode: structure

Besides the linguistic and other features discussed above, narratives often follow particular patterns or structures. Structure is not typically included as a defining dimension of discourse modes, since aspects of structure are more usually considered as part of *genre knowledge*, but in the case of narrating and narratives it has been argued that there is a prototypical structure which should therefore be taken into account in any discussion of the *narrating* mode. This is why it is considered here.

Narrative structure in various media has received a great deal of attention (see for example, Toolan, 2001; Bamberg, 1997; Chatman, 1989), and in full narratives we can see various patterns which seem to be typical. To illustrate this, look at an invented narrative which is somehow 'odd', and consider how it might be corrected:

A The boy ran after it.
B One day a boy was playing football in the park.
C The dog let go of the ball and the boy got it back again.
D He carried on playing football.
E Then a dog ran up to him, snatched his ball and ran away.
F It was lovely and sunny.

Two points can be made about our reading of this story. The sentences are in the wrong order and it is easy for us to recognise the 'correct' order of the sentences, but what is it which allows us to carry out both of these actions? We have never seen this exact story before, so how can we see that it is wrong and how is it that we are able to correct it? To put the question another way, what is it that we *know* (thinking back to Figure 1.1 in Chapter 1) which enables us to identify an odd narrative structure, and to alter it to our and everyone else's satisfaction?

First of all we make use of what could be called *discourse signals*, since they are signal sequences, beginnings and ends, among other things. These make up part of the knowledge which helps us to rearrange this story sequence correctly; for example, we know that *'One day'* is a typical narrative opening phrase, so we guess that sentence B is the first of the story. A second aspect of our knowledge which helps us to sequence the story correctly is the fact that certain *parts of speech* can act as discourse signals, so we make use of adverbs such as 'then' in sentence E to help us to reconstruct the sequence of events. Thirdly, we draw on aspects of *cohesion*, and also, fourthly, of our *world knowledge*, to identify, for example, that the word 'it' in some of the sentences refers to the ball and in others to the dog. In short, we use 'lower order' and also 'higher order' elements shown in Figure 1.1, to help us both to see that the story sequence is wrong, and to correct it.

Nonetheless, in this short story there are few of these signals, cohesive devices and other features to help us, certainly not enough to tell us the order by themselves, so what other knowledge do we use in order to sort the sentences correctly? In essence, we draw heavily on our knowledge of *typical story structure* in the process. This is a *mental script* of the sort we discussed previously since we know that typical stories start by establishing a sort of setting, a status quo in which things seem to be stable. Next, as we know, we often get an event of some sort which upsets that stable situation. Our *script* tells us that the characters often then try hard to overcome the problem or the disruption. Finally, we know that often they succeed and we get a happy ending.

This 'script' of how narratives work, like other mental scripts, is largely subconscious but nonetheless powerful in shaping our expectations of stories, films and other narratives which we come across, and is therefore a part of our expectation of many genres in which narrative is involved, such as jokes. Using our shared mental script, we would probably agree to arrange the sentences like this:

1 B One day a boy was playing football in the park.
2 F It was lovely and sunny.
3 E Then a dog ran up to him, snatched his ball and ran away.
4 A The boy ran after it.
5 C The dog let go of the ball and the boy got it back again.
6 D He carried on playing football.

We are able to reconstruct this story and agree on it partly because we all agree on a basic *narrative structure*. When discussing narrative structure most commentators refer back to the ancient Greek philosopher Aristotle (born 384 BCE) who was the first known critic (in his *Poetics*, ed. Atchity, 1998) to work through the basic pattern we see in the story above:

1. A stable beginning or setting.
2. A disruption of some sort.
3. A return to stability and equilibrium.

This is a simplified version of the scheme, of course, and we need to recall that Aristotle was concerned in the relevant passages of his work with the genre of tragic drama in particular, so we need to be cautious in applying what he said to all narratives. His particular aim was not to set a template for narrative, but to argue the reasons why some dramas are particularly effective. However, this has not prevented writers through the centuries using what Aristotle said almost as a prescription for how stories should be, sometimes extending his ideas in ways which were not in his original text. Other writers have proposed significant and interesting additions and developments, and one who made useful and well-known contributions is Todorov. In his *Poetics of Prose* and other writings, Todorov tried to compare the structure of a story with the grammatical structure of a sentence so as to develop what he called a 'grammar of narrative', in order to identify what he considered an 'ideal' narrative plot structure. We can see from some of his conclusions that his idea was close to what Aristotle was suggesting, but offers a slightly different perspective:

> An 'ideal' narrative begins with a stable situation which is disturbed by some power or force. There results a state of disequilibrium; by the action of a force directed in the opposite direction, the equilibrium is re-established; the second equilibrium is similar to the first, but the two are never identical. (Todorov, 1977 [1971]:111)

This fits quite well with our simple story above: the boy playing on a sunny day in lines 1 and 2 is our *stable situation*, then a power comes to *disrupt* that state (the dog in line 3), then the *action* of the boy himself serves as the force in the opposite direction (line 4), leading to the *reinstatement of the equilibrium* as he starts playing again. Of course, Todorov applied this analysis to more complex narratives, but in essence this is an outline of his scheme. I have applied it to a simple invented example, but if we stop to consider how this applies to more complex stories, written or on film, it seems to fit quite well, although each story naturally emphasises different stages in different ways.

Todorov's analysis was then developed (1990 [1978]) towards what is arguably his major contribution to narrative theory. After analysing a traditional Russian story called *The Swan-Geese* Todorov identified, beside the classical elements we mentioned above of *setting – disruption – return to equilibrium*, two more which he considered to be important:

> If we analyze 'The Swan-Geese' this way, we shall discover that the tale includes five obligatory elements: (1) the opening situation of equilibrium; (2) the degradation of the situation through the kidnapping of the boy; (3) the state of disequilibrium observed by the little girl; (4) the search for and recovery of the boy; (5) the reestablishment of the initial equilibrium – the return home. If any one of these five actions had been omitted, the tale would have lost its identity. (Todorov, trans. 1990:29)

Where this differs from the classic scheme is in *(3) the state of disequilibrium observed by the little girl* and *(4) the search for and recovery of the boy,* or in more general terms, the *recognition* that something has been disturbed or gone wrong, and the *attempt* to put it right. If we consider most narratives which are successful or well-known it appears that whereas they might have a setting, a disruption and a final equilibrium, it is frequently the two middle elements identified by Todorov which are the most significant and powerful. For example, although many have (1) a setting, (2) a disruption and (5) a final equilibrium, large parts may in fact be taken up with Todorov's stage 4, the efforts taken by the hero(es) or heroine(s) to resolve the problem. Every James Bond film, for example, offers the setting and disruption within the first few minutes, then a brief stage 3 (recognition) when his boss might explain with a worried frown how serious this issue is, but almost the whole film, in effect, represents stage 4, the attempt to resolve the situation, before the final stage of equilibrium, with a few digressions for flirtation and fun along the way.

Stage 4 seems important then, but what of stage 3, the *recognition* of the disruption? At first it may seem insignificant, but in practice it is often the main way of distinguishing less effectual narratives from more successful ones. This is the stage where the main character not only *realises* and *feels* the loss or problem or reversal, but also when we as the reader or audience notice and appreciate that suffering or worrying or crying – we feel the pain or the problem, sometimes at great length. Lesser narratives or films often do not show much of this stage, but greater ones often do. If we think about classics like Shakespeare's tragedy *Hamlet,* the character spends large parts of the action bemoaning his fate, so we get a full sense of his suffering. In fact, even if we add this stage to our simple example story we can see that it does make a difference:

		Stage in narrative structure
1	One day a boy was playing football in the park.	1 *Setting and equilibrium*
2	It was lovely and sunny.	
3	Then a dog ran up to him, snatched his ball and ran away.	2 *Disruption*
4 (new)	**The boy cried out and shouted after the dog, worried that he might lose his ball for ever.**	3 *Recognition of disruption*
5	The boy ran after it.	4 *Attempt to resolve the disruption*
6	The dog let go of the ball and the boy got it back again.	5 *Return to equilibrium, (though not the same as at first)*
7	He carried on playing football.	

This illustrates the value of Todorov's analysis, and of the elements he identified.

Breaking with the script

It is worth thinking about the role of this third stage when we consider other narratives, for example films and stories we know well, to reflect on how they deal with it. It is also important to note that the stages above are a sort of mental *script*, like other mental scripts we mentioned in Chapter 3, which means that genres and texts are not bound to follow it; indeed some will deliberately go against or contravene our expectations for various purposes. Many genres, for example, begin not with the *setting* but with the *problem or disruption* – a gun going off, perhaps. This is a common literary technique which is given the Latin name *in medias res* (in the middle of things) for obvious reasons, and serves to hook the reader or viewer into the story. Such narratives then either let us guess the setting or else offer a flashback or explanation to elucidate the setting in more detail.

A good example is the 'Three men' joke given earlier. In the first sentence this joke gives the first two narrative stages together, because it starts with stage 2, the disrupted situation itself ('There are these three men abandoned ...') and then tells us the setting very briefly after it ('on a desert island'). There is then a second *disruption* to the already disrupted scene, this time a positive one, because one man finds a possible solution to their problem in the form of the magic lamp – a sort of new stage 2. This is followed by a very brief stage 3, *recognition of disruption* when the man smiles – he recognises that there is hope. However, the main and longest part of the joke is stage 4, the attempt to resolve the disruption, which in fact happens three times. As is common with this sub-genre of jokes, it does not end happily.

Do these differences, and this sad ending, mean that Todorov was wrong? On the contrary, this exemplifies the important point that the general narrative structure outlined above is often altered in different genres, as it is here in this kind of joke. Furthermore, when Todorov noted that narratives typically end with an equilibrium, he did not mean by this that there is usually a happy ending. In fact this joke fits his scheme well because it offers a sort of grim equilibrium, in which the men end up back where they began. This reminds us that there is no necessity at all for genres to follow *script* expectations and a genre might even achieve its purpose precisely by contradicting our expected script or schema. This is exactly what this joke does. Although it certainly requires us *to know* the standard narrative script, its humour comes precisely from its *overturning* of those expectations through the actions of the foolish man, and then the failure of all of them. So as readers, and also as analysts, we need first to know the script, and then to appreciate how a genre or text adheres to or diverges from it.

Some texts offer even more radical digressions from the standard narrative sequence we have outlined above. An interesting example is the film *Memento* (2000), directed by Christopher Nolan, in which the whole story is told backwards. Even examples such as this, however, typically include all the elements we have noted above, but in a different order and quantity.

By contrast, unsuccessful films or books are sometimes weak partly because they omit or reduce one or more of the expected stages, or devote too much attention to one stage. Stages 3 and 4 are frequently less developed in weaker plots. We can see in children's stories that they often omit one of the stages, and the story can sometimes seem weak as a result. The way in which texts can diverge in this sort of way from the 'normal' sequence for various effects is important to several genres to be discussed in the chapters to come.

Is this narrative structuring universal?

Todorov was not the first to suggest that the third and fourth elements are crucial to successful narratives. Propp (1968), for example, in his work on folktales in the 1920s, had also seen these elements as important, but Todorov was arguably the analyst who brought them most to our attention, focussing in particular on the various types of what he called the *transformations* which a narrative depicts, whether it is a transformation in the character of the hero, or in some other element. However, he also at times made claims for his elements of narrative structure which now seem excessive. For example he suggested of the elements he had identified that 'this cycle belongs to the very definition of narrative: one cannot imagine a narrative that fails to contain at least a part of it' (Todorov. 1990: 29).

The assumption that all narratives will follow this scheme now seems rather ethnocentric, since other non-Western narrative traditions exist which do not conform to this pattern. To take just one example, Hoey (2001:1–2) reproduces a fascinating Anangu aboriginal story from Australia which is structured quite differently from Western expectations, appearing to 'contravene' many of the structural patterns set out above. In other words, it is risky to assume that this pattern is a human universal.

Notwithstanding, we must admit that the structure does seem to be deeply rooted in many cultures and traditions. Analysts have often argued for the longevity of such narrative patterns. For example, when Todorov (1977) discusses what he calls 'primitive narrative' he makes extensive reference to Homer's narrative poems, but even earlier human narratives, for instance the Mesopotamian story of Gilgamesh, which dates from over 3,000 years ago

(George, 2003), show remarkable similarities to the narrative pattern outlined above. This suggests that even if the structure outlined above is not universal, it does seem to have a long history in human societies, and to be common to many cultures.

Spoken Narratives

Aristotle's work revolved primarily around dramatic tragedy, and Todorov's around written stories, but what of spoken narratives? There is evidence that these follow rather different structural patterns. The most well-known early research on spoken narratives is that by William Labov (Labov and Waletzky, 1967; Labov, 1972; and see Pridham, 2001) in which he and his colleagues analysed the spoken narratives of black New York teenagers, identifying six broad stages, rather than the five identified by Todorov. His aim was to identify 'the structural schema underlying spontaneous conversational narrative' (Johnstone, 2002:82).

As a way of looking in detail at the structural patterns which Labov identified, take a story told by a schoolboy called Michael. Here he reports an incident in which he and a friend called Fred were doing a task at school which involved designing and making model chairs for his schoolteacher, Mrs. Taylor. I have transcribed it broadly to make it as clear as possible to read, while trying to preserve some of the sense of his natural speech such as significant stresses. As you read, try to identify the *stages* of the story, to see if they resemble the pattern identified by Todorov, including the setting, the disruption and the other three stages:

¹ At school we we did.. these chairs and, and, well I, me and Fred, a, did this really,
² a..a, hard thing up and then suddenly it pinged back and all went loose.. a..and it was
³ really tough and we all had to do it <u>again</u>.
⁴ And.. and then Mrs Taylor said it was too loose, so we had to undo it.....and do it <u>again</u>.
⁵ And then she still said it was too loose and we di.... we had to do it <u>again</u>. But in the
⁶ end we got it but we had to do that a lots of times.... for it and it took ages,.... all day.

It is clear that although Michael is only nine years old, he has already learned the socially expected structure of a narrative. He starts with the *setting*, giving some basic context (the place, the task and the participants) and then moves on to the incident itself. The *disruption* comes in line 2 when the unexplained 'hard thing' suddenly 'pinged back and it went all loose'. The *recognition of the disruption* stage comes when he says 'it was really tough', which is emphasised in Michael's intonation and stress in the original recording. It is interesting to note that Michael reports *three* attempts to repair the problem, since repetition three times (the 'Rule of Three' Atkinson, 1984): is an important feature of many genres (see Chapter 9). Finally the disruption gives way to the *resolution* stage in lines 5–6: 'But in the end we got it'. An important point to note is that the narrative sequence in Michael's telling of the story follows exactly the actual sequence of the events in real time, which Labov identifies as a feature of spoken narratives (unlike, for example, news reports which often report events in a different order – see Chapter 8).

This appears at first to fit Todorov's analysis of written stories quite closely, but as it is spoken, not written, it contains other features which Labov's analysis of spoken narrative helps to elucidate. In Labov's analysis spoken narratives frequently start with an *abstract*, summarising the story the speaker is about to tell. For example Michael might have said, 'We had this big problem with this chair today which kept breaking'. In fact Michael does not offer any 'abstract' of this kind (and of course Labov does not say that *all* spoken narratives will contain *all* features), but in many spoken narratives this 'abstract' does occur.

Secondly, Labov noticed what he called an *orientation* stage (which resembles Todorov's *setting* stage), followed by what he calls a *complicating action* (which is in effect the same as the *disruption*). Whereas at this point Todorov saw a 'recognition of disruption' as a frequent feature in written narrative, Labov sees instead an *evaluation* aspect in which the speaker explains the point of the narrative. In our example this is not prominent – Michael simply says, 'it was really tough' – and it is not clear whether this is more like Todorov's 'recognition of disruption' or Labov's 'evaluation'. Perhaps both interpretations are plausible. Labov notes, by the way, that 'evaluation' can be scattered throughout the narrative (Labov, 1972:366).

A curious feature of Labov's scheme is that there is no stage for *attempt at resolution*. In the discussion of Todorov's scheme above this was taken as an important stage in many narratives and one which is at the heart of many films and novels and possibly the most original part of Todorov's analysis. Furthermore there is a clear example of it in Michael's story when he reports three attempts to repair the chair, and it is placed at the centre of the story. Even so, Labov does not identify this as a separate stage, but in effect includes it as part of his fifth stage, the *result* or *resolution*.

Finally, Labov identifies a part which does not seem so common in written narrative and which does not enter Todorov's scheme – namely the *coda*, which serves to signal an end to the story and a return to the present moment, such as 'That was that', or 'That was the most dangerous moment in my life' In fact at the end of his story we see Michael saying, 'but we had to do that a lots of times...for it and it took ages...all day' and this seems to serve partly as a *coda* in Labov's terms, signalling the end of the action, and also as *evaluation*, showing the main point of the narrative. This tells us firstly that Labov was perhaps correct to suggest that spoken narratives might

Table 4.1 Elements of spoken narrative structure

Stage (adapted from Labov, 1972, and Pridham, 2001)	Example from Michael's story
Abstract	
Summarizes the central action and the main point of the narrative. Narrators often begin with one or two clauses summarizing the whole story.	None
Orientation	
Sets the scene. At the outset it is necessary to identify in some way the time, place, persons and their activity or situation.	At school we we did...these chairs and, and, well I, me and Fred, a, did this really, a...a, hard thing up...
(Complicating) action	
What happened (then)?	and then suddenly it pinged back and all went loose...
Evaluation	
Answers the question: 'so what?'	a...and it was really tough
The means used by the narrator to indicate the point of the narrative, why it is being told and what the narrator is getting at.	
Result or resolution	
What finally happened to conclude the sequence of events.	and we all had to do it <u>again</u>. And... and then Mrs Taylor said it was too loose, so we had to undo it...and do it <u>again.</u> And then she still said it was too loose and we di...we had to do it <u>again</u>. But in the end we got it
Coda	
At the end of the **narrative**. Signals end and return to the present. 'And that was that.' 'And that was one of the most important ...'	but we had to do that a lots of times...for it and it took ages,...all day.

be slightly different from written ones, and also that in any actual text we might find the elements which Labov and Todorov identified in slightly different sequences and quantities. The point is, of course, that neither of the two schemes should be treated as a complete description of all narratives, but both are useful when we actually seek to analyse and understand what a speaker or writer is trying to do when narrating.

To summarise, we can set Labov's scheme out with the examples from Michael's story alongside (see Table 4.1).

A general scheme of narrative structure

This example has illustrated some valuable aspects of the scheme broadly set out by Todorov, and also some interestingly different aspects identified by Labov. It is useful at this stage to combine the two interpretations, to give the following eight possible stages or slots for narratives. This could then serve as a guide to possible stages of both written and spoken narratives, though of course these will probably not all occur in any one text.

1. **Abstract:** Summarizes the central action and the main point of the narrative
2. **Setting or orientation:** Sets the scene
3. **Disruption or complicating action:** What happened next?
4. **Recognition of disruption:** Showing the effect of the disruption on participants
5. **Attempt at resolution:** How the issue was resolved (may be repeated or complex)
6. **Result or resolution:** What finally happened to conclude the sequence of events
7. **Evaluation:** Used to indicate the purpose of the narrative, why it is being told and what the narrator is getting at (could occur at other points in the sequence)
8. **Coda:** At the end of the narrative. Signals end and return to the present: 'And that was that.'

As noted above, this narrative structure should not be treated as inevitable or universal, as individual storytellers and even whole cultures may not follow this pattern closely or at all (as in the example of the Australian folk tale). Furthermore some elements will occur more often in spoken or written narratives. Nonetheless, in many cultures this pattern has become part of our narrative expectation, and in the next chapters when we look at jokes and other texts which draw on the *narrating* discourse mode it will be useful as a way of understanding how various texts follow or diverge from this 'standard pattern' to achieve various effects.

Before turning, then, to consider the *interacting* discourse mode, Table 4.2 provides a summary of elements of the *narrating* discourse mode. My examples are from English; other languages will of course use different patterns to achieve similar effects.

Table 4.2   Features of the narrating discourse mode

1. Presentation of 'a sequence of events and states that have the same participants and/or causal and other consequential relation' (Smith, 2003:26).
2. Events reported predominantly in the past tense, although other tenses can be used. Frequent use of finite verb forms (Jeffries, 2006:87).
3. Frequent use of adverbs of sequencing and consequence.
4. Frequent use of pronouns (Jeffries, 2006:93) and other co-referencing devices (Almasi, 2002).
5. Events typically draw on or follow a standard narrative structure, frequently with a setting, a disruption, a recognition of the disruption, an attempt to resolve the disruption, and a final equilibrium.
6. Spoken narratives often also include other features such as an abstract, a coda and evaluation.

4.3 Interacting

It was noted above that the *interacting* discourse mode is characterised by its 'dialogic' two-way nature, as is the *instructing* mode, since both of them imply more than one active participant. In *instructing* mode the other participant is typically silent and implied, supposedly following the instructions, whereas in *interacting* mode, by contrast, each participant offers written or spoken contributions.

This section, then, considers some aspects of interaction central to the *interacting* discourse mode. Many of them draw for their examples on work done in the Conversation Analysis (CA) research tradition, but it must be borne in mind that *interacting* discourse mode as defined here operates at a relatively abstract level, and can enter into written discourse (for example, in texting and online gaming) as well as spoken discourse, so the discussion of the *interacting* mode in this chapter is not intended to be a discussion of conversation *per se*. Conversation will be discussed in Chapter 6 as one example of a genre which uses the *interacting* discourse mode.

Adjacency pairs

During the analysis of the 'Window' exchange in Chapter 1 it was suggested that Ann's opening remark, namely 'It's cold with that window open', might typically be understood not as a simple statement of fact but as a request requiring a particular response, that is, the first part of a pair of utterances between speakers. In a series of now well-known lectures on conversation delivered in the 1960s, the linguist Harvey Sacks discussed such paired utterances. Drawing on the work of Harold Garfinkel from the 1960s onwards, in a broad research area which came to be known as 'ethnomethodology' (discussed in Garfinkel, 1984[1967]; 2002), linguists such as Sacks set out to understand the ways in which conversational interaction is managed by participants. Their work developed into what is now known as Conversation Analysis (CA). They were interested in more than simply language, indeed language was not their central focus: 'CA is only marginally interested in language as such; its actual object of study is the interactional organization of social activities' (Hutchby and Wooffitt 1998:14).

Sacks, among others, noted that adjacency pairs were an important mechanism by which such 'social activities' were organized. He characterised them in his lectures as follows: 'Aspects of certain sequences that occur in conversation can be isolated, for which the following features obtain: They're two utterances long, and the utterances that compose them are adjacently placed to each other' (Sacks, 1995, Vol. 2:521). For this reason he came to call these utterances 'adjacency pairs' (Sacks, 1995, Vol. 2:521; Levinson, 1983), although it was later accepted that the two parts need not be strictly adjacent to each other, as will be discussed below. Sacks noted that the first part of the pair of utterances calls for a particular answer, since 'given a first pair part, not anything that could be a second pair part goes, but given some first, only some seconds are admissible' (Sacks, 1995, Vol. 2:521). In his original lectures Sacks identified a number of such adjacency pairs, and it is interesting to see his original formulation of these types:

> Now, characteristically there are names for the components of such pairs, for example, greeting-greeting, question-answer, 'goodbye-goodbye' (whatever you want to call that), complaints followed by an excuse or a request for forgiveness or an apology or a denial, offers followed by acceptances or refusals, requests followed by acceptances or rejections, compliments followed by acceptances of a compliment, etc., etc. (Sacks 1995, Vol. 2:521)

Sacks was quoted above as saying that 'given some first, only some seconds are admissible'. To put this another way, 'a first pair part is typically made in the expectation of a certain second pair part; for example, an apology is typically made in the expectation of an acceptance. It is, however, possible that an apology is met with a refusal' (Cheng 2003:19). In the case of an apology, acceptance would be termed the 'preferred' response whereas refusal would be considered a 'dispreferred' response or 'dispreferred second' (Schegloff *et al.*, 1977:362). Cheng suggests ways of identifying such 'dispreferred' responses in terms of their structure: 'Structurally, a dispreferred response differs from a preferred response. A dispreferred second pair part is marked and made structurally complex, while a preferred second pair part is unmarked and typically structurally simple' (Cheng, 2003:19 citing Schegloff *et al.*, 1977). Since the preferred response is expected by both interlocutors it is frequently shorter and less complex, 'whereas the 'dispreferred' alternative can be marked by pauses, hesitations, excuses, mitigations and justifications' (Jupp, 2006:43). To put it another way:

> responses which agree or are congruent with the expectation projected by a first pair-part are produced contiguously and without mitigation. Responses which diverge from that expectation – which in some way disagree – tend to be prefaced by hesitations, discourse markers such as Well... and, unlike congruent responses, are accompanied by accounts for why the speaker is responding in this way. (Hutchby 2001: 67)

Jupp has summarised the status of adjacency pairs as follows, and several of these key dimensions will be revisited in the chapters to follow:

a) the sequence is composed of two adjacency turns issued by two different speakers;
b) given the first, the second is expectable (conditional relevance rule)
c) when the second part is missing (for example, the answer in the 'question/answer' pair), its absence is pointed out by one of the speakers;
d) this mechanism provides a frame for interpretation: by producing a second pair, speakers display their understanding of what the first pair is actually doing.

(Jupp, 2006:43)

The conditional relevance rule refers to 'the way in which particular types of utterance can be made conditionally relevant by prior turns' (Clift *et al.*, 2009:48). The same writers then explain how this operates:

> The production of a first pair-part, such as a greeting, sets up a constraint that a next selected speaker should follow directly by producing

the relevant second pair-part—in this case, a return greeting. Moreover, whatever does follow a first pair-part will be monitored for exactly how it works as a response to that move. (Clift *et al.*, 2009:48)

The first speaker, in other words, is attentive to the way in which the other participant either follows the 'rules' by offering a preferred response, or breaks the rules by not offering it. From this, he or she draws inferences which guide the next utterances.

It will be appreciated that this process involves – indeed depends on – shared expectations on the part of speaker and hearer, and shared understandings of how a discourse interaction is supposed to work. In that sense it is 'normative', meaning that participants are 'expected' to follow certain social 'norms' or tacit rules. This shared set of understood rules is important because it means that participants can on this basis make reasonable deductions about the feelings and aims of other speakers in the interaction. In other words,

motivational inferences can be drawn from the non-occurrence of a second part following the production of a first. For instance, not returning a greeting may be taken as a sign of rudeness; not providing an answer to a question may be taken as indicative of evasiveness; while not proffering a defence to an accusation may be taken as a tacit admission of guilt. (Clift *et al.*, 2009:48)

Types of adjacency pair

It may be helpful at this point to list some of the most common adjacency pair types. The list which is offered in Table 4.3 includes those identified by Sacks and a number of other writers, with some illustrative examples of preferred and dispreferred responses.

It was noted above that dispreferred responses are often structurally different from preferred responses. In spoken language we can also use a range of other indicators to 'apologise' for giving a dispreferred response, including some of these: 'delay/hesitation, preface, expression of doubt, token 'yes', apology, mention of obligation, appeal for understanding, making the dispreferred response non-personal, giving an account, hedges and mitigators' (Cheng, 2003:19 citing Yule, 1996). In other words, preferred responses tend to be swift and brief: 'Broadly, responses which agree or are congruent with the expectation projected by a first pair-part are produced contiguously and without mitigation' (Clift *et al.*, 2009:49). By contrast, dispreferred responses tend to be signalled as such, for example by the various markers in the

Table 4.3 Types and examples of adjacency pairs

Type /function of adjacency pair*	Initiation move (examples)	Response move (examples)	
Greetings	Good morning	Good morning	*Preferred*
Leavetaking formulae	A: Goodbye	B: Goodbye	*Preferred*
Complaints	A: Isn't he dreadful?	B: Yes, but he's not all bad.	*Dispreferred*
Offers	A: Would you like some carrots?	B: Yeah	*Preferred*
Compliments	A: Why?, it's the loveliest record!	B: Well, thank you. (Pomerantz, 1978:84)	*Preferred*
Invitations	B: Uh if you'd care to come over and visit a little while this morning I'll give you a cup of coffee.	A: hehh Well that's awfully sweet of you, I don't think I can make it this morning - hh uhm I'm running an ad in the paper and -and uh I have to stay near the phone. (Heritage, 1984, p. 266)	*Dispreferred*
Requesting information	A: What's the name of that color?	B: Blue. (Merritt, 1982:235, in Duranti, 1997)	*Preferred*
Requesting action	Sara: Barbara I have to go to a lecture in a few minutes and Joan isn't back from lunch ... could you take over the desk for me?	Barbara: erm (tut) well I – I could but it would be better if you could find someone else cos I have to leave at two. (adapted from Holmes, 2008:380)	*Dispreferred*

*From Sacks (1995) unless otherwise indicated.

dispreferred responses in Table 4.3, such as 'erm (tut) well I – I...' in the example of Requesting action.

It is worth noting that when a response is said to be 'preferred' this has nothing to do with the personal preferences of the speakers. As Duranti explains it:

> Sacks and other conversation analysts did not think of preferences as psychological properties, residing in an individual's consciousness. Rather, they saw preferences as tendencies provided in the system and by the system ... Preferences are interpretive frameworks within which

members must operate at the very moment of engaging in the mediating activity of talk. (Duranti 1997:260)

So any first pair-part sets up an expectation within the system which implies in itself a preference, no matter what the speaker actually wants.

Teaching exchanges

One common type of exchange has three parts rather than two, and is known as the *IRF* sequence because of the initials of its three parts: Initiation, Response and Feedback/follow-up (Seedhouse, 1996). This IRF sequence, which for convenience we could term an 'adjacency trio', is common and important in teaching situations and some situations with parents and children, and will be discussed in greater detail in Chapter 6. However, it is not so common in other situations. If someone offered us the third 'feedback move' in certain everyday situations we would be confused, and might suppose the speaker to be either joking or arrogant, as in this invented example:

Edward: Excuse me, what time is the next bus?
Flavia: It's due in five minutes
Edward: Excellent! Well done!
Flavia: *(Thinks: Well why did you ask me if you knew already?!?)*

We could explain this more technically by saying that Flavia took Edward's move to be part of an Information Request adjacency pair and responded accordingly, drawing on her prior knowledge to offer what she took to be the appropriate response, only to be surprised to find that his question was not genuine, as he knew the answer already. In other words, the IRF sequence is not appropriate in all situations.

Adjacent and not adjacent

The term 'adjacency pair' suggests that the response will necessarily be 'adjacent' or near to the 'initiation'. However, this is rather misleading because frequently in practice the response move can be at some distance from the initiation move. Look at the following example, which contains as many as three adjacency pairs, and notice how the pairs are structured.

1   A: Can I borrow your car?
2   B: When?

3   A: This afternoon
4   B: For how long?
5   A: A couple of hours
6   B: Okay.

(Silverman, 1998:106)

The conversation starts in line 1 with an initiating move which is a request. However, the response is delayed until line 6 when B eventually agrees. In line 2, instead of immediately responding to line 1, B begins his own new adjacency pair, which in this case is a request for information. This move is termed an *insertion sequence* Schelgoff, 1972; Levinson, 1983–84 because it is inserted between the two parts of the initial adjacency pair. Lines 4 and 5 are another insertion sequence. However, consider this example:

A: that wasn't the guy I met, was it – when we saw the building? -
B: saw it where –
A: when I went over to Chetwynd Road
B: yes

(Clark, 1996:200)

When the sequence which is inserted is not directly related to the main pair, as is the case here, it is termed a *side sequence* rather than an insertion sequence.

These examples illustrate a number of important points about adjacency pairs. Firstly, they can be combined in real discourse in quite subtle ways, with one or more parts inserted between the parts of another pair. Secondly, what is fascinating is that speakers (and indeed writers) can for the most part expertly (but instinctively, without conscious awareness of what they are doing) follow these quite complex operations so as to achieve what they want in discourse and society. This means, thirdly, that if we as analysts look closely for and at adjacency pairs in real interactions, they can offer a valuable insight into what the conversants are doing and seeking to do. For this reason adjacency pairs are an important part of the analytical toolkit, and will be seen again in the analyses in later chapters.

A final point which this example illustrates is that, as noted above, the two parts of a pair might not be 'adjacent' at all. In fact, since adjacency pairs occur in writing as well as in speech (for example, in emails, text messages, birthday greetings cards) there might be a considerable time lag in the answers. For example, there is frequently a lag of hours between text message pairs, and I have received Christmas cards with messages replying a year later to my previous year's greeting, a time lag of a full year between initiation and response! These are no less adjacency pairs than those we find in oral interaction, so the discussion of such pairs can contribute to our understanding of written as well as spoken interactions. (Indeed we will draw on them when analysing courtroom discourse in Chapter 7, and online discourse and text messaging in Chapter 8). This again illustrates how important adjacency pairs are to language behaviour, as an essential part of the *interacting* discourse mode, which is in turn a significant part in many *genres*, and therefore of central importance to the discourse analyst.

Turn-taking

Another important part of the *interacting* discourse mode is the way in which speakers and writers take and give *turns* as they interact. Turns have been described as follows:

> Turn is the fundamental unit of description in conversation analysis. It can be defined as the length of time a speaker holds the floor. Length and turn constructional units are constantly negotiated by speakers as they interact. A turn can be anything from any audible sound, to a single word, a clause, a sentence, a narrative. (Jupp, 2006:42)

In practice speakers (and also writers in some written interaction, though not in the same ways) are sensitive to the moments when turns might be given and taken. Jupp puts it as follows, referring to the 'turn-taking system', and explaining what is known as the *transition relevant place*:

> Another feature of this type of organization is projectability. Through the turn-taking system, hearers can detect first possible completion of the current speaker's turn. This point is called <u>transition relevant place</u>, that is the moment at which change of speaker may take place. Turn-allocational techniques centre around three options:
>
> 1. a current speaker may select a next speaker (for example, asking a question);
> 2. if (1) is not used, then parties may self-select in starting to talk;
> 3. if (2) is not used, then the current speaker may continue to talk.
>   (Jupp, 2006:42 emphasis in original)

Just as analysis of adjacency pairs is a useful tool for the discourse analyst, so the analysis of turn-taking behaviour can also can give insights into patterns of language behaviour. Both are important *features* of many texts, spoken and written, which help to achieve the text's function.

Perceptions and reality in analysing interaction

When writers invent dialogue they tend to present it as relatively ordered and neat, in stark contrast to the apparent chaos of transcripts of real-life interaction. This contrast is illustrated in the two texts below. The first is an attempt at representing a job interview, in a book designed for language learners, while the second is a transcript of an authentic interview. The first arguably represents our mental model or genre of how interviews 'should' work, whereas the second shows how participants in practice negotiate inter-actively, drawing on their genre expectations but also achieving other social purposes. This is the first text; note how orderly it is:

Job Interview 1

	Mr. Richards:	Good morning Mr Plant. Do sit down.
1	Christopher:	Thank you.
2	Mr. Richards:	First of all I'd like you to tell me a bit about what you've been doing.
	Christopher:	Well, I left school after I'd done my A levels.
3	Mr. Richards:	What subjects did you take?
4	Christopher:	French, German and Art.
5	Mr. Richards:	Art?
6	Christopher:	Well, I really wanted to study art. But a friend of my father's offered me a job. He's an accountant in the City.
7	Mr. Richards:	I see. In your application, you say that you only spent nine months with this firm of account-ants. Why was that?
8	Christopher:	Well to be quite honest, I didn't like it – so I got a place at the Art College.
9	Mr. Richards:	Did your father mind?
10	Christopher	Well, he was quite disappointed at first. He's an accountant too, you see.
11	Mr. Richards:	Have you any brothers or sisters?

(Abbs *et al.*, 1979:49–50, quoted in Cook, 1989)

The authors of this interview (perhaps to help the language learners) have made the turns and turn-taking very neat and organised. There are no side sequences or insertion sequences here (though to be fair it is true that in a formal job interview there might be fewer than in everyday conversation).

Furthermore, each speaker completes his turn perfectly, with no hint of hesitation or interruption. Each turn offers a perfect answer to the previous – this time the parts of the adjacency pairs are indeed neatly 'adjacent' to each other. In terms of 'topic placement', again we see a high level of organisation, with the interviewer succeeding in guiding the topics exactly according to our idealised notion of the genre. In short, the text matches an ideal, commonsense idea of how interaction in general works, as well as our stylised sense (our genre) of the job interview. But is discourse in *interacting* discourse mode really as neat as this?

The second interview, below, gives the lie to this impression of order and neatness. This is an authentic text, unlike the invented one above, and it shows the ways in which our *genre schema* of the job interview, our stylised ideal representation of it, (similar to the invented example above) meshes with the reality in some areas, but diverges from it quite starkly in others.

Job Interview 2

12	Interviewee:	Hallo
13	Gilbey:	Hallo. Do have a seat
14	Interviewee:	Thank you very much.
15	Gilbey:	Well thank you very much indeed for coming today. Very pleased to see you
16	Interviewee:	*(inaudible)*
17	Gilbey:	Perhaps I ought to start by introducing us all . em my name's Mr Gilbey I'm Assistant County Personnel Officer
18	Interviewee:	mhm
19	Gilbey:	This is Mr ... Tibbles who's a ... personnel officer and this is Rob Woodhull who's the administrative officer who would be your immediate
20	Interviewee:	Ah yes
21	Gilbey:	superior... if you were to get the job ... did you have any trouble getting here today
22	Interviewee:	No *(inaudible)*
23	Gilbey:	Car parking OK?
24	Interviewee:	Well I came on the bus today actually
25	Gilbey:	Did you?
26	Interviewee:	And the bus was on time yes
27	Gilbey:	That's a bit of a walk up is it it it's raining out there? Did you...
28	Interviewee:	Oh no
29	Gilbey:	manage to keep dry
30	Interviewee:	It's not it's not far from the bus stop actually
31	Gilbey:	Fine . Right – now ... just to start by em asking you
		(Cheepen, 1988: 31, transcription as in the original)

The formal greetings and other formulae in the opening lines do seem to conform to our expectation of a job interview genre. However, the actual interaction quickly diverges from the genre expectation because one of the participants, Mr. Gilbey, chooses to add some friendly informality to the daunting formal situation, perhaps to relax the job candidate (lines 17–32). In other ways also this example demonstrates how authentic interaction patterns, such as use of adjacency pairs, turn-taking behaviour, actually operate in interaction. It offers examples of straightforward adjacency pairing (lines 12 and 13), and of interesting negotiation and *repair* (lines 23–26 and 27). The point to make here is that the analyst can start by identifying the discourse mode as interacting, and on that basis can draw on tools such as analysis of adjacency pairs, turn-taking behaviour and so on, so as to explain the main purposes of the participants.

Summary: interacting

In brief, then, the interacting discourse mode as we define it here has the following features. Note again that although the discussion above has focussed on speech, this discourse mode could also apply to written interaction.

Whereas with other discourse modes it is possible to predict particular verb forms and other grammatical features as typical (for example, in *narrating* discourse mode we expect frequent past tense forms), in *interacting* discourse mode it is not so easy to identify particular grammar or lexis characteristic of the discourse mode, apart from question forms, since interaction can be in written form or spoken, and can in effect use any grammar or lexis. It is characterised more by participant behaviour than by aspects of grammatical or lexical form, so its characteristics are largely confined to those identified in Table 4.4.

Before turning to look at other discourse modes, we could usefully ask ourselves how the interacting discourse mode operates in practice. If you think about a university lecture, we can see that it mostly consists of one person speaking (one turn) and therefore not many adjacency pairs. However, at the end there may be a period of questioning and answering, in which we

Table 4.4 Features of the interacting discourse mode

1. Turn-taking and turn-giving behaviour, including turns, pauses, overlaps.
2. Sequencing patterns typified by the frequent use of adjacency pairs.
3. A high incidence of question forms (part of turn-giving strategies).

could see more adjacency pairs and more turn-taking and turn-giving. The Lecture genre, as we typically conceive it, could therefore be characterised in terms of one of its defining features, namely by these particular patterns of turns and turn-taking, quite different from the pattern we see in other forms of linguistic interaction. To put it another way, each genre which makes use of the *interacting* discourse mode will deploy different patterns of turns and turn-taking and different uses of adjacency pairs, and this in part is what allows us to define it and to distinguish it from other genres.

In the next chapter, when we look at examples of spoken texts, we will see in greater detail how these features work in practice, in other words how turn-taking, adjacency pairs and other features of the interacting discourse mode are used in different genres and help to define those genres. For example we will look in more detail at a sample of conversation, so as to illustrate more clearly the complexities of adjacency pairs and of turns, as well as repairs, and our skills in dealing with them as we speak.

4.4 Describing

The third discourse mode to be discussed is that of *describing*. Consider the text from a charity leaflet, focussing on a girl called Vestina, in Illustration 4.1.

The *function* of the text is clearly *persuasive*, attempting to encourage us to donate money. One of the main *features* of the text is its extended use of the *describing* discourse mode. A few *events* are mentioned briefly (for example, that her parents died when she was small), in a nod towards *narrating* discourse mode, but here they are designed to explain what is predominantly a description of Vestina's situation.

The description is achieved by frequent use of structures typical of this discourse mode, such as the Subject-Predicator-Complement (SPC) clause structure described by Jeffries (2006:129,138), as in these examples:

Subject	Predicator	Complement
Vestina Gundy	is	14, HIV positive and from Zambia
She	's	a bright spark
...she	's	tiny for her age
...Vestina	's not	a statistic
She	's	a child

This use of *intensive* verbs (such as *be, seem, become, appear*) along with verbs of change (such as *make*) and verbs of perception (*think, believe, consider*), (types discussed in Jeffries, 2006) is common in this discourse mode. We recall the earlier example of the travel webpage text about Sydney using *describing* mode

For Vestina, shoes mean school. And school means a future

Vestina Gunda is 14, HIV positive and from Zambia. She's tiny for her age. Poor health means she coughs constantly. But she's a bright spark. And an education could transform her chances in life.

Both Vestina's parents died of HIV-related illnesses. Now she lives with her grandparents, who adore her. But they are struggling to look after Vestina, her sister and six of her cousins – all orphans.

Our partner organisation, the Arch Diocese of Lusaka (ADL) has been working with the family to make sure she can go to school.

Vestina's background could easily condemn her to a life of poverty and exploitation, bad health and an early death. But if she can get an education, her chances will improve dramatically. Statistically, every year of education causes life expectancy to rise.* Of course, Vestina's not a statistic. She's a child. And you could help a child like her by giving just £2 a month.

* Ricci & Zachariadis, Longevity and Education: A Macroeconomic Perspective, 2007

Can £2 a month really send a child to school?

Illustration 4.1   Excerpt from a Christian Aid fundraising leaflet (2007)

in similar ways. As Jeffries puts it – and the point applies also to other descriptive texts as well as travel brochures: 'One of the reasons why such structures are common in travel brochures is that they enable the writer to make quite bold statements without being at risk of contradiction. The intensive verb acts as an equals sign, making the sentence appear to be stating a given truth whereby the subject and the complement are clearly identical'. (Jeffries 2006:133). Smith offers further characterisation of this mode in general, which can apply to the Vestina text and also, as she notes, to travel writing. Her point about the time dimension in describing mode is also pertinent:

Descriptive passages tend to focus on specifics: particular objects, people, mental states…Time is static or suspended. There are no significant changes or advancements. The entities introduced in descriptions are usually states, ongoing events, athelic events. Description is predominant in travel writing; it appears in fiction, and most other genres. Descriptive passages progress spatially through a scene. (Smith, 2003:28)

Table 4.5   Features of the describing discourse mode

Features of the describing discourse mode	Examples from the text
1. Frequent use of intensive verbs such as be, become, seem, appear (Jeffries, 2006; cf. 'Relational Processes' in Bloor and Bloor 2004)	Vestina Gunda is 14... She's tiny for her age...
2. Frequent use of the verb 'have' to describe features: 'She has brown hair'	-
3. Verbs in the Present Simple and Past Simple, to describe current situations, or other verbal forms such as the Present Progressive to describe ongoing situations or activities	Now she lives [Present Simple] with her grandparents, who adore [Present Simple] her. But they are struggling [Present Progressive] to look after Vestina, her sister and six of her cousins ...
4. Frequent use of descriptive adjectives	HIV positive, tiny, poor, bright
5. Adverbs of frequency used to describe actions or verbs	constantly

So in the *describing* discourse mode there is less of a focus on events than in *narrating,* and more focus on people, places and things. To summarise, this discourse mode is typically characterised by the existence of the features set out in Table 4.5. (Examples again come from English. Other languages will of course use different structural and lexical resources.)

In Chapter 8 we will see that other genres, such as Lonely Hearts advertisements, also draw extensively on the *describing* discourse mode as one of their features.

4.5 Reporting

Chapter 8 provides an extensive discussion of News reports, at which point I will address a number of issues related to the *reporting* discourse mode as used in practice. In this chapter, then, it is necessary only to set out the essential features of this mode, in particular to distinguish it from *narrating.* Again, Smith offers a useful account of what she terms 'reports':

> Reports give an account of situations from the temporal standpoint of the reporter. They are, like narrative, mainly concerned with events and states. The significant difference between these modes is that, in Reports, the relation to Speech Time determines temporal advancement.

Situations are related to Speech Time, rather than to each other.(Smith, 2003:29–30)

The main difference, then, between *narrating* and *reporting* discourse modes relates to what Smith calls *Speech Time*, since a report is assumed to be relating events from the point of view of the person doing the reporting. Situations in this mode, in other words, are set out in relation to Speech Time and not in relation to each other, as they are in narrating. One result of this is a high frequency of verbs, adverbs and other forms with 'deictic' reference:

> Reports conform to the basic speech situation, in which the speaker is central. This centrality is signaled by adverbials such as here, now, last week, which take Speech Time as their orientation, or anchor. Such forms are known as 'deictic'. 'Deixis' is the term for linguistic forms that are anchored to the time of speech. The present tense conveys that a situation holds now, the past tense conveys that a situation precedes now. (Smith, 2003:29–30)

In her earlier book in this series, Jeffries describes *deixis* as follows: 'Deixis refers to the capacity of some words to shift their reference, depending on who says (or writes) them and/or the speaker's position in space and time' (Jeffries, 2006:190). This is an important concept in language as a whole; as Chapman puts it, in English 'the whole grammatical system of verb tenses is deictic' (Chapman, 2006:123). In the discourse mode of *reporting*, since the events are conveyed from the speakers' 'here and now', or from Speech Time as Smith calls it, the result is a high frequency of forms with deictic reference to that particular place and time. Such expressions occur in almost every printed news report, with clear deictic reference to the time and place of writing (though this is less true of online reporting, which could be read many days later). A particularly important feature in this respect in English

Table 4.6 Features of the reporting discourse mode

Features of the reporting discourse mode	Examples
1. Deictic verbs with implicit reference to the place of speaking	'come' 'go' (Jeffries, 2006: 190)
2. Deictic use of the Present Perfect tense	the government has announced
3. Deictic noun phrases	'this man', 'that boy' (Chapman, 2006:123)
4. Deictic adverbs of time	tomorrow, yesterday, on Wednesday, last week
5. Deictic adverbs of place	here, there

is the use of the Present Perfect tense, since it is often employed to imply a direct relationship between the recent past and the current time of speaking, as in 'the government has announced...'

I summarise some of the features of the *reporting* mode in Table 4.6.

4.6 Instructing

The last of the discourse modes to be considered in this chapter is termed *instructing*, not included in Smith's discussion but nonetheless quite common. An example of a text which uses this discourse mode extensively is the 'Washing Clothes' text discussed earlier:

> First you arrange items into different groups... If you have to go somewhere else due to lack of facilities that is the next step; otherwise, you are pretty much set. (Bransford and Johnson, 1972:400)

The same text offers a good instance of switching between discourse modes, since besides its extensive use of *instructing*, it also includes aspects of *describing* in the phrases 'it is better to do too few things at once than too many' and: 'A mistake can be expensive as well'. It therefore demonstrates how texts can mix discourse modes for various purposes, and also how attention to the discourse modes could potentially allow the analyst to identify interesting textual patterns.

A genre which makes extensive use of the *instructing discourse mode* is the Recipe. We all have in our minds an idealised *genre* of Recipe, which is probably similar for most of us, albeit with individual and cultural differences here and there. Most people's genre schema of recipes would probably include a picture of the completed food, a list of the ingredients, then a sequence of instructions as to how to prepare the dish. It might also include other information such as the number of hungry people which the dish will provide for, and so on.

If we think about this genre we can see that there are various elements of *describing discourse mode* (for instance the list of ingredients is a sort of description) but that the main element of recipes is drawn from the *instructing discourse mode* in the steps which the cook needs to follow. Here again, then, we see how a genre can draw primarily on one discourse mode, but make use of others in various flexible ways. The key is *flexibility*, and the key aim is that the genre, and then the text itself, will achieve their intended *functions*.

We can now turn to consider an interesting example, a recipe (Ilustration 4.2), but not quite what we would expect. What the charity is doing here is

Life FOOD

A recipe for disaster

Ingredients
1 World Trade Organisation
1 International Monetary Fund
1 World Bank
A handful of rich countries
As many poor countries as you can get

First take the international organisations (WTO, IMF, World Bank) and use them to force open the markets of poor countries. Next cut off the support poor-country governments give their farmers.

Using plenty of subsidies, prepare the following in the rich countries, and pour generously over poor countries.

• Frozen chicken from Europe and the US – ship to Ghana where it will be sold more cheaply than Ghanaian chicken.

• Rice from the US – dump on Honduras where it will force local farmers out of business.

• Plenty of European tomato paste – smear over west Africa's markets until locally grown tomatoes have turned rotten.

This one always comes out nicely for us. World's richest countries

International trade rules are destroying the livelihoods of millions of people in the world's poorest countries. Join the Trade Justice Campaign and help make trade work for the world's poorest communities.

Get cooking – send off these cards today.

 Christian Aid is campaigning as a member of the Trade Justice Movement – calling for trade justice, not free trade – with rules weighted to benefit poor people and the environment.

Illustration 4.2 Excerpt from a Christian Aid fundraising leaflet: recipe

offering us a 'spoof' or parody of a recipe, in what is actually a leaflet, part of a charity campaign. It draws on our genre expectations (and it would not work without them) and then ironically places different elements in the various parts of the recipe. The text is therefore highly intertextual, since it relies heavily on knowledge of the Recipe genre for its effectiveness. At first sight it looks like a recipe we might have at home in the kitchen – it is apparently torn out of a magazine; it has a small yellow reminder note on it which ironically says 'This one always comes out nicely for us. World's richest countries', parodying a note which might be added to a recipe as a reminder, or a note to a friend about a genuine recipe. It then follows the pattern we expect from recipes in having the ingredients at the top, then the procedure in *instructing discourse mode*, followed by other elements. In other words, this text draws

Table 4.7 Features of the instructing discourse mode

Features of the instructing discourse mode	Examples
1. Frequent use of the imperative form of the verb	Cut the onions
2. Frequent use of the Present Simple tense to describe typical actions – avoiding the imperative so as to sound less dictatorial	'First you arrange items into different groups.' ('Washing' text)
3. Use of adjectivals to specify aspects of the elements to be used	*Fresh* parsley, *runner* beans, *coconut* milk
4. Adverbs of sequence to tell us the order of events	First, then, next, thirdly

on our genre schema, and on the typical recipe *instructing* discourse mode, to make an ironic intertextual point.

To summarise, some of the key features of the *instructing discourse mode* are set out in Table 4.7, again focusing on texts in English.

4.7 Summary

This chapter has discussed some of the main discourse modes so as to allow for their identification in some of the texts to be analysed in the chapters to come. It has not been possible to describe all of the discourse modes exhaustively, but the discussion here should at least facilitate their identification in various texts in ways which can open up possible avenues for analysis. For example, if a text appears to make use of the *reporting* discourse mode, the analyst can look in particular for deictic features; if the text appears to be in *narrating* mode, the analyst can look for patterns of verb tenses and adverbs; if the text appears to use extensive *interacting*, then an approach looking at adjacency pairs and turn-taking (in speech or writing) could be fruitful.

The discourse modes are offered, then, as potentially useful indicators of the kinds of features which a text might employ in order to achieve its functions or purposes. They can be used in order to open up a text for analysis, if the text is of a kind suited to this kind of approach. However, they are not intended to constitute an all-embracing method, or to be employed in any rigid way. This will become clearer in the next chapter, where I draw on the discussion so far on the nature of discourse, genre and discourse modes so as to set out a broad heuristic approach to discourse analysis in general, in which attention to genre and discourse mode have their place, as preparation for the more detailed discussion of spoken and written texts in the second half of the book.

Analysing Discourse 5

The analyst seeking to develop a fully comprehensive methodological approach to discourse would face at least two major obstacles, namely the sheer variety and also the 'hybridity' of texts in the real world (Chouliaraki and Fairclough, 1999), both of which any proposed approach would have to address. It is noteworthy, in this regard, that those approaches to discourse which have made most progress in recent years have confined themselves to relatively clearly defined domains of discourse and relatively non-hybrid texts, for example work in Conversational Analysis and academic writing. While scholars in these and other specialist areas have made progress in developing methodological procedures and approaches which serve to illuminate the particular texts, genres and domains on which they focus, none would claim that those approaches can then straightforwardly be applied to the full range of other texts, spoken and written, encountered around us.

This sheer heterogeneity and hybridity of textual data, then, in conjunction with the fact that each analyst approaches her or his data from different viewpoints and with differing intentions, means that it is illusory to hope for a single 'Discourse Analysis Method' or a set of 'hard-and-fast rules or methods' (Rapley, 2007:5) which can lead us step-by-step into the analysis of every text we wish to examine. For this and other reasons it seems more satisfactory on methodological and indeed on practical grounds to avoid attempting any such single approach to analysis, but to consider discourse analysis more like a 'craft skill', as some writers have suggested (Potter, 1997; Rapley, 2007). This suggests the need not for any fixed method of doing discourse analysis but for what is sometimes called a 'heuristic', a procedure through which each analyst can interrogate each text in a systematic way, drawing on a range of approaches, techniques and procedures to suit the text and context at hand.

Johnstone argues for such an approach, describing her preferred method as 'a set of discovery procedures for systematic application or a set of topics for systematic consideration' (Johnstone, 2002:9). These, she continues, 'do not need to be followed in any particular order, and there is no fixed way of following them. A heuristic is not a mechanical set of steps to follow, and there is no guarantee that following it will result in a single ideal explanation.' Furthermore, a heuristic 'is not a theory. It is a step in analysis which may help you see what sorts of theory you need in order to connect the observations about discourse you make as you use the heuristic with general statements about language, human life, or society' (Johnstone 2002:9).

Johnstone's heuristic for approaching discourse begins with a set of six aspects which in her view help to shape texts, many of which have also been addressed in Chapter 2 above. For example the first aspect which she invites the analyst to address is: 'Discourse is shaped by the world and discourse shapes the world' (Johnstone 2002:9), an essentially constructionist position. She then illustrates ways in which the analyst can follow up this insight when approaching a text. However, given that my approach to discourse differs in several ways from Johnstone's, particularly in my focus on genre and discourse modes as one way of approaching texts, and also given my preference for basing my model on a set of questions rather than a set of statements, the heuristic which follows will draw on her broad approach, but will not borrow from her framework directly.

5.1 Discourse analysis as a research method

It might be assumed, from Johnstone's description of a heuristic above, that it represents a relatively *laissez-faire* attitude to research, as if any approach will do. This would be a mistake. A heuristic does not insist on 'a mechanical set of steps to follow', but it does nonetheless insist on 'systematic application'. In this regard discourse analysis is taken to resemble other broadly qualitative, interpretive research methods in the social sciences in allowing a degree of interpretive flexibility, but always on the condition that the researcher operates within strict and rigorous boundaries in all areas of research approach and procedure. In qualitative research in general, according to Holliday (1997:213), '[t]he scientific rigour and system are in the discipline of researcher procedure which comprises tight rules concerning how the researcher relates to and writes about the research environment'.

So too in the analysis of discourse, the analyst is expected not only to operate systematically and in a balanced way with regard to the discourse data, but also to describe the approach to analysis in a transparent, full and systematic manner, and to set out the findings with no less transparency, 'showing its workings every single time' (Holliday, 2001:8) in such a way that other researchers can fully appreciate the weight of evidence and the validity of the conclusions drawn, to the extent that they can even repeat some or all of the analysis to ascertain its credibility (see Gee, 2005).

The upshot of this is that although the set of guidelines to be outlined here may appear to be less constraining than a more directive method, it nonetheless expects the analyst to set out fully, in any account of his or her research, the precise way in which the analysis was conducted and in which the conclusions were drawn from and warranted by the discourse data. If the analyst is disciplined and transparent in carrying out and presenting the analysis, there is no reason why the approach taken should not form the basis of an in-depth analysis of quality and credibility.

5.2 Approaches to discourse

As was noted in my introduction, a central aim of this book is to assist in and facilitate the practical analysis of texts. As I also noted in the introduction, this approach is based on a set of questions concerning

- *What* the particular text under analysis does or achieves;
- *How* it achieves it; and
- *Why* it seeks to do so.

Having considered in the last four chapters the nature of comprehension, discourse, genre and the discourse modes, these three initial questions can now be developed and expanded so as to offer a fuller set of procedures for dealing with texts under analysis.

This heuristic is laid out here as a set of broad questions for the analyst to consider, with an emphasis on clarity and usability, in the expectation that the approach will be given rigour and transparency through the way in which it is adopted by the researcher, and through the discipline of the researcher who uses it. In the account below, the heuristic is glossed with notes on how it can be used in the practice of analysis, and its use will then be illustrated in more detail through the partial analysis of one example, before serving as the basis for the fuller analyses of the wide variety of texts in the coming chapters. Given that an analyst frequently studies patterns across more than one text the heuristic will refer to texts in the plural, assuming that the analyst is concerned with a corpus, although the approach can equally be used for a single text.

5.3 A broad heuristic for analysing discourse

In line with the broadly functional view of genres outlined in Chapter 3, the heuristic adopted here starts from consideration of what the texts in question achieve or aim to achieve, which means their function or functions, broadly speaking. To put it simply, the first question for the analyst is 'What do these texts do or aim to do?' In practice, of course, the two parts of this question might not give the same answer, since a text or author might aim to do something and in fact fail, or achieve something else. That is a possibility which the analyst will bear in mind, but nonetheless it is taken as a viable starting point that the main initial question relates to the texts' function, impact and effect, in general terms.

That is the *what* question; the second question then concerns *how* the texts achieve this. This could be answered narrowly, in terms of linguistic features alone for example, but given the emphasis in our definition of discourse in Chapter 2 on context, a fuller answer will usually seek to include a range of non-linguistic factors also, such as aspects of the context, visual appearance and so on. To put it another way, the analyst will look at all the aspects of the texts in their context (broadly understood) so as to explain *how* they achieve their impact or function.

The third question, then, is *why*. This concerns consideration of the social, political or ideological positioning of the texts in the world, asking why they seek to do what they do, and how that relates to broader social and ideological considerations.

I have set these questions out in a particular sequence, but this is not to imply that the analyst must always take each one strictly in turn. It may happen that in practice the question of *what* a text does will be revisited and re-addressed after consideration of *how* and *why*. The heuristic can now be set out for easy reference in a more schematic format.

A *The analyst first considers the texts in context, so as to identify their impact or effect in broad terms.*

   1. **What do the texts achieve or aim to achieve?**
      - What is the impact of the texts on the readers or listeners, cognitively, socially and in other ways?
      - What is the function of the texts, or what do they *do*?
      - In the case of texts with more than one participant, e.g. texts in *interacting* mode, what is the function of each participant's contribution?
      - What is the wider impact of the texts, beyond the individual reader or listener?
      - What other impacts or functions can be identified?

B *The analyst can then consider how the texts achieve their impact or effect. In essence, the analyst seeks to identify the ways in which particular features of the texts relate to their function(s)*

2. *How* do they achieve their impact or function? Consider these questions, as relevant.

- What are the core *features* of the texts, and how do they relate to the overall *function(s)*? These features might include reference to the following:
  a. What specific *genre* or *genres* do the texts draw on?
  b. What aspects of text *structure* do the texts employ so as to achieve their function(s)?
  c. What *discourse modes* do the texts draw on, and in what combinations?
  d. What *layout, auditory* or *visual* resources does the text or texts draw on?
  e. What *intertextual* links or relationships are significant?
  f. What other strategies or techniques do the texts employ, either as part of the genre or discourse mode, or apart from them?
  g. What *phonological, lexical* and *grammatical* resources do the texts draw on in achieving their effects?
- What other resources do the texts employ in order to achieve their effects?

C *At this point the analyst could consider why the texts do what they do, including the following questions as relevant.*

3. *Why* do the texts seek to do this?

- What are the socio-political and ideological underpinnings of the text?
- What do the texts seek to foreground and why?
- What do the texts seek to obscure or 'background', and why?

D *This last stage may afford opportunities for linking the discussion with theoretical considerations in the way which Johnstone outlined, seeking 'to connect the observations about discourse you make as you use the heuristic with general statements about language, human life, or society'* (Johnstone, 2002:9).

This heuristic is designed to be seen in the light of the fuller discussion on the nature of discourse and genre in earlier chapters, and also in the light of the examples to come in later chapters. In line with the discussion in this chapter, it offers an approach to discourse which includes consideration of the discourse modes, but only in conjunction with consideration of the full range of other possible features which might be part of the texts' impact or function.

Table 5.1 Illustration of the heuristic in the analysis of a sample text

Questions	In analysing the sample text ('Vestina', p. 89), the analyst could consider these issues:
1. What does the text achieve?	
• What is the impact of the text on the readers or listeners, cognitively, socially and in other ways?	-cognitive dimensions: e.g. the informations conveyed -emotive dimension: feelings evoked -impact on reader's sense of self, identity and relationship with the characters
• What is the function of the text, or what does it do?	-persuasive / promotional / to attract funds
• What is the wider impact of the text, beyond the individual reader or listener?	-possible impact on societal awareness, global issues, political structures etcetera
• What other impacts can be identified?	-impact on education?
2. _How_ does it achieve it?	
What are the features of the text, and how do they relate to the overall function?	
a. What aspects of text _structure_ does the text employ so as to achieve its function?	-Possible modified problem-solution structure
b. What main discourse modes does the text draw on?	-Describing, narrating
c. What layout, auditory or visual resources does the text draw on?	-Photos, colours, layout etcetera.
d. What _intertextual_ links or relationships are significant?	-no obvious specific intertextual references
e. What other strategies or techniques does the text use, either as part of the genre or discourse mode, or apart from them?	-Use of characters, emotive appeal, reasoning
f. What _phonological, lexical_ and _grammatical_ resources does the text draw on in achieving its effects?	-analysis of verb tenses and lexical choices to support the main function/aims of the text
3. _Why_ does the text seek to do this?	**- social aims, political aims**
• What are the socio-political and ideological underpinnings of the text?	- the ideology behind the text
• What does the text seek to foreground and why?	-poverty, inequality, children
• What does the text seek to obscure or 'background', and why?	-other dimensions of the context, such as the adult participants

Sample analysis

It will by now be clear that the above heuristic and its constituent questions are not intended to be applied in a rigidly mechanical way to any piece of discourse, but offer a general approach to analysis which can, it is argued, offer a useful means of addressing discourse if used intelligently and flexibly. The heuristic will be employed in a general way in the chapters which follow, in the course of which the proposed approach should become clearer, but at this point it is also worth offering a brief illustration of how it can be used when approaching a text for analysis.

The way in which the set of questions can help the analyst to approach a text is therefore set out schematically in Table 5.1 with reference to the charity leaflet about Vestina which was discussed on p. 89. This is not an analysis in itself, but rather an illustration of how the procedure described above can be employed in broad terms, by focusing first on the *impact* and *function* of the text, as assessed by the analyst, then on its *features*, considering how these achieve the function or not. Finally it addresses the issue of *why* the author or text attempts to achieve its impact, which aims to relate the text to its sociological and ideological context and intentions.

In this illustration the questions in the heuristic have therefore been followed in sequence, so that in the second column are suggested ways in which the analyst might answer each question in relation to the 'Vestina' text. However, as has been noted above, the heuristic does not in fact require any particular ordering of questions, since – in tune with its status as heuristic rather than method – it allows for flexibility in terms of what questions can be considered and when. For this reason an analyst confronted with a different text might decide to pose the questions in a different order altogether.

In the chapters to come this heuristic will be used on texts from a variety of domains, spoken and written. One aim of this will be to show the way in which the heuristic outlined above can assist in the analyses of a variety of texts. However an important additional aim of the next chapters is to extend and add to the heuristic as it stands. In this chapter it has been set out in its barest bones, in terms of how to approach texts in the broadest terms. As it is applied to the analysis of a variety of texts in the next chapters, however, numerous questions and issues will emerge, discussion of which should enrich and expand it in a number of ways. Using the heuristic in these sample texts will therefore both exemplify how it can be used in the actual analysis of discourse, and will also sharpen and extend it in the process.

6 Spoken Genres: Conversations and Classrooms

The first half of this book considered the nature of language comprehension, the nature of discourse and the nature of genre in principle. It surveyed the literature and the state of thinking in the field of discourse and genre, and on that basis it elaborated a set of working definitions of the main concepts. In the previous chapter, on the basis of the discussion in the first four, I then set out a broad approach to the analysis of discourse, proposing that we start with *what* those texts are doing, that is, the impact or function of the text or texts as understood in their context, then examine *how* they do it, by looking at the various features of those texts to see in general terms how they achieve those effects, and also considering *why* those texts are operating in this way. This is the heuristic on the basis of which we can now proceed.

Although efforts were made throughout those chapters to illustrate the discussion through authentic examples of actual texts, and to work inductively as far as possible in line with the aims set out in the introduction, the first half of the book was, of necessity, relatively theoretical. The second half will offer a contrast, since now the focus of attention will be on an array of (I believe) interesting and varied texts, with a view to analysing them in accordance with the heuristic.

The range of texts is deliberately broad, covering conversation, legal texts, classroom discourse, lonely hearts ads, advertisements, newspaper reports, sports reports, political speeches and more besides. The sheer variety of examples might mean that in places I have sacrificed analytical depth for the sake of breadth, but my aim is not to offer full analyses of any of the texts discussed, even if that were possible. Instead the aim is to examine each text only to the extent that it illustrates my approach, and raises for discussion issues central to discourse analysis as a way of enriching the heuristic set out in Chapter 5.

For example, in this chapter the discussion begins with a sample of conversation, but the aim is not exhaustively to analyse one conversational text in all its details, but rather to use the examination of that text in order to set out some of the possible approaches to conversations of this type, and to draw out some useful lessons for anyone wanting to analyse such texts in future. For a fuller analysis of each type of text the reader will then be able to go to the specialist literature, for example the vast literature on Conversation Analysis, since here the main purpose is instead to prepare the toolkit, in other words to establish, chapter by chapter, a set of *approaches, tools and techniques* which can potentially be used in future analyses. Chapter 10 will then set out a summary of the approaches and tools which have been discussed throughout the book, and will discuss, in conclusion, two case studies of fuller analyses and how they were carried out in practice.

6.1 Conversation

Turning to conversation, not everything which is commonly understood by the term would be classified by linguists as such. Cook considers that talk can be termed 'conversation' only if it has these features:

1. It is not primarily necessitated by a practical task
2. Any unequal power of participants is partially suspended
3. The number of the participants is small
4. Turns are quite short
5. Talk is primarily for the participants not for an outside audience

(Cook 1989: 51)

By this definition, the discourse on a TV chat show would not be classed as conversation as it does not meet the last criterion (Cutting, 2002). Let us look at an example of genuine conversation.

Buying dress material

In the text below two young women are discussing some material which they have recently bought in the market. I will present it almost exactly as it appeared in the original (Cheepen, 1988:102–3), the aim being to show some of the complexities of authentic transcript data and also to offer a flavour of real analysis. There is little punctuation, reflecting the speed of the flow of conversation, and only a few markings such as <.> and <+> to indicate short and long pauses, <* *> around a word to show when it overlaps with another word or words from the next speaker's turn (also surrounded by <* *>), and the abbreviation *inaud.* to indicate an inaudible part. I have given only the first part of Cheepen's text, and I have also given the women invented names to make the discussion easier.

Turns

1. *Clare: I've got some stuff to show you. I went and bought this this morning cause my mum said she'd treat me she wants me to do a couple for her she's going to America (inaud.)*
2. *Karen: yeh I've just made one yeh*
3. *Clare: I was rather pleased with that*
4. *Karen: yeh have you made it already*
5. *Clare: no no I've just bought it this morning*
6. *Karen: haven't you got the straps*
7. *Clare: come off the bottom*
8. *Karen: oh which one d'you get it on*
9. *Clare: I got it on the one opposite Woolworth's*
10. *Karen: yeh yeh if you get it from the other one he gives you the straps as well*
11. *Clare: yeh but that other one wasn't there today I saw it Wednesday*
12. *Karen: oh mind you I've just made one and I don't need the straps*

(Cheepen, 1988:102)

Following the procedure set out in Chapter 5, an initial question to ask (the *what* question) concerns the *function* of this text. However, it is immediately apparent that in the case of interactions such as this one each participant might well have a different aim and intention, and each utterance might have a slightly different function. This means that although we could talk generally about the function of this text as a whole (like most conversations it is arguably mostly *phatic*, that is, it concerns social relations between the two speakers) it is often more appropriate in texts which involve more than one participant to think about *each speaker's particular aim* in the discourse, and how they all manage the interaction towards achieving their aims. This means that a useful initial strategy when dealing with texts which include more than one participant is to consider not only the *function of the text as a whole*, but the aims and intentions of each participant and how those interconnect through the discourse. In our approach to discourse, in other words, initial consideration of *text function* might be complemented, when considering texts with several participants, by careful attention to *participant intentions and aims*.

   The next question is the *how* question: how does the text achieve its func-tion? This now needs to be framed in terms of each participant, to give the questions: how does each participant achieve or seek to achieve his or her aim? What *features* of the discourse contribute to the fulfilment (or failure) of these aims or intentions?

We have already seen, in relation to the text in which Gilbey was conducting a job interview (p. 86), that genuine spoken discourse is often more complex than we imagine, when we are not participants and when we do not have paralinguistic clues (such as gestures and facial expressions) or contextual clues to help us. As we read what the two women say here we need to draw on all the types of knowledge we identified in Figure 1.1, and even then we might not find the exchange fully coherent. One problem is that the participants are operating quickly and flexibly, and drawing on knowledge of each other and of the context in sometimes opaque ways. Take lines 8 and 9 when Karen asks:

> Karen: oh which one d'you get it on
> Clare: I got it on the one opposite Woolworth's

I suspect from my own knowledge of such shopping situations that she is referring to a market stall in the street, opposite the shop called Woolworth's. I assume this partly because in my home town there are just such stalls in the street in very similar situations, so I can draw on personal knowledge. This is also plausible because it fits with a later utterance in line 11, since when Karen has said in line 10 that the 'other one' is better, Clare replies: *'yeh but that other one wasn't there today I saw it Wednesday'* which suggests that she bought it not in a normal shop, but on a temporary stall which is there some days and not others. Whether or not this is true, what is clear is that the participants *themselves* have enough shared knowledge so as to be able to operate with it quickly and telegraphically, without needing to be specific – a behaviour which gives spoken interaction a speed and flow which is remarkably effective for participants, but which can cause problems for the analyst.

Topic placement and manipulation

The special point of interest in this exchange, however, is the way in which the participants manipulate and manage *topic* in order to achieve their own ends. This is the kind of area which Conversation Analysis considers particularly important, along with adjacency pair and repair analysis. A superficial view of the exchange up to this point might consider that Karen has been cooperative and even offered to give Clare some straps, but closer analysis suggests that this is not an adequate explanation of the exchange. As Cheepen notes when analysing the text, 'It is clear, just from this extract, that potential trouble has arisen here between the interactants' (Cheepen, 1988:103). Because both participants make efforts to appear friendly and positive, however, and relatively casual, this 'trouble' is not immediately apparent. Nevertheless, if we look more closely, an analysis of the adjacency pairs reveals not only the tension between them but also the strategies which each woman – very rapidly and probably only half consciously – adopts, in a kind of elaborate dance or game, to achieve certain social ends.

Clare starts the conversation with what we can call a 'fishing for compliments' strategy. This strategy appears to have received scant discussion in the CA literature, but is nonetheless quite common in real life – when I buy a new shirt I want my friends and family to admire it, so the *preferred response* to an utterance such as 'I bought this shirt today' is typically a compliment of some sort. In this case Clare has bought some dress material to make 'a couple' of dresses for her mother, and probably her mother has paid for it as a treat (though this is not very clear). The key point is that she is angling for Karen to congratulate her – the preferred response would be something like 'Wow, that is great! It's lovely, and so much of it! What a bargain! You are a genius in the material buying department!' However, Karen does not offer any such compliments. In a move reminiscent of grumpy Brian in the 'Window' dialogue (see p. 6), she withholds consent except in the briefest word 'yeh', almost as if she has not heard what Clare said. Furthermore she even tries to change the topic to talk about her own activities: *'yeh I've just made one yeh'*. Clare, rather like Ann in the 'Window' dialogue, seems not to be affected by this apparent diversionary tactic but persists, still trying to get the compliment she wants. For her part, Karen appears to refuse it, and assumes an apparently casual and relaxed air in doing so, as we can gauge from her frequent use of 'yeh' and 'oh' at the start of her responses. We could set out one partial analysis of this part of the conversation like this:

Turns	Text	Analysis
1.	Clare: I've got some stuff to show you. I went and bought this this morning cause my mum said she'd treat me she wants me to do a couple for her she's going to America (inaud.)	Adjacency opener: fishing for a compliment, praise or appreciation
2.	Karen: yeh I've just made one yeh	Displacement (or Dispreferred response?): withholds praise and attempts topic switch
3.	Clare: I was rather pleased with that	Repeats opener, still fishing!

4.	*Karen: yeh have you made it already*	*Displacement (or Dispreferred response?):* still withholds praise and attempts another topic switch with an *Adjacency opener:* information question
5.	*Clare: no no I've just bought it this morning*	Karen's topic switch has been successful. Clare cooperates with a *dispreferred response (no, instead of yes)* and justification
6.	*Karen: haven't you got the straps*	Presses her advantage with yet another topic adjustment. *Adjacency opener:* information question
7.	*Clare: come off the bottom*	*Preferred response*: explains that the straps can be made from surplus material at the bottom of the cloth
8.	*Karen: oh which one d'you get it on*	Continues to press her advantage with another enquiry. *Adjacency opener:* information request
9.	*Clare: I got it on the one opposite Woolworth's*	*Preferred response:* gives information
10.	*Karen: yeh yeh if you get it from the other one he gives you the straps as well*	*Adjacency opener:* statement of fact, but also an implied *criticism*
11.	*Clare: yeh but that other one wasn't there today I saw it Wednesday*	*Preferred response:* accepts criticism but explains
12.	*Karen: oh mind you I've just made one and I don't need the straps*	*Adjacency opener:* Offer to give the straps

In lines 2 and 4, how could we analyse Karen's responses? Clare wants a compliment or some affirmation; however, Karen does not give it, but offers another adjacency opener in each case. Some analysts would treat this as a dispreferred response; for example Schulze-Wenke suggests that 'Counter-suggestions clearly constitute a dispreferred response to a first speaker's suggestion, as they do not go along with the suggestion, but instead propose a different course of action' (Schulze-Wenke, 2005:343). Cutting also considers it a dispreferred response in cases where 'the second part does not follow on from the first' (Cutting, 2002:30), as is the case in lines 2 and 4. By contrast, other analysts would say that there is no dispreferred response here, but rather a behaviour which we could term 'displacement' (Schegloff, 2007), since rather than actually criticising the material, Karen merely avoids any response at all. The upshot of this is that Clare's 'fishing' for a compliment or support has in effect been completely bypassed by Karen's refusal to give it, or rather by Karen's successful move to sidetrack the discussion down different paths. Karen appears to have successfully used a number of discourse strategies so as to withhold the praise or support which Clare was seeking, and has then succeeded in turning the conversation to other areas. Clare, by contrast, comes across as rather more cooperative and perhaps less forceful, offering *preferred responses* and/or apologies at each stage.

The power relation appears clear – Karen is dominating the discourse and doing so by clever, subtle management of the *adjacency pairs* and of *topic placement* and adjustment. Such is the nature of natural conversation, however, generally carried out without conscious awareness, that Clare is probably only vaguely aware of what exactly is happening, and of why she is not quite getting the responses she want.

Validity and warranting

It might be thought that this analysis is extreme. Does Karen really do this? Perhaps it is unfair to suggest that Karen is so devious? This is a central question for any discourse analyst: how do we know that our interpretation is valid?

One of the central precepts of the Conversation Analysis (CA) group of researchers is that we should avoid reading into any exchange our own preconceptions of what is happening, but should be sure to *warrant* everything we deduce about any text by reference to actual elements of the exchange itself. As Heritage puts it, 'there is a strong bias [in CA] against a priori speculation about the orientations and motives of speakers and in favour of detailed examination of conversationalists' actual actions. Thus the empirical conduct of speakers is treated as the central resource out of which analysis may develop' (Heritage, 1984:243). Although this is a view typical of the CA approach in particular, and not shared by all discourse analysts, it can be a useful principle, worth remembering whenever we analyse discourse, since it prevents us from inserting our own preconceptions, or reading into texts aspects which may not be valid. So before examining Clare and Karen's interaction further, it is worth considering what exactly this 'warranting principle' means for our analysis here, and for discourse analysis in general.

When Karen made her first comment in the exchange, in line 2, we could understand it in several ways. Depending on her intonation, her facial signals, and so on she might have been understood as being very supportive or else (as I have suggested) withholding her praise and therefore being rather unsupportive. Which is correct? The important point which CA researchers would emphasise is that the only way of interpreting the exchange correctly is by seeing how the actual participants themselves responded and behaved, in other words, we must ground our interpretation solidly in what the participants themselves do and say. This means, amongst other things, looking closely at how Clare answered Karen.

Hutchby and Wooffitt (1998:15), in their discussion of the principles of CA, term this approach the 'next-turn proof procedure', and consider it to be 'the most basic tool used in CA to ensure that analyses explicate the orderly properties of talk as oriented-to accomplishments of participants, rather than being based merely on the assumptions of the analyst.' This means that we need to look at how the talk is managed by the participants themselves as a way of interpreting it in a valid way. In short, for any analysis to be considered valid and credible in the CA tradition it must demonstrate that its conclusions are drawn closely from various features of the exchange itself: it needs to be *warranted* by the data. If we want to interpret Karen's behaviour as being potentially disruptive (as Cheepen concluded) then we need to show *from evidence in the text* that the other participant, Clare, showed signs of feeling that way. In this particular case we see that in line 3 Clare in fact responds: 'I was rather pleased with that'. If she was not very concerned with getting any praise or a compliment, she could instead have followed Karen's new lead and started talking about Karen's dress, and *never returned* to her own topic at all, so the fact that she persists, albeit rather timidly, is significant.

As Hutchby and Wooffitt point out, what they call the 'next-turn proof procedure' is therefore important for determining how to analyse any utterance in interaction. However, we must be aware that this alone may not be enough – and I suggest that a better name for it might be a 'next turns proof procedure' in the plural, since in some cases in conversation it is only much later in the exchange that we can say for certain how the participants have understood an earlier comment. In this dialogue, for example, it is only after seeing Clare try several times to get the compliment she wants that we can say for certain that a conflict is apparent.

This demonstrates two important points about analysing conversation in the CA tradition, or indeed any written or spoken discourse which uses the *interacting* discourse mode. The first point is that we need to withhold our personal interpretation of any particular utterance or turn and instead focus on the evidence from the wider exchange as a whole. In a well-known passage, Sacks *et al.* point out that participants in talk themselves signal their intentions to a great extent:

> while understandings of other turns' talk are displayed to co-participants, they are available as well to professional analysts who are thereby afforded a proof criterion (and a search procedure) for the analysis of what a turn's talk is occupied with. (Sacks *et al.*,1974: 729)

They continue to explain that it is participants' understandings and not analysts' understandings which are to be given priority: *'Since it is the parties' understandings of prior turns' talk that is relevant to the construction of next turns, it is their understandings that are wanted for analysis'* (Sacks *et al.*, 1974: 729, original emphasis).

It is useful to keep in mind, therefore, that in general when analysing discourse it is not *'our* understandings' that matter but *'their, the participants'* understandings', and it is worth making efforts to unearth the latter. Not all approaches to conversation or to discourse in general would insist on this as strongly as CA does, but it is nonetheless a useful general precept. A second important point is that in our analysis we need to look not only at the utterance in question, nor even at the next utterance, but at all later (and even earlier) utterances, since these might significantly alter our understanding of the turn we are seeking to interpret. We need to make use of a 'next turns proof procedure', as well as a 'later turns proof procedure' and even at times a 'previous turns proof procedure' to warrant our interpretation of any exchange.

If we now look at the second part of the dressmaking exchange we can see how valuable it can be to follow this kind of approach if we are to interpret discourse in a valid and convincing way. Will Clare succeed in getting her compliment? Will she insist? Will Karen praise her, or change the topic completely? We can see from the next stage that Clare does indeed try repeatedly to extract the response she wants, but Karen is unyielding.

Turns

13. *Clare:* *well I mean look how much*
14. *Karen: yeh*
15. *Clare: see there's tons*
16. *Karen: I know they're ever so good*
17. *Clare: I'm ever so pleased*
18. *Karen: yeh I made one for Shirley and one for me and Shirley doesn't it's a bit too small I didn't quite have enough material four ninety nine*
19. *Clare: four four ninety*
20. *Karen: oh well mine was four *ninety**

21.　　*Clare:* *yeh* yeh
22.　　*Karen:* and +nine p+
23.　　*Clare:* +yeh+
24.　　*Karen:* for the *straps*
25.　　*Clare:* *yeh*
26.　　*Karen:* there you are
27.　　*Clare:* I was really pleased

In line 14 Karen offers the minimal 'yeh', and in line 16 she praises not Clare but something or someone else (it is not clear who – perhaps the market stalls or stallholders, or the rolls of cloth themselves), and then in line 18 succeeds in switching topic again. Clare follows this topic thread but still at the end (line 27) she is persisting politely but doggedly in her attempt to get some form of compliment. Our interpretation of the behaviour of the two participants seems therefore to be warranted by the weight of evidence from various parts of the exchange.

This is all the text we have, so it is not clear how it continues or if they come to blows. It is interesting partly because it is unusual – as Heritage (1984:249) notes, it is often from such 'deviant' cases rather than from samples of 'smooth' discourse that we find the most illumination. In a fuller analysis, for each utterance, '[the] CA researcher would examine what comes before and what follows [the utterance], together with attention to pauses, hesitations, false starts, intakes of breath, intonation, and similar clues, to help interpret what is going on' (Holmes 2008:387).

As a general policy within a CA framework, ten Have (following Schegloff) recommends that the analyst do the following:

1. Check the episode carefully in terms of *turn-taking:* the construction of turns, pauses, overlaps, etc.; make notes of any remarkable phenomena, especially on any 'disturbances' in the fluent working of the turn-taking system.
2. Then look for sequences in the episode under review, especially *adjacency pairs* and their sequels.
3. And finally, note any phenomena of *repair,* such as repair initiators, actual repairs, etc.

(ten Have, 1999:104)

This affords a useful set of approaches to analysing conversation within the CA tradition, as well as some pointers as to what an analyst might focus on when examining such texts. However, other types of spoken discourse might lend themselves to different approaches, as can be demonstrated by examining a more formal example, namely Classroom discourse.

6.2 Classroom discourse

Conversation was once thought to be chaotic and mostly unstructured, and difficult to analyse. In 1975 Sinclair and Coulthard noted that they had left off the attempt to study what they saw as 'desultory conversation' (1975:4), because from their standpoint at the time it simply appeared rather random, chaotic and not amenable to clear analysis. We can now see, with hindsight, that this was perhaps overly pessimistic, since CA and other approaches have since made headway in explicating the mechanics of conversational interaction.

Sinclair and Coulthard, for the reasons they stated, then turned instead to analyse what they considered a more structured area of discourse, namely the discourse of the classroom, and the result was a now well-known and often-cited study, sometimes considered the first significant discourse analysis on any large scale. They looked initially at a relatively small number of transcripts of primary school classroom lessons, and here is part of one of them:

1. Teacher: What are Pyramids?
2. Pupils: (no answer)
3. T: Why did they build Pyramids?
4. T: Paul.
5. Pupil: When they were dead they put all their riches and
             everything they owned in their Pyramid.
6. T: Yes they did, yes.
             (adapted from Sinclair and Coulthard, 1975:82–3)

In terms of the first step of the heuristic mapped out in Chapter 5, it is obvious that the *function* or purpose of this text is educational. The next step in the analysis is to consider *how* it achieves that function or purpose, and which *features* of the text assist in that overarching aim.

This educational function may be the main reason why this sample of classroom discourse is apparently far more structured and organised than the 'Dressmaking' conversation we saw above. Sinclair and Coulthard (1975:6) went on to examine a wider variety of lessons in different schools, and their approach is characterised by an analysis of what is called the *exchange structure* of discourse, since they looked at how participants were managing the exchanges they made with each other.

One significant finding which Sinclair and Coulthard made was precisely how regular the patterns and structures of classroom interaction and lessons are. If we consider classrooms uncritically we might think that every one is quite different owing to the subject matter and the different behaviour of individual teachers and students. However, what Sinclair and Coulthard demonstrated through close analysis of their classroom discourse data was a surprisingly consistent set of patterns in teacher and student behaviour, whose 'well-ordered nature' surprised even the researchers themselves (p.112).

The patterning of classroom discourse

The 'Pyramid' lesson was offered by Sinclair and Coulthard as an extended example of their analysis. I reproduce it more fully here below, slightly rearranged and divided up for ease of analysis. Their transcript did not include the intonation and other useful features of the context, but it still gives a sense of the original lesson. As we read it, it is useful to reflect on how we could *analyse* and *explain* the precise function of what is happening at each point – in particular at lines 4, 6 and 12, in bold.

1. Teacher: What are Pyramids?
2. Pupils: (*no answer*)
3. T: Why did they build Pyramids?
4. T: Paul.
5 Pupil: When they were dead they put all their riches and everything they owned in their Pyramid.
6. T: Yes they did, yes.
7. T: Right in the depth, in the heart of the Pyramid there was a special little room where they had their personal belongings. Precious special things that belonged to them.
8. T: Can you suggest the sort of things that might be with them?
9. Pupil: (*Pupil puts hand up*)
10. T: Yes.
11. Pupil: Jewels.
12. T: Their own special jewels.
13. T: The ones that they liked the best.
14. Pupil: Their robes.
15. T: Clothes.
16. T: Yes
17. Pupil: The couch they liked best.
18. T: Yes, their favourite chair or throne or couch.
(adapted from Sinclair and Coulthard, 1975:82–3, emphasis added)

If we look at the teacher's strategies here, we see that the first question goes unanswered, so she tries a slightly different approach in line 3. This too seems at first to fail, so she then uses a name (nomination) 'Paul' and this time does

Table 6.1 Nested hierarchy of categories

Lesson					
Transaction			Transaction		
Exchange		Exchange		Exchange	
Move	Move	Move	Move	Move	Move
Act Act Act	Act Act Act	Act Act Act	Act Act	Act Act Act	Act Act

Source: adapted from Sinclair and Coulthard, 1975

get a response from a pupil (line 5). She then gives the simple feedback: 'Yes they did, yes', some more information (line 7), and so the lesson continues.

This is the beginning of a section which Sinclair and Coulthard class as a Transaction. In their scheme Lessons and Transactions are the two highest levels in the 'nested hierarchy' as illustrated in Table 6.1. In this table the Lesson happens to contain only two Transactions (for reasons of space), but it could well include more in practice. For example, the 'Pyramid' lesson above is about two thirds of a transaction, and in that lesson as a whole there are a total of 12 transactions in Sinclair and Coulthard's analysis.

From Table 6.1 we can further see that each transaction can be divided in their scheme into smaller pieces, which are called Exchanges. These in turn are divided in their analysis into even smaller units called Moves, and these in turn are divided into smaller units called Acts. Acts are the smallest unit, and could include a single word, a gesture or even 'heavy breathing' and 'clicking' (Sinclair and Coulthard, 1975:41).

Sinclair and Coulthard found that the lessons they analysed could be divided up satisfactorily into these units, each one nested inside each other. However, how clear are these units in practice? We can answer this by looking back at the transcript to see if we ourselves can identify the parts of the lesson which they identified, namely the Exchanges, Moves and Acts. A clue is that Exchanges typically consist of one, two or three Moves, called Opening, Answering and (if they exist) Follow-up moves, reminiscent of the adjacency pairs we discussed in Chapter 4. In particular recall the IRF sequence which we called an *adjacency trio* (p.82, which also involves three parts, an Initiation, a Response and Follow-up – a *pattern* identified as a 'Teaching Cycle' as long ago as 1966 (Bellack *et al.*, 1966). In essence this IRF pattern (see p.82), is identical to Sinclair and Coulthard's *Teaching Exchange*, and not surprisingly, the Opening Move of an Exchange (or the *initiation* in IRF terms) often consists of a question.

This is the case in the 'Pyramid' lesson, in fact, as the Opening Move in this case is the question in line 1. However, because this time the teacher does not get any Answering Move (*response* in IRF), she does not give any Follow-up Move – and so the Exchange is ended rather abruptly:

1. Teacher: What are Pyramids?
2. Pupils: (*no answer*)

Since the whole Exchange has failed it stops at that point. (As Sinclair and Coulthard would put it, only the Opening Move is *obligatory* in an Exchange – whereas the Answering Move and the Follow-up Move are *optional*.) For this reason the teacher starts on a second Exchange of this transaction, again with an Opening Move which is again a question. This time, after she resorts to a Nomination Act by saying the pupil's name (line 4), she is more successful:

3. T: Why did they build Pyramids?
4. T: Paul.
5. Pupil: When they were dead they put all their riches and every-thing they owned in their Pyramid.
6. T: Yes they did, yes.
7. T: Right in the depth, in the heart of the Pyramid there was a special little room where they had their personal belongings. Precious special things that belonged to them.

So this time the Exchange does include a clear Answering Move (line 5) and also a Follow-Up Move, which is when the teacher accepts the answer (line 6). She then emphasises the point she wishes to make by adding a *comment* in line 7 – still part of the Follow-Up Move, but an additional, optional part. Her next step is to start the third Exchange with another question, and again she is successful, this time getting several Answering Moves and giving several Follow-up Moves:

8. T: Can you suggest the sort of things that might be with them?
9. Pupil: (*Pupil puts hand up*)
10. T: Yes.
11. Pupil: Jewels.
12. T: Their own special jewels.
13. T: The ones that they liked the best.
14. Pupil: Their robes.
15. T: Clothes.
16. T: Yes
17. Pupil: The couch they liked best.
18. T: Yes, their favourite chair or throne or couch.

In short, this example offers us three clear Exchanges, the first one very short, as it included only the obligatory Opening Move and nothing else, and the second and third being rather longer and more developed, with all three Moves observable.

This is at the level of Exchanges and of Moves, but it was noted above that Sinclair and Coulthard's scheme used the term Acts for the lowest level of units in their scheme, and they identified more than twenty of these in their data, each of which was given a code such as 'ch' for a 'check'. We do not need to look at all the Acts they identified, but the commonest are things like *starter* (coded as 's'), *elicitation* (el), *prompt* (p), *clue* (cl) and *nomination* (when a pupil is named – n). We can see how this operated by looking in greater detail in Table 6.2 at how they coded the second of the three exchanges we have seen above. (I have explained the codes for each Act in the last column, to make the analysis easier to follow.)

Table 6.2 Analysis of the 'Pyramid' Teaching Exchange

Line			MOVES	ACTS
3.	T:	Why did they build Pyramids?	Opening	el = elicitation
4.	T:	Paul.		n = nomination
	Pupil:	When they were dead they put all their riches and everything they owned in their Pyramid.	Answering	rep = reply
5.	T:	Yes they did, yes.	Follow-up	e = evaluate
6.	T:	Right in the depth, in the heart of the Pyramid there was a special little room where they had their personal belongings. Precious special things that belonged to them.		com = comment

Source: adapted from Sinclair and Coulthard, 1975:82–3.

This does not do justice to the detail of analysis which Sinclair and Coulthard offered, but it is perhaps sufficient to show the way in which their analysis operated. Here we have a good illustration of an Exchange, in this case what they call a Teaching Exchange, and we have seen already that this is identical to the IRF pattern we discussed in Chapter 4 (see p. 82). This means that the Exchange has three Moves, the Opening, the Answering and the Follow-up, which correspond exactly with the IRF pattern. Within each of the Moves we then have one or several Acts in their analysis; for example the Follow-up Move can have an *evaluating act* and also a *comment act*, in which the teacher gives more information to make the point clear.

It might seem at first sight as if this is describing something quite straightforward, an everyday lesson activity. However, the key contribution of Sinclair and Coulthard's analysis is that it demonstrated the remarkable extent to which the discourse is *rule-governed* – far more than we might expect. This includes the insight that only a small number of the possible range of events can actually occur in each level, and certain acts, and combinations of acts, seem never to happen. Sinclair and Coulthard saw this as similar to the way in which grammar operates. In grammar some combinations of words are possible and common while others are apparently impossible – for example, among structures which seem to be 'illegal' in English is the invented combination 'Ate cat the big mouse the.' Likewise Sinclair and Coulthard demonstrated that in the classroom discourse they studied, only certain patterns of Acts seemed to occur in certain places within Moves, and so on, and other combinations seemed not to occur, as if the participants were following various discourse rules without conscious awareness of their behaviour.

Sinclair and Coulthard's work also demonstrates the value of the close study of discourse in laying bare patterns which may not be obvious, but which are nonetheless intrinsic parts of our social and linguistic behaviour. For education, of course, seeing such underlying patterns in classroom discourse can be of great value, since it might show up, for example, ways in which one teacher succeeds while another does not, or ways in which teachers in a certain setting might change their questioning or naming strategies, and so on.

Incidentally, Sinclair and Coulthard's analysis also raises the question of how discourse relates to power. As was noted above when discussing conversation, researching discourse in more formal settings can offer insights into the broader ways in which people wield power and influence through discourse strategies. The teacher in their example, for instance, is the one in control of the turn-taking and turn-giving, and the transcripts suggest that pupils 'agree' tacitly with this power dynamic.

In this case the wielding of power-through-discourse perhaps serves some social good, namely education. However, this might not always be the case; in other contexts this power relation might lead to disadvantage for some participants. By analysing such discourse in a variety of settings, we can therefore learn how power and control can be manipulated and used for good or evil through discourse techniques – and we can therefore be better equipped to deal with such discourse strategies in our own lives. This relation between discourse and power will be considered in greater depth in later chapters.

6.3 Approaches to analysis

Sinclair and Coulthard were based at the University of Birmingham in England, and what is therefore known as the Birmingham School's approach to classroom discourse has been influential both in demonstrating the value of analysing discourse carefully and systematically, and also in demonstrating important regularities about classroom discourse in particular. This approach to discourse – now sometimes called an *exchange structure* approach, since it focuses on the structure of the exchanges which participants carried out – has, however, been criticised by some analysts who point unfavourably to the practice of taking a pre-determined set of categories and then analysing the data to see to what extent it fitted those categories. This approach is sometimes then contrasted unfavourably with a CA (conversation analysis) approach which tends to *prioritise the data,* refusing to set up predetermined categories but seeking to draw them from actual authentic examples. For example one critic discusses Sinclair and Coulthard's approach as follows:

> The exchange structure approach looked at discourse as a predeter-mined sequence. It started with the theory of a patterning of units, and showed how what people say fits the model, thus viewing conversation as a product. Conversation analysis (CA), on the other hand, takes a 'bottom-up' approach: starting with the conversation itself, it lets the data dictates its own structure. (Cutting, 2002:27–8)

This criticism revolves around a central point of principle, since it concerns the approach we should take whenever we carry out any discourse analysis. Should we start with a clear idea of fixed categories, perhaps taken from linguistics, and then see if the real discourse fits into those categories? For example, could we take a checklist of genres perhaps and then test that check-list against a set of texts to see if they fit? Is that a valuable and proper way of proceeding? This is in essence a *deductive* research approach, as Chapman explains in some detail (Chapman, 2006:16–23), since it considers it impor-tant to offer a general theoretical framework and then evaluate the data in that light. It could be called a 'top-down' approach as it starts with pre-set ideas and them imposes them as if 'from above'.

Or should we take the opposite approach and *start with the texts themselves* and then try with an open mind to see if there are any patterns we can observe, for example any observable groups of genres? The second approach would be called a 'bottom-up' approach – as Cutting said in the quotation above – as it starts with the data sets themselves, and then works upwards from them to try and establish patterns and categories. The difference in approach seems to be fundamental. This is what would be termed an *induc-tive* research approach, collecting data – again in ways discussed by Chapman (2006) – and then drawing a theory from that accumulated evidence.

In her comment quoted above Cutting suggested rather critically that Sinclair and Coulthard's approach, which she calls the *exchange structure* approach, is 'top-down' as she considers that it applied preconceived notions or hypothetical categories rather than letting the data speak for itself. This kind of criticism may derive from the fact that Sinclair and Coulthard themselves stated that they were trying to align the presentation of their analysis to other linguistic work on grammar (Sinclair and Coulthard, 1975:24), even borrowing their terminology from such work. This might certainly suggest at first sight that they were trying to squeeze their analysis into preset frameworks in the way which Cutting implies in her critique.

However, although their terminology and presentation certainly seem to follow previous work on grammar, the evidence from their actual analysis suggests that Sinclair and Coulthard are perhaps not as 'guilty' as they might appear. In the first place they were not intending their work to be applied to conversation but to classroom discourse, and secondly they explicitly wrote that '[w]hen we began we had no preconceptions about the organization or extent of linguistic patterning' of the data (Sinclair and Coulthard, 1975:19). If we then look closely at how they proceeded, it is clear that they did indeed attempt to derive their scheme carefully from the data as they worked through the lessons. For this reason it is perhaps unfair to suggest that their approach was 'top-down', imposing categories on the data in advance. Furthermore, there is in any case nothing inherently better or worse in a deductive approach as opposed to an inductive one. As Chapman notes in her discussion of deductive and inductive approaches to language study:

> it is not a case of one being necessarily right and the other wrong, or of deciding conclusively which is better... The important thing is to be aware of what type of method an individual linguist is using, and to remember the limitations of this method and its possible implications for the resultant account of language. (Chapman, 2006:23)

It is true, however, that Sinclair and Coulthard's resulting scheme of Transactions, Exchanges and so on does come across as rather restrictive and closed. This is perhaps because classroom language is different from conversation in tending to be relatively controlled in its topic switching and in the power relations of the speakers. In a classroom, unlike in conversation when any participant can take the topic in almost any direction, within understood boundaries, the teacher generally has power over the planning of the discourse and is generally in control of the topics and themes. This was apparent in the 'Pyramid' examples from the way the teacher handled the discourse, exercising clear control over the taking and giving of turns and the management of topics.

For these reasons of power and of topic management then, amongst others, it seems that the broad approach to analysis used in the Birmingham work is perhaps most usefully applied in relatively formal situations where one person exercises power over topic switching and over the planning and management of the discourse, such as in formal meetings, in the law courts and so on. However, it is probably true to say that in more informal discourse situations, any such attempt to identify clear-cut categories for chunks of the discourse data might be less straightforward.

6.4 Conversation versus classroom discourse

Both Conversation and Classroom lesson genres use the *interacting* discourse mode, which means that both show adjacency pairs, turn-taking and so on. However, the patterning of these features is very different in the two, for reasons just mentioned. In terms of *adjacency pairs*, *topic management* and *turn-taking* Classroom discourse shows far greater apparent regularity than Conversation, probably owing to the fact that one participant (a teacher) has been granted greater power to control these elements, and the other participants acquiesce and (usually) cooperate in that control.

One further and significant difference between the two genres is that Classroom discourse contains as a central feature the IRF pattern. In recent years, although the concept of IRF in education has been re-examined, so that it is accepted that its functions can vary more widely than was once thought, it is nonetheless 'constant across instructional settings' (Hicks, 2003:17). The pattern may be relatively infrequent in other genres, as it can appear impolite if we give feedback on what someone says to us in situations when they do not want it or see any need for it, but it does exist in other genres where there is a situation of unequal power, such as certain business meetings and doctor–patient encounters (Berry, 1981) or in parent–child discourse (Seedhouse, 1996).

6.5 Summary

This chapter has examined two examples of important spoken genres which involve the *interacting* discourse mode, and has also identified a number of techniques and approaches for analysis.

The first part of the chapter addressed Conversation, and showed how a conversation can be approached in practice by examining patterns of *turn-taking*, *topic management* and patterns of *adjacency pairs*. The analysis of the transcript of conversation, as well as the line-by-line analysis of parts of it, exemplified one approach to this kind of discourse. A full analysis in the CA tradition would also examine *repair* and would take account of a wider range of features, including intonation, gestures and so on, as can be seen in the literature specialising in CA (see, for example, Hutchby and Wooffitt,1998).

The second part of the chapter considered, by way of comparison, a more formal spoken genre. This was the genre of Classroom lessons, distinguished from Conversation in part by formality and more formalised power relations. Here also we looked at *turn-taking and turn-giving* (for example, through questions), and at an example of *exchange analysis* which involved categorising classes of Move and Act and then identifying them in subsequent discourse. A particular feature of classroom discourse, related to the power dynamic, is the use of the three-part IRF pattern, which was considered as part of the broader examination of classroom turn-taking patterns.

Discussion of these two areas of discourse led to a comparison of two different approaches to analysing discourse, broadly characterised as a CA or Conversation Analysis approach ('bottom-up') as opposed to a DA or Discourse Analysis approach ('top-down'). The point was made, with reference to Chapman (2006) that neither is inherently better than the other, but that it is important to be aware of which is being used in any analysis, and of the limitations of both.

7 Spoken Genres: Legal Discourse, Jokes, Sports Commentary and Advertising

Conversation and classroom interaction mainly involve the *interacting* discourse mode. This chapter will start by examining an example of legal language which also draws on *interacting* and will then turn to examples such as jokes, sports commentary and advertising which use other discourse modes such as *describing*, *instructing* and *narrating*.

7.1 Courtroom discourse

A lawyer defending an alleged rapist is questioning the alleged victim. As we examine the extract we might first consider how the lawyer *constructs* the witness through his questions, and how we ourselves might perceive the woman if we were on a jury considering this case. (The length of pauses is indicated in brackets, a dot for a short pause with longer pauses in seconds; overlapping speech is indicated with square brackets. Otherwise the text, including the 'spelling', is as in the original.)

1. Defence lawyer:	O.K. you went outside and you waited for at least ten minutes for one of these friends to emerge, is that correct?	
2.	(1.2)	
3. Witness:	Mmhmm	
4. Defence lawyer:	Who were you waiting for?	
5.	(3.9)	
6. Witness:	I dont remember who it was.	
7. Defence lawyer:	Aren'tchu just trying tuh come up with an excuse for why you had to wait outside there?	
8.	(0.6)	
9. Witness:	No	

10.		[[
11.	Defence lawyer:	Weren't you in fact waiting outside for somebody to go pardying with (.) anybody
12.	Prosecution lawyer:	Objection yer honour
13.	Judge:	Overruled
14.	Witness:	No

(adapted from Matoesian, 1993: 161)

Forensic linguistics: language and power

Before we look in detail at this exchange, we can consider where it stands in terms of genre. Courtroom discourse could be said to be a general *register*, with the use of legal jargon, formal ways of turn-taking and so on, but within it we can also identify particular *genres* with clear beginnings and ends. A whole court case could in fact be analysed as a genre in these terms, and so could the exchange on which the text above appears to be modelled, which we could call a Cross-Examination, in which a lawyer has a chance to question a witness.

The linguistic approach to studying such legal discourse comes under what is now called Forensic Linguistics (Coulthard 2000; Coulthard and Johnson, 2007). This area of study, which began with the work of linguists such as Malcolm Coulthard, (whose work with Sinclair on classroom discourse was discussed in Chapter 6,) has expanded in recent years to cover many aspects of language and the law, including police interviews (see Heydon, 2005), police language in other areas (see Rock, 2007), the language of law reports, or the ways in which various participants (such as judges, lawyers and the public) interact linguistically inside and outside the courtroom.

One reason why this area is of increasing interest is the intrinsic relation in legal matters between *language* and *power*, a relationship whose importance can be seen in the exchange above. This link between language and power has surfaced at various times during the analyses in this book. We have already noted, for example, that power relations operate in Classroom lessons and in Conversation, and later chapters will consider its role in News reports, in Political Speeches and in numerous other genres and discourse settings. In the law court it can be pivotal, of course, in the sense that poor uses of or responses to language could mean imprisonment or worse. To take the courtroom exchange above, which will be examined in more detail shortly, the power is clearly in the hands of the lawyer, and the woman is relatively powerless (at this point in the trial) to put her point of view as she would wish to.

Cross-examination

If we examine the sample text more closely, we can usefully start with the function of the genre, which in the case of the Cross-Examination is essentially to *persuade* a judge or a jury in a law court. Even though some of the background is unclear, it is apparent at once from the exchange that the lawyer is attempting to persuade the jury essentially by 'constructing' the woman as promiscuous and irresponsible through the focus and content of his questions. Furthermore, his strategy is to present events in such a way that the woman cannot easily contradict him, for example:

> O.K. you went outside and you waited for at least ten minutes for one of these friends to emerge, is that correct?

This of course is only the first part of the lawyer's plan, leading the witness towards a particular point. Instead of asking an open question, he frames his utterance rather as a statement with a short question tacked on, in a common strategy in legal language, known as a Confirmation question (Gibbons, 2003:102), and furthermore it is what we would call a Yes/No question because the witness can only answer 'yes' or 'no'. Both of these aspects of the question, its structure or syntax as essentially a statement, and the Yes/No element at the end, serve to restrict the woman's freedom to speak, and therefore have significant power implications. If the lawyer had instead asked the woman freely to describe what she did, she might have put it in a way which did not suit his case – which is exactly why lawyers adopt such strategies in their questioning.

The lawyer then pursues the strategy of constructing the woman as 'loose' and 'partying', so as eventually to put part of the blame for the rape on her, and thereby get his client acquitted. He comes eventually to this question:

> *Weren't you in fact waiting outside for somebody to go pardying with (.) anybody*

This constructs her as someone out for fun, and even promiscuous, since she is depicted as waiting for 'anybody' to go partying with. Of course it is put as a question, because the rules of a cross-examination imply *interacting*, but the lawyer in fact means it to come across as a description which he hopes will stick in the jury's mind. The opposing lawyer tries to object, but the judge allows the question to stand, so that although the woman answers 'No', the damage is already done. The lawyer has succeeded through his questioning strategies in creating a negative impression of the woman's behaviour in the jurors' minds.

Questions and questioning

This is a short examination of a small piece of data with relatively little context, but it serves to make the point that questioning strategies are an aspect of turn-taking and turn-giving which can be used to gain power.

Table 7.1 Questioning strategies and power

	Type of question	Power and effect	Example
1	**'WH' questions** – questions constructed with the question words who, where, what, why, how	Relatively free, allowing a wide range of responses, but can contain presupposition	Who owned or took weapons to the hotel? (Gibbons, 2003:104) Would you care to tell me how the heroin came to be in your house tonight? (Gibbons, 2003:103)
2	**Yes/No** questions, or polar questions	To restrict and channel the listener to the questioner's advantage	Did you burgle a house last night? (Gibbons, 2003:104)
3	**Either/or** questions	To restrict options to suit the questioner	Was it a large club or a small club? (Gibbons, 2003:104)
4	**Referential** questions	To teach or show knowledge. This question is not a genuine request for information since the questioner already knows the answer, and it is common in classrooms and education generally.	Why did they build Pyramids? (Sinclair and Coulthard 1975:82)
5	Questions as **command**	Not a genuine question	Are you going to keep interrupting me? (Coulthard and Johnson, 2007:15)
6	**Confirmation** questions, i.e. seeking confirmation (statements with positive agreement tag; see Gibbons, 2003:102)	Restrictive, as the questioner is able to construct the situation to her or his advantage.	You started work at 7 am. Is that correct? (Coulthard and Johnson, 2007:15)
7	**Rhetorical** questions, i.e. questions posed for effect, which do not expect and do not usually have, an answer	Restrictive, as no answering move is allowed or expected	Where is the evidence in that case, that a 14 minute stop on the road after three and a quarter hours is sinister? (Author's data from lawyer's final summing-up)

Table 7.1 summarises the ways in which certain types of questions allow certain answers, and therefore involve different power strategies, varying from open questions to closed confirmation questions. Other question types also exist, of course, beside these, but this sample suffices to illustrate some of the main ways in which questions can control, restrict or guide listeners in particular directions. Although they can do so in a wide range of genres and situations, of course, each one is illustrated here with an example from legal settings, with the exception of Referential questions, where we see again the teacher from the lesson analysed on pp. 113ff.

Ideology in language

The discussion above centred around a lawyer accusing the woman witness in a rape case of waiting for somebody 'to go partying with', with the implication that this activity was somehow problematic. But why is it so bad to go partying? The reason of course is that the lawyer was drawing on a particularly conservative *set of ideas* about women's behaviour, namely that they should not go partying with 'anybody', they should not drink too much, they should not have many sexual partners – and if they do, it is implied that they are somehow partly to blame if they are raped. This is obviously unfair, and raises a number of serious questions about the legal system, about the position of women and about equality, but it is undoubtedly a set of ideas which does exist in many societies and which is powerful.

The very reason for its power is because of the connected *set of ideas* which it appeals to, the naturalised *ideology* about women's behaviour. The word 'ideology' is often seen to relate to politics, but such networks of ideas can relate to any aspect of society, not only the political. The lawyer in that example used language to 'ignite' this set of ideas, hoping that the ideological framework itself would then impact in powerful ways on the minds of the jury. In these ways, language can gain its power by calling up in its support a whole system of ideas, beliefs and values like a military general summoning up an invisible army.

What is an ideology?

The reason for this is that *ideologies* are rather like the schemas and scripts considered in Chapter 3, because they are complexes of concepts which we accept implicitly to be true, and act on them accordingly. As was discussed in Chapter 3, schemas and scripts can seem to be neutral mental devices to help us understand the world, but of course they can also include implicit *values* and *beliefs* which affect our world view in powerful ways, and ideologies are no different. They are sets of concepts which can act on us powerfully, and they intersect with language in interesting ways.

To use the classic example, if we hear the word 'terrorist' our mind brings up pictures of aggressive, unhinged men causing mindless violence, whereas if we hear the word 'freedom fighter' we imagine strong, courageous people fighting for right and justice, defending the poor and oppressed. Each word conjures up, in these ways, not only one picture, but a host of values, emotions and beliefs, a complex mental network which then affects our whole view of the person being described. The implication of this for a newspaper journalist, say, is that by choosing one of these two words instead of the other, s/he is not simply choosing a bland descriptor, but is calling up a powerful *ideology* in support of one world view or the opposite, influencing the reader to love the individuals concerned or fear and loathe them. Choice of language can therefore evoke powerful ideological forces to influence readers and listeners and it is this link between *language choice* and *ideologies* which obliges the discourse analyst to take ideology into account.

Ideologies are 'the taken-for-granted assumptions, beliefs and value-systems which are shared collectively by social groups' (Simpson, 1993:3). In other words we treat them as if they are obviously true, and 'just common sense'. We do not usually critique them. Part of their strength lies in the fact that they are an invisible *and assumed* network of beliefs and values. To the people who hold these ideologies, they are not only 'the basic principles that govern social judgement' (van Dijk, 1998:24–5), but they also 'appear to be logical and natural' (Jones and Peccei, 2004:38), and they appear logical and natural partly because they are socially shared. 'Everybody knows' that terrorists are evil, so if a man is described as a terrorist, he 'must be' evil. If no-one else questions the pattern of beliefs and ideas, we take them as true. In short, one of the reasons why language is a loaded weapon is that, when we read and listen, we tend to respond to the language and its associated ideological networks of values and beliefs without questioning them.

We can set out some of the features of ideologies as follows, so as to help us to take account of them in future analyses:

1. Ideologies are mental networks of ideas and notions, linked with *values* and *beliefs*.
2. Ideologies are shared by groups of people, and this implicit *consensus* is part of their power.
3. Because they are shared, ideologies are often assumed and *invisible* – accepted as 'just common sense', 'naturalised'.

4. Ideologies tend not to be often questioned; anyone questioning them is treated as being crazy or a troublemaker.

5. Ideologies are frequently polarised into 'Them' versus 'Us' (van Dijk, 1998:25).

6. Ideologies are central to group identity because they frequently help to 'constitute the social identity and define the interest of a group' (van Dijk, 1998:25).

7. Ideologies are not necessarily logical, for example we can often hold *several different competing ideologies at once*, and operate with them differently in different situations.

8. Our *behaviour* relating to ideologies can be contradictory. We may have a strong set of beliefs about the need to save the environment, for instance, but we might at the same time use the car for unnecessary journeys without a second thought, because 'I'm in a hurry'.

9. Some ideologies can be clearly *political* in nature (so we can speak of Marxist ideology, for example) but at the other end of the scale they can be relatively apolitical notions.

10. Ideologies can be invoked in language by terms such as 'terrorist' or 'Nazi', but everyday words can also carry ideological implications (for example, 'housewife', 'chairman').

It is important in particular to note that language and ideology are closely intertwined, to the extent that we could analyse any text to discover its ideological underpinnings, looking, for example, at particular patterns of words, particular metaphors, and other clues as to the ideological position of the text. We have seen a simple example in a legal context, and will consider other examples as we proceed.

Presupposition and implicature

Would you care to tell me how the heroin came to be in your house tonight? (Gibbons, 2003:103)

In this piece of legal questioning, there is an interesting example of presupposition at work. The speaker is making an assumption or *presupposition* – there was heroin in the house – and this is then embedded into the question in a way which makes it very difficult to deny. As with ideologies, *presuppositions*, when embedded in this way into statements and questions, are powerful precisely because they are not explicit, but relatively invisible and assumed. 'Presuppositions are background assumptions embedded within a sentence or phrase. These assumptions are taken for granted to be true regardless of whether the whole sentence is true' (Jones and Peccei, 2004:44).

The jury in the heroin case has therefore been manipulated, by means of this embedded presupposition, into assuming – believing without question – that there was heroin in the house. If the witness wants to contradict this, she or he must say something like: 'No, there wasn't any heroin in the house'. However, because by doing so s/he will have failed to offer the *preferred response* to the initial question, which was expecting a factual answer, it will then appear to the jury as if s/he is being aggressive or unreasonable – so either way the witness is at a disadvantage. This is the power of embedding a presupposition into an apparently simple question. (Incidentally, the most well-known example of this linguistic device is the question 'Have you stopped beating your wife yet?', because if the respondent answers 'yes', it means he did beat her before, and if he answers 'no', it means he still beats her, so he is guilty either way. The question is 'loaded'.)

Presuppositions (or 'presumptions', as some writers call them; see Chilton 2004:81) occur not only in questions. Definite noun phrases also presuppose the existence of their referents, and comparative adjectives, such as *fairer*, may logically presuppose a current state of unfairness (Jones and Peccei, 2004: 42). This sentence from a police interview contains an obvious presupposition:

> What I intend to ask you is some questions about the murder of P Q about 11 o'clock on the 16th of November. (Gibbons, 2003:144)

Clearly, this statement *presupposes* that there was a murder, and that all the details which are mentioned about it are true.

Implicatures are different from presuppositions. They are the result of speakers deviating from interactional norms ('Gricean maxims'; see Grice, 1975) with the result that the hearer draws some inference from this behaviour. Implicatures are 'much more dependent on shared knowledge between the speaker and hearer and on the surrounding context of the discourse' (Jones and Peccei, 2004:44). The important point for us is the way in which writers make use of such assumed knowledge, whether it is *presupposition* or *implicature*, in ways which can conceal power strategies (as in the law court.) The analyst must be aware of such features when dealing with texts.

So far this chapter has examined courtroom discourse, which we discussed in terms of ideology and presupposition. Many of the examples were relatively serious, sober and legalistic, so it is perhaps time to consider something a little lighter – namely jokes.

7.2 Jokes

Having looked at *interacting* as used in Conversation, in Classroom lessons, and in Courtroom Exchanges, we turn to a genre which can draw also on other discourse modes, namely Jokes. Jokes are of interest in our discussion of genres because they are hugely varied, which means that they offer insights into the flexible ways in which listeners and readers deal with genres and texts in practice. They also illustrate several of the features of genres we have discussed in previous chapters. Here is an example, reminiscent of the joke cited on p. 65:

> There were these three men lost in the desert, hot and tired, when one of them saw a lamp in the sand. He picked it up, rubbed it and out popped a small genie. 'I am the genie of the lamp', it said 'but I am only a little genie, so I can't take you out of the desert. I can give you each only one small wish.'
>
> 'Well', said the first man, 'please can I have a water bottle which never runs dry?'
> So the genie clicked its fingers and the water bottle appeared.
> 'Well', said the second man, 'please can I have an electric fan which never stops?'
> So the genie clicked its fingers and the fan appeared.
> 'Great', said the third man, 'please can I have a car door?' The genie stopped and looked at him. 'A car door?'
> 'Yes please', said the man.
> 'OK' the genie shrugged, then clicked its fingers and a car door appeared in the sand.
>
> When the genie had vanished the three men set off through the desert again, the first man sipping his water, the second cooling his face with the fan and the third man carrying the car door. The first man looked puzzled and turned to the third man. 'I don't understand. Why did you want a car door?' he asked.
>
> 'Well', said the man, 'When it gets hot I can open the window.'

Why is this joke funny? What genre and sub-genre does it relate to? A similar joke, about three men on a desert island, was discussed in Chapter 4, and although the first one was in the present tense and the second in the past tense, they clearly share several features, including the fact that:

- they both involve three men, one stupid and two normal
- they both concern a tricky situation

- in both, a possible solution presents itself
- both end in an unexpected or sad or foolish way.

This demonstrates the fact that jokes, like other texts, can share 'family' features with each other and can therefore be put into 'family groups' according to those resemblances. At a very general level, it is therefore useful to refer to the *genre* of Jokes and then to divide the class into what could be called various *sub-genres*, according to the characteristics which they share. The joke above, for example, could be seen as drawing on the sub-genre of 'Three men' jokes, as we can call it, since texts which draw on this sub-genre seem to share the features we identified above. *Genre,* in other words, is a broad overarching category mainly linked with a particular function, but then within any broad genre there might be other more detailed family resemblances which could be identified as *sub-genres*. As is the case with genres, the boundaries of the class of sub-genres will be necessarily 'fuzzy'. The central point is that they share a main function (humour in this case) and that each sub-genre will share enough prototypical features to allow us to recognise them and respond quickly. The key is not 'fit with analytical categories' but utility and function in the real world.

Jokes and discourse modes

Besides again illustrating the essential 'fuzziness' of genres and sub-genres, jokes also illustrate the ways in which the various *discourse modes* operate in respect of genres. Part of the way in which we respond to jokes derives from the various discourse modes which they draw on. For example, when my son comes up to me and says 'Knock, knock', I draw on my prior intertextual knowledge, and realise that this is an opening move and part of an *interacting discourse mode* which calls for my response. For this reason I respond at once, saying 'Who's there?', and then the joke continues. If I fail to realise that the mode is *interacting*, the joke will fail.

However, when someone says to me 'There were these three men on a desert island', it would be socially wrong of me to stop him and interact, asking him exactly which desert island it was, or who exactly the men were. If I did so I would miss a joke and lose a friend. I do not do this because when I hear the opening line I again draw on my intertextual knowledge, this time of texts in *narrating* mode, and jokes in particular, and know that I should just listen. If I start to *interact* I will be breaking an unwritten social and discourse rule, as well as risking personal injury.

This points again to the value of drawing on discourse modes as a way of understanding, explaining and even organising genres. It is clear that a central characteristic of some genres and sub-genres is the discourse mode they draw on.

Other discourse modes in jokes

Here is another example – which discourse mode is involved here?

How to cook a steak

First you place a steak in a large frying pan, and set it to low heat. Then while it is cooking, add two cups of apple cider with a dash of cinnamon. You then add a cup of best brandy, a dash of vodka, and cook the steak gently in the sauce for five minutes. Finally add a cup of whisky, then throw away the steak and drink the sauce.

When we read the title of this text we draw on our intertextual knowledge to expect a recipe. Our suspicion is then apparently confirmed by features of the *instructing* mode, including discourse signals such as *'first'*, *'then'*, *'finally'*, along with jargon and grammar typical of recipes. The last line, however, surprises us. The humour (as with the Zombie text discussed on page 44) comes from the surprise when our genre expectations are overturned – it is not a recipe for the steak, but for a drink, albeit an odd one. Jokes frequently derive their humour from setting up expectations in this way, deriving either from settings we know from elsewhere or from other genres, and then confounding those expectations in a humorous way. As Alexander (1997:15) puts it,'a crucial process for the joke … may be the perception, on the part of the listener, of an incongruity between the punchline and what comes before'. To put it in terms of the heuristic, the *function* of the joke is humour, and the main *feature* in the text which works towards that function is the disruption of our genre expectations.

Responding to jokes

We have already noted (see p. 67) that although narrative structure typically contains a setting, then a *disruption* of some sort, and finally some sort of *resolution* which is typically happy, a defining feature of jokes is that they may contravene this structure in systematic ways. With this in mind, here is a third joke of the 'Three men' sub-genre. Consider to what extent it fits or does not fit with the 'standard' narrative structure set out on p. 70:

There were three men in prison, due to be executed. The first man said 'I have an idea – copy me.' The next morning he was led out by the soldiers and was standing by the wall. The soldiers raised their rifles ready to execute him, but the man suddenly shouted out 'Flood, flood', at which the soldiers took fright and threw down their rifles. The man jumped over the wall and ran away.

The two other men saw what happened, and the next morning the second man was led out and put against the wall. Just as the soldiers were ready to fire he shouted out loudly 'Earthquake, earthquake'. Again the soldiers took fright and dropped their guns, so the man was able to escape.

The third man thought carefully about this and smiled to himself. The next morning he walked out cheerfully and stood against the wall. When the soldiers raised their rifles, the man shouted out 'Fire!'... So they did.

This joke is similar to the 'Desert Island' joke in obvious ways – it has three men, one of them stupid, whose plan fails. When we hear it we therefore have expectations of what will happen (if we know this type of joke), and the humour comes from the third man's (expected) stupidity.

In terms of narrative structure, this type of joke shows part of the classic pattern we discussed in Chapter 4, but there are also differences. It does not start with a stable situation which is then disrupted, but with an already 'disrupted' problem situation – the men are in a difficult situation already, looking for a resolution. One analysis of this type of joke can be set out as follows:

	Classic narrative structure	'Desert island' joke / 'Prison' joke
1.	Stable initial setting introduced	-None given
2.	Disruption of setting	-Both jokes start at this point (no background information)
3.	Realisation of disruption	-Minimal
4.	Attempt at resolution	-Plan or possibility of escape -(This stage is repeated three times)
5.	Resolution and equilibrium	-None – both end in failure

Part of the joke's humour is because we already know, from our intertextual knowledge and our knowledge of the *narrating* discourse mode that these jokes diverge from 'normal' narratives. The stupid third man also diverges from our expectation of 'normal' behaviour, and it is these types of divergence which help to generate the humour. In short, the humorous effect depends entirely on both our prior knowledge of human behaviour and on our intertextual knowledge of other stories and other jokes.

If we attempted, then, to define this sub-genre of jokes, we could do so by reference to their content (three men, one of them stupid, a tricky situation and so on) and also by reference to aspects of their narrative structure, in that amongst other things they omit the classic first stage (the setting) and then repeat the *attempt at resolution* stage three times. This example demonstrates therefore the way in which *genres* can be defined in relatively broad terms, by means of their function, (in the case of Jokes it is the function of humour), whereas when we look at the level of *sub-genre* we can often be more precise and detailed about the content and structure of the class, including the precise *configuration of the discourse modes* and other features they draw on.

7.3 Discourse signals revisited

Part of our response to texts is to identify – speedily and without conscious awareness – the discourse mode genre, so that we can respond appropriately, and we do this partly by spotting discourse signals, in ways discussed earlier (page 67) . To take some further examples, can you guess which genres are signalled by these opening discourse signals?

1. Here is the news
2. Silence in court!
3. First, chop the onions finely
4. Chapter 1
5. Hello, can I speak to Jim please?
6. Dear Sir

As I typed the last of these, my computer immediately put a message on screen asking me if I wanted help in composing the letter, which demonstrates the way in which many discourse signals are clear clues as to the genre in question, even to the extent that machines can now recognise them. The others are of course from the radio or television news, from a hearing in a court of law, from a recipe, from a book (perhaps a novel), from a telephone conversation and from a formal letter.

It would be straightforward to generate further examples – signals which indicate the opening of a genre, or a particular stage in a genre, or a topic switch, or a conclusion. These signals are a constituent part of the genres of which they form a part. We recognise and create genres in part through finding and using such discourse signals, and when we analyse discourse in any actual text it is useful to look out for and identify patterns of discourse signals which may be typical or atypical of one or other genre.

7.4 Sports commentary

Although different genres may draw on different modes, one is frequently dominant. In recipes, for instance, the *instructing* discourse mode plays the major part. We can now examine a spoken genre whose main aim is *describing*. It seems quite typical of the genre – which is not difficult to identify – but a number of features are perhaps unexpected. I have emphasised parts of the text.

1. And welcome to the horse racing extravaganza here **at number 12 Cheltenham Terrace** and the runners and riders for the **Reservoir Nags** Handicap are under starter's orders...
2. ...and they're away!
3. ...and it's **Mr Red, Mr Orange, Mr Green, Mr Yellow and Mr Black** carrying the hopes and dreams of so many as they come up to the first foot marker now...
4. ...and Mr Red has the early running closely followed by Mr Green, Mr Red the favourite as they come round this **superbly crafted course**, the going officially described as a **bit plasticky** and Mr Orange struggling now on the far side..
5. ...and Mr Red is down!...Mr Red **being dragged** by Mr Green, this is dreadful...
6. ...and Mr Orange is really being **quite crap** now! Make sure you don't put your money on him **when you buy this fantastic racing game!**
7. ...and Mr Red is back on his hooves and steaming ahead putting the rest of the field to shame now!...
8. ...and here's the finish line **helpfully marked 'Finish'.**
9. ...and at the line it's Mr Red the winner, half a length ahead of Mr Yellow!

(www.iwoot.com)

This text clearly draws on the genre of Sports Commentary, but it also has a number of odd features. If we have ever heard such race commentaries we will have certain expectations. Its *function*, of course, is to inform us about a race as it happens, and also to motivate us and to add excitement – its aim is more than purely descriptive. In terms of its *features* – how it achieves that function – it has a clear structure, beginning at the start of the race and ending soon after, with standard *discourse signals* indicating the start (line 2: *and they're away!*) and the end of the race (line 9: *and at the line it's Mr Red the winner*). In terms of the linking of actions, it is also typical. 'A ... characteristic of commentary is the way in which clauses are linked together. A very small number of conjunctive elements are used to link clauses together, often rather loosely' (Delin, 2000:40). In this text this is achieved by the additive conjunctives (Jeffries, 2006:186) '...*and*...*and*...*as* ...*and*...*as*...' The text draws primarily on the *describing* discourse mode but it also has elements of *narrating*, as the description is of an ongoing event rather than a static person or a place. We therefore expect the following features, and to some extent, as listed in the column on the right, they are apparent in this text:

Description of the setting before the event begins – Where are we? Who are the participants? What is the atmosphere and context?	*And welcome to the horse racing extravaganza here at number 12 Cheltenham Terrace and the runners and riders for the Reservoir Nags Handicap are under starter's orders...* *Names of runners during race*
Discourse signals	l.2: *...and they're away! (start)* l.9: *and at the line it's Mr. Red the winner*
Use of **deictic reference** to highlight the 'here and now' (see p.91)	*here, now, this*
Additive conjunctions	*...and...and...as...and...as...*
Emotive, exaggerated **lexis and phrasing** to generate excitement	*extravaganza, carrying the hopes and dreams of so many, this is dreadful!*
Extensive use of **progressive participles** (Jeffries, 2006:88) to emphasise current ongoing action	*carrying, struggling, being dragged*
Highly varied **intonation**, extensive variation in **pitch** patterns and movement (high to low and low to high), breathless phrasing	*Not observable in this transcript*

It is apparent from the analysis summarised here that this text fits the genre of Sports Commentary fairly closely. However, the text also has a few oddities, as it is not really a genuine horse racing commentary at all. In fact it is part of a television and web advertisement for a children's plastic horse racing game which humorously parodies real commentaries (and can be found on the YouTube website). What alerts us to the fact that it is a spoof or parody is precisely the features which deviate from the genre norm. The deviations, highlighted in bold in the text above, signal that it is a parody and not a genuine commentary, in a sort of *intertextual style-mixing*:

a. the odd location – a home address (but an intertextual pun on a real horse racing track at Cheltenham)

b. the unusual name of the race – 'Reservoir Nags Handicap' (perhaps an intertextual pun on the film 'Reservoir Dogs')

c. the unusual naming of all of the horses by their colours

d. humorous references to the fact that the course is made of plastic ('superbly crafted', 'plasticky')

e. odd events – a horse being 'dragged' by another, as the plastic horse falls over

f. Lexis from the wrong register and genre ('crap' is an informal and mildly 'dirty' word and would not be used in authentic race commentaries to describe a horse)

g. explicit reference to the product being offered: 'this fantastic racing game'

So just as it can be useful to study 'deviant' examples of conversation, as was noted in Chapter 6, it can be illuminating to study parodies like this one because they not only highlight what is typical of the genre – as there must be enough features there for us to recognise the genre clearly – but they also offer clear features which are not typical of the genre, and may even come (intertextually) from other genres, for humorous or other purposes.

7.5 Summary

The previous chapter examined two genres which predominantly use the interacting discourse mode, namely Conversation and Classroom lessons. This chapter has examined three other spoken genres which use a mix of modes, namely courtroom Cross-Examinations, Jokes, and Sports Commentary, as well as elements of Advertisements. We have considered the ways in which texts combine modes for different effects and borrow intertextually from other genres in creative ways, for example in parody. This serves to reinforce a central theme of this book, namely the inherent flexibility and dynamism of everyday texts in their attempt to achieve their main functions, as well as the ways in which they draw flexibly on our genre expectations.

In addition, the discussion has progressively introduced and expanded on a range of approaches, issues and tools which are important when analysing types of discourse. Issues addressed in this chapter included the following:

• question types and patterns, for example in legal settings
• presuppositions and implicature

- ideology
- narrative structure, and deviations from narrative expectations
- intertextual style-mixing

These form part of the analytical toolkit which will be discussed in full in Chapter 10.

Written Genres: News Reports, Personal Ads, Texting and Online Gaming

Chapters 6 and 7 have examined a variety of spoken texts, and drawn out the range of features which such texts employ in order to achieve their various aims or functions. This chapter turns to examine written texts, starting with News Reports, which naturally employ the *reporting* discourse mode, then turning to Personal Advertisements, and finally to two written genres which are highly interactive, namely Texting and Computer Gaming.

8.1 News Reports

In Chapter 4 the *reporting* discourse mode was characterised in terms of its deixis, since (unlike *narrating* mode) its principle time reference is what Smith (2003) called Speech Time, referring to the time (and indeed place) at which the speaker or writer is currently located. Events in *reporting* mode are then reported in relation to that Speech Time, giving rise to frequent use of deictic expressions which have full meaning only with reference to knowledge of the reporter's location in time and space.

Given that different News Reports often present contradictory accounts of what is happening in the world, it is of value for all readers to develop the ability to critique and evaluate the ways in which such stories present the news. The apparent *function* of such reports is to inform, and examination of the *features* could arguably elucidate how the information is conveyed. But often the information is contested, so the analyst has the additional task of analysing how reports offer divergent accounts of disputed events, and then of asking the third question (*Why?*) which has until now remained somewhat in the background. In simple terms, the analyst needs to develop critical tools to tease out conflicting approaches and representations of events, so as to identify any bias or distortion through language.

To illustrate these points I have chosen a topic which is controversial, namely a series of incidents in the conflict in Gaza between Hamas, the Palestinian political party, and the Israeli armed forces, in February 2008, as reported by the *New York Times* in an article on 28 February 2008. I start by considering simply the article's discourse features in general. A closer analysis will then examine how it presents each side of the conflict.

The *New York Times* article begins like this. Try to work out the sequence of the events as they actually happened.

Hamas and Israelis Trade Attacks, Killing Several

> Picture of an Israeli woman being carried down some stairs with the caption:
>
> *An Israeli woman was carried after a rocket fired by Palestinian militants in Gaza landed in a factory in the southern Israeli town of Sderot on Wednesday.*

By ISABEL KERSHNER

Paragraph 1, sentence 1	JERUSALEM – In a sudden surge of violence, an Israeli civilian was killed Wednesday in a rocket attack by Hamas militants from Gaza, the first such fatality in nine months, and at least eight Palestinians, militants and civilians, were killed in Israeli airstrikes before and after the rocket attack.
Paragraph 2, sentence 1	Israel carried out the first airstrike in southern Gaza on Wednesday morning, hitting a minivan on a road west of Khan Yunis and killing five members of the Hamas military wing, Qassam Brigades, Hamas said.
Paragraph 2, sentence 2	Southern Israel then came under heavy rocket fire, with more than 25 rockets launched in two hours, the Israeli Army said.
Paragraph 2, sentence 3	Hamas, the Islamic militant group that controls Gaza, claimed responsibility for the rocket barrage, saying it had been retaliating for the Israeli strike.

Analysing news stories: attribution, abstract and story

A useful approach to analysing the structure of news stories has been set out by Allan Bell, (Bell, 1991; 1998). In developing his approach he drew on work by Labov on spoken narratives (see p. 73).

In Bell's analysis, newspaper articles typically include three main parts, an *attribution*, an *abstract* and the *story* proper. The *attribution* tells us who wrote the piece, where and when, and this is evident at once in our example, since it offers the name of the author, the date and the place (Jerusalem). In Bell's analysis a news story then typically gives an *abstract*, which 'consists of the lead sentence or "intro" of the news story and – for press news – also a headline' (Bell, 1998:67). This too is clear in our example; the headline provides part of the abstract, then the first sentence completes it by presenting the whole story in brief. Greater detail is then provided in the third part, in Bell's analysis, namely the *story* itself, which begins in paragraph two and continues through the rest of the article.

News reports draw extensively on the *reporting* discourse mode since they typically describe sequences of events from the point of Speech Time. The first sentence here, whose function as part of the abstract is to set out the whole story in brief, has two main parts, the first concerning the Israeli who was killed, and the second concerning the Palestinians who were killed. The other elements of the same sentence are supporting and adding information in various ways, all of which will later be expanded in the full story to come. Bell (1998:103) notes the importance in news reports of 'the journalist's 'five Ws and an H', namely the *who, what, where, why, when and how* of any story, suggesting that a good news story will typically answer these questions as quickly and directly as possible. If we take this as a starting point, an initial analysis can be set out as follows, incidentally showing an interesting symmetry within the sentence:

1	In a sudden surge of violence,	*Comment on the context*
2	an Israeli civilian	*Who?*
3	was killed	*Main event*
4	Wednesday	*When?*
5	in a rocket attack by Hamas militants from Gaza,	*Who by? (agent)*
6	the first such fatality in nine months,	*Adjectival comment, modifying or describing the victim. Also setting this event into a wider context.*
7	and	*Conjunction, joining the two parts of the sentence together*
8	at least eight Palestinians	*Who?*
9	militants and civilians	*Noun, describing the victims*
10	were killed	*Main event*
11	in Israeli airstrikes	*Who by? (agent)*
12	before and after the rocket attack.	*When?*

This answers some, but not all, of Bell's *who, what, where, why, when and how* questions. In terms of sentence structure, apart from the contextualising comment in segment 1, the first element in each part of the sentence is the main actor or actors (in Bell's terms), in this case the Israeli and the Palestinian victims (segments 2 and 8). As Bell points out (1998:74), it is typical in news reports to focus on people by foregrounding them, putting them at the front of the sentence, exactly as we see here, and this often means that the verbs related to those people are put into the passive voice, again exactly as we see them here (3: 'was killed'; 10: 'were killed'). Bell's comment on this is interesting as it illustrates a distinctive feature of news reporting as opposed to narrative forms – people are often foregrounded even if that means that other elements of the sentence must be moved around and altered:

> The stress on personalisation and elite news actors guides the order of constituents within the sentence, even if this will result in a passive-voice verb. News-writing mythology holds that verbs should be active, but passivisation is quite common as the only means of getting the main news actors to the start of the sentence. (Bell, 1998:74)

However, this foregrounding might also attribute blame, as van Dijk notes from a different perspective, related to the Critical Linguistics tradition (see, for example, Fowler 1991; Fowler *et al.*, 1979):

> If negative acts are attributed to people appearing in the Agent role, they are held (more) responsible for these actions than if they appear in other roles. Moreover the syntactic structure of the sentence expressing such propositions may vary such that the agency of a particular person or group is de-emphasized, as is the case in passive constructions. (van Dijk, 1998:33, emphasis in original)

This alerts us to the important ways in which syntactic structuring, for example through passivisation, can serve to *attribute* more or less blame to particular 'actors' in any story, a point to which we will return when analysing the main story. In addition, this example neatly illustrates and supports Bell's analysis in terms of the existence of both *attribution* and *abstract* parts.

Turning now to the main part, the *story* itself, Bell's analysis of the event structure of the text can also illuminate ways in which the events of that day are depicted. Here is the second paragraph of the story again, and in addition the third paragraph, with the foregrounded actors, highlighted in bold:

Paragraph 2, sentence 1	**Israel** carried out the first airstrike in southern Gaza on Wednesday morning, hitting a minivan on a road west of Khan Yunis and killing five members of the Hamas military wing, Qassam Brigades, Hamas said.
Paragraph 2, sentence 2	**Southern Israel** then came under heavy rocket fire, with more than 25 rockets launched in two hours, the Israeli Army said.
Paragraph 2, sentence 3	**Hamas**, the Islamic militant group that controls Gaza, claimed responsibility for the rocket barrage, saying it had been retaliating for the Israeli strike.
Paragraph 3, sentence 1	In a second Israeli airstrike carried out amid the rocket fire, **two Palestinian youths** were killed and **12 other civilians** were wounded, Dr. Muawiya Hassanein, director of emergency medical services in Gaza, said.
Paragraph 3, sentence 2	**An Israeli Army spokeswoman** said the strike had been aimed at a rocket-firing squad, and **witnesses** in Gaza told Palestinian news media that the civilians had been hit while watching Hamas militants fire the rockets.

Besides the fact that again many of *who, what, where, why, when and how* elements of the story are present, and that human elements have been foregrounded in almost every case, it is noticeable that as the text continues we tend to get more detail about *what, why* and *who*, because the text unpacks the information which it had condensed together in the abstract in paragraph 1. A clearer sequence of events is now presented, along with more discussion of what exactly happened, and why. In this last aspect, the comments are then attributed to various witnesses and other speakers.

Paragraph structure in news reports

A news editor with limited space, who regularly needs to cut articles to make them fit, will naturally prefer her journalists to write their texts so that they can be cut most efficiently *from the bottom*, paragraph by paragraph, until they fit the space available. In other words each paragraph and each sentence should ideally be able to stand on its own, rather than being linked closely with other paragraphs with cohesive devices. This to some extent explains why news reports are commonly written in this style – with a series of standalone sentences and paragraphs, with relatively few devices linking them together. As Bell expresses it:

> News stories are standardly written as a series of one-sentence paragraphs, and commonly express little linkage between the sentences... There is routinely no flow of time sequence from one sentence to the next, and a lack of devices such as adverbs expressing linkages between sentences. (Bell, 1998:90)

In the *New York Times* example this appears to be largely true. An editor could cut any of the paragraphs starting from the bottom and the remaining story would still make sense. This also explains again why news reports have a lot of the basic information (the *what*, *who*, *when* and *where*) immediately, with slightly more detailed information (perhaps the *why* and *how*) often left until later.

Constructing the facts

The *New York Times*, in the analysis above, apparently attempted to put both sides of the conflict. However, if we look again at how that news report presented the situation, a number of questions might be raised, including these:

1. *Graphics:* Why has the newspaper headed the report with a picture of an Israeli woman being carried? A second picture further down is also of Israelis taking cover in a shelter, and there are no pictures of Palestinians.
2. *Sentence structure:* If the attacks began with an Israeli airstrike which killed Palestinians, as we learn in paragraph 2, why did the abstract in paragraph 1 lead syntactically with the death of an Israeli civilian and leave the deaths of the Palestinians until the end?: 'an Israeli civilian was killed Wednesday in a rocket attack by Hamas militants'.
3. *Lexis:* Why has the reporter chosen the word 'civilian' to describe the Israeli victim, and chosen the word 'militants' for the Hamas fighters, instead of (for example) 'freedom fighters' or 'soldiers'?
4. What effect do these choices of image, syntactic positioning and of lexis have on the reader?

This is not to imply that the *New York Times* was deliberately biased, or sought to project a particular picture; it is merely to say that it is important for discourse analysts to examine the images, syntactic patterning and lexical patterning and then ask these kinds of questions. Roger Fowler and a number of his colleagues are known for their work on what is called Critical Linguistics (for example, Fowler *et al.,* 1979), a forerunner of Critical Discourse Analysis (CDA). They raised questions such as these about news reporting in general and offered tools and approaches for analysing news reports critically. One key point which is prominent in their work is the fact that each writer makes a series of choices, consciously or otherwise, which means that analysts always need to ask the question: 'why did the writer choose to put the case in this particular way?' The issue concerns the choice of *focus* – the writer can choose to focus our attention on one aspect or one side or one person, as opposed to another, and this choice of focus is expressed through the language.

Another term often used in this regard is 'topicalisation' or 'topic control' (Bloor and Bloor, 2007:107) in which the writer or speaker tries to control the topic which they wish to receive the most focus. The reporter in this case, for example, could have chosen to begin the article differently, for example by foregrounding the Palestinian victims like this: 'Innocent Palestinian civilians were killed Wednesday in an attack by the Israeli airforce'. Another newspaper, the *International Herald Tribune,,* effectively did foreground the Palestinian victims with its headline on the same event : '7 Palestinians die in Israeli airstrike; Hamas rocket kills Israeli civilian.' So the fact that the *New York Times* chose not to do so is interesting, and worthy of investigation. Similarly every other sentence in the report could have been expressed syntactically and lexically in a different way – the writer made choices – so it is part of our role as discourse analysts to examine possible alternatives and then ask why the writer chose *this* way of linguistically constructing the situation rather than any other.

News time and events

Another way of expressing this is to say that in any part of any news report the reporter can choose what to give most prominence to, and the resulting choices can have a significant impact on the impression given to the reader. A particularly significant choice which has to be made is the *order* in which to present the events – whether it is the actual order in which they occurred in real life, or a different order. We saw earlier (see p. 73) that, according to Labov, spoken narratives typically follow the real time sequence very closely – we recall the schoolboy Michael's story about making a chair – but Bell alerts us to the fact that '[n]ews stories, by contrast, are seldom if ever told in chronological order' (Bell, 1998:96). Frequently they operate with what Bell terms 'news time', presenting events in a sequence quite different from the actual chronological sequence of real life events.

To ask the *why* question from the heuristic in Chapter 5, why is this? Why do news reports frequently tell the story in a different order? Bell and others (see, for example, van Dijk, 1995:82) note that one general reason for changing the order of events is the importance of *recency* in news reports, so that the most recent chronological event is often put first as it is seen as most newsworthy. This makes sense – we want to read what has just happened first, and the background can be filled in later. However, we need to be aware that such simple 'neutral' explanations might not be the whole story, and that other reasons can also come into play, for example political or moral decisions.

What about the approach of the *New York Times* in this text? If we follow Bell's basic approach to analysing the *event structure* in news reports we can see that the sequence of events as presented in this text is different from the sequence in real life. We then need to ask why this is so. It is clear that there were essentially three events – the Israeli attack (which we can call Event 1), the Hamas rockets (Event 2), and – during the rocket attacks – a second Israeli air attack (Event 3).

Event sequence	Chronological sequence of events in real life
Event 1: **Wednesday morning**	Israel carried out the first airstrike in southern Gaza on Wednesday morning.
Event 2: **Later**	Southern Israel then came under heavy rocket fire, with more than 25 rockets launched in two hours, the Israeli Army said.
Event 3: **During Event 2**	In a second Israeli airstrike carried out amid the rocket fire, two Palestinian youths were killed and 12 other civilians were wounded, Dr. Muawiya Hassanein, director of emergency medical services in Gaza, said.

However, if we look at the most prominent parts of the *New York Times* text, namely the *headline* and the first sentence (the *abstract*) we see in fact that Event 2, the Hamas rocket attack, is clearly given prominence in both.

Headline and abstract	Event sequence
Hamas and Israelis Trade Attacks, Killing Several	Event 2 (Hamas), then Event 1 and 3 (Israel)

In a sudden surge of violence, an Israeli civil-   Event 2
ian was killed Wednesday in a rocket attack by   Events 1 and 3
Hamas militants from Gaza, the first such fatality
in nine months, and at least eight Palestinians,
militants and civilians, were killed in Israeli air-
strikes before and after the rocket attack.

In these prominent parts of the text, the reporter (or perhaps a newspaper sub-editor) has chosen to *foreground* the Hamas attacks and *background* the Israel ones, contrary to their actual sequence in real life. As discourse analysts we therefore need to ask two questions:

a. *What is the effect of this on the reader?* (For example whom does this strategy favour, and who comes out worse from it?) To my mind this particular event order, along with the photographs, tends to construct Hamas as more aggressive and more to blame, even though the first attack in fact came from the Israeli side.
b. *Is this a regular pattern in this newspaper and others?* If so, and if we have clear evidence for such a pattern, we might start to see an element of bias for one reason or another.

My analysis here is small in scale, intending only to show in microcosm the way in which we can use Bell's approach to investigate *the event sequence* chosen in a news report, and how we can then question *what effect it has on the reader* and furthermore *why the news reporter might have chosen to do it in that way*. It would not of course be fair on the basis of such a small piece of evidence to criticise the *New York Times* or this reporter. For one thing, the reporter might argue in her own defence that in the full story she clearly set out the exact sequence of events as they happened. However, the work of Fowler makes us sensitive to the fact that fair construction and representation is not simply a question of what is in the text as a whole, but also of *how* it is presented, *what is made prominent*. As we analyse any text we need to be aware of this.

8.2 Lonely hearts ads

We can turn now from news reports to a very different kind of written text, namely small advertisements designed to attract a partner, often called 'lonely hearts ads'. Here is an example from the internet, adapted and ano-nymised, but with the original spellings and punctuation:

Age: 19 From: B... United Kingdom
The fun, loveable me!

I'm Isabelle but mainly known as Izzy! I am 19 years old and looking for a fun guy between the ages of 20–23. I have long brown hair, hazel eyes and 5ft3". I am fun, love going out and i am a good listner.

This is a good example of how a text can 'construct' people, in ways discussed in Chapter 2 (see p. 31). Here a young woman constructs an image of herself which she hopes will attract someone to respond. As with all advertisements the general function is primarily to *persuade*. Crane and Michie Ino (1987) suggest these are similar to advertisements for other commodities such as second-hand cars, reflecting in their view wider patterns of 'market exchange processes found in capitalist societies' (1987:233) as if people in such societies see themselves as commodities to be bought and sold. However, lonely hearts advertisements also have their own particular features, which we can now consider.

In terms of *discourse mode*, we can see that lonely hearts advertisements draw more on *describing* discourse mode, in this case describing the writer herself and making use of typical describing features, such as the use of the intensive verb 'am', the verb 'to have' to identify features she possesses such as her hair colour, and frequent use of adjectives.

The *structure* of lonely hearts ads differs from publication to publication; in this example the format on this particular website requires the age and location to be at the top, probably as they are key pieces of information for readers. They are followed by a short summary in the form of a sort of 'byline', *('The fun, loveable me!')*, then by the more detailed description. These are all features which clearly support the main function of the text.

Izzy's self-construction revolves around the idea of fun; not only is the word mentioned 3 times, but the sense of relaxation and 'rule-breaking' is reinforced by the numerous exclamation marks, the abbreviations ('Izzy', I'm',) the informal punctuation and capitalisation ('i' for 'I') and even the misspelling 'listner' for 'listener', as well as aspects of the content (for example, she loves going out). She therefore comes across as someone not worried about conventions and rules. Because we associate this kind of attitude with young people (!), she successfully constructs herself as youthful.

It might appear as if Izzy has simply sat down and written freely, but closer analysis shows that her text conforms closely to a standard pattern for this genre. The genre of lonely hearts ads might appear to be informal, but in fact they follow a remarkably restricted and formalised set of parameters, to the extent that there are guides available on how to write them. The trick of the writer – as with many genres – is to conform to the genre norm but also to stand out as different. Crane and Michie Ino (1987) point out that beside the basic information such as name, age and location, such ads are typically expected to include the following features, which I set alongside examples from Izzy's ad:

Typical contents of a lonely hearts ad (partly adapted from Crane and Michie Ino, 1987:233–4)	Examples from Izzy's ad
basic information	Age: 19 From: B... United Kingdom I'm Isabelle but mainly known as Izzy!
physical attributes	I have long brown hair, hazel eyes and 5ft3.
personality attributes	I am fun..... i am a good listner
relational statuses (e.g. information on work, marriage, health, education, finances, religion and so on) tastes	- ...love going out
qualities sought in the Other (i.e. what she is looking for in a partner)	looking for a fun guy between the ages of 20–23.

It will be clear that Izzy follows the genre expectation quite closely, giving us all the expected information with the exception of the 'relational', possibly because those features would make her seem too conventional.

Here is a different ad, adapted and anonymised from a similar website. Note that it follows a similar structure, for the reasons we identified above, but with some significant differences.

Happy times
Hi, I am a 45 year old divorcee who suffered a stroke 4 years ago.

I am tall and slim and pretty attractive. I live with my three teenage children and two old cats and a pet rabbit (although I've never seen it – my children say it's still definitely still alive!!)

We are happy together and all live in harmony. I work locally part-time and have lots of friends and on the whole have a great social life.

But someone is missing; it would be nice to share some special times with a soul mate.

I love eating out or in! I prefer red wine to white and I love all sorts of music. So you can see that in spite of life's ups and downs I am a happy and fun person.

Hope to hear from you.

This woman, whom we can call June, is older than Izzy and at a very different stage of life. This may in part determine the way she constructs herself through her advertisement. If we analyse it as we did in Izzy's case, we can see that it does fulfil the genre expectations, but at the same time emphasises different aspects.

Typical contents of a lonely hearts ad (partly adapted from Crane and Michie Ino, 1987:233–4)	Examples from June's ad
basic information	...I am a 45 year old divorcee I work locally part-time
physical attributes	I am tall and slim and pretty attractive.
personality attributes	...I am a happy and fun person
relational statuses (e.g. information on work, marriage, health, education, finances, religion and so on)	...who suffered a stroke 4 years ago I live with my three teenage children and two old cats and a pet rabbit. We are happy together and all live in harmony...and have lots of friends and on the whole have a great social life
tastes	I love eating out or in! I prefer red wine to white and I love all sorts of music.
qualities sought in the Other (i.e. what she is looking for in a partner)	...a soul mate

This shows that her ad also fits closely with the genre expectation as analysed by Crane and Michie Ino (1987). However, where it significantly differs from Izzy's ad is in the amount of 'relational' information which June offers. June gives a lot of information about her health, her relationships, her family and so on, in ways which project her as older and more 'attached' than Izzy, presumably so as to attract someone for whom those traits are also of importance.

When we construct ourselves in such ads we can of course choose which aspects to emphasise or neglect, and this in turn impacts on the image we offer to the reader. In wider terms this also illustrates the fact that when we write we can draw on a standard genre, but within its general parameters we can be flexible and individual in ways which then make the text itself individual and different. We can also offer embellishments and extra features such as humorous comments ('although I've never seen it – my children say it's still definitely still alive!!'*). In short, good writers strike a balance between conforming to the genre, but also embellishing and changing it creatively.

8.3 Discourse and new technology

Recently researchers have shown considerable interest in the types of language behaviour displayed on the internet and on mobile phones. Some commentators suggest that such language is driving a decline in traditional forms of language use, while others (see, for example, Crystal, 2008) see it more as a manifestation of the natural dynamic of language development. Some researchers (see, for example, Herring, 2004) have argued that analysing what they term 'computer mediated discourse' calls for a particular set of approaches – termed computer mediated discourse analysis or CMDA. In any case, as this area is of increasing interest, it is worth now looking at two forms of 'digital discourse', namely text messaging and online gaming discourse.

8.4 Text messaging

Has there ever been a linguistic phenomenon which has aroused such curiosity, suspicion, fear, antagonism, fascination, excitement, and enthusiasm, all at once? (Crystal, 2008: 3)

Crystal is here referring to text messaging. If we look at an example, you will probably be familiar with the kind of language it uses, and will recognise immediately its function and style:

Safe -Angie + Lucy had words last nite-stood
there arguing 4 ages,loads of people outside cobarna.Bit
obvious they... ...werent gonna fight tho cos they were
there 4 so long!I was a bit pissed (woh!) Good nite tho!Spk
2u lata xxBeckyxx

(from Thurlow and Poff, 2009:13)

As Crystal implies in the comment quoted above, text messaging is a relatively new form of language use, and has aroused controversy deriving from the fear that it might affect other more standardised forms of writing. This is largely because of its use of odd abbreviations, symbols, exaggerated punctuation, and a 'creative attitude to spelling', making the words sound like colloquial speech. To the observer these features may seem random and chaotic, not amenable to analysis in any way. However, as in the case of conversation, it is possible through close analysis to discover *patterns and regularities* which texters assimilate through practice, and then make use of just as they do with other forms of discourse.

The first step in the procedure, as previously, is to identify the *function* of the discourse, and then to identify particular *features* of it. Thurlow and Poff (2009:14) have argued that the main function of texting language is what they call the 'principle of sociality', related to 'solidary' behaviour or what other writers call 'solidarity'; in other words, people text mainly for social interaction. As with conversation, one defining feature of texting is its emphasis on *interaction* rather than *transaction* (achieving some sort of exchange). Although of course we do use text messages to arrange meetings or to get information (transactions) it is probably true that their main function is to ease and develop social contact with other people.

In terms of its *features* Thurlow and Poff suggest that this main function of texting is underpinned by three main maxims. These can be summarised as follows, and illustrated with examples from the text message we saw above:

Three main maxims of texting	Examples
(1) *Brevity and speed*: text messages are driven by the need to be brief and quick	Abbreviated greetings and leave-taking: *Hi babe!...Spk 2u lata xxBeckyxx* Shortened spellings and use of symbols: *nite, 4 ages, tho , +, 2u*
(2) *Paralinguistic restitution*: normally when we speak with someone we have 'paralinguistic' clues such as facial expression, intonation and gestures to help us understand. With text messages we do not have these so we use various devices such as exaggerated punctuation (!!!??!), emoticons and other symbols in order to overcome the absence of such visual and auditory clues – so as to give 'paralinguistic restitution'.	Symbols and other language used to replace actions or gestures: *xx (woh!)*
(3) *Phonological approximation*: where the standard spelling is changed to fit closely with colloquial speech, e.g. 'gonna, 'bin', 'coz', 'girlz'	*gonna, cos, lata*

(adapted from Thurlow and Poff, 2009:14)

It may seem as if the use of abbreviations is for purely technical reasons, in other words because using the keypad is cumbersome. However, this is not the whole story, since it also allows for efficient, rapid turn-taking sequences resembling face-to-face speech. To put it more formally: 'the need for both brevity and speed appears to be motivated less by technological constraints, but rather by pragmatic demands such as ease of turn-taking and fluidity of social interaction' (Thurlow and Poff, 2009:14). This in turn links with the point that texters may adopt these three practices primarily for social cohesion, to create social bonds. Texting language has its practical side, in short, but what drives the phenomenon is the fact that many texters also use these language devices as an expression of *solidarity*; they want to 'fit in' with a particular social group, and they show their solidarity with that in-group by adopting a particular shared set of language norms.

Is text messaging a genre?

Thurlow and Poff argue that 'what gives text messages a distinctive (though not necessarily unique) generic feel is the <u>combination</u> of:

- (a) the <u>comparatively</u> short length of text-messages;
- (b) the <u>relative</u> concentration of non-standard typographic markers; and
- (c) their <u>predominantly</u> small-talk content and solidary orientation.'
  (Thurlow and Poff, 2009:13, emphasis in the original)

I would add a fourth important element, the fact that text messaging draws on the *interacting* discourse mode, since each message is typically either an opening move in an adjacency pair, expecting a response, or in some way a response to a previous message.

Although Thurlow and Poff also note on the same page that none of their three generic features 'is individually sufficient to characterize text-messaging' it is convincing to suggest that the combination of all of these features, including the fourth one we have added, entitles text messaging to be considered a genre. A further compelling point in favour of this is that many people can easily recognise what is meant by text messaging, and can identify its main features, to the extent that books have been written about it in its own right, and this suggests that it has earned its place in general recognition as a genre. To conclude our discussion of Text Messaging we can do no better than to quote Crystal's argument that the practice is no bad thing in itself:

All the popular beliefs about texting are wrong, or at least debatable. Its graphic distinctiveness is not a totally new phenomenon. Nor is its use restricted to the young. There is increasing evidence that it helps rather than hinders literacy. And only a very tiny part of the language uses its distinctive orthography... Texting has added a new dimension to language use, indeed, but its long-term impact on the already existing varieties of language is likely to be negligible. (Crystal, 2008:9)

8.5 Computer gaming

To turn to another form of 'digital interaction', the language of online computer gaming offers some unusually dense and difficult discourse. Here is part of one such interaction, taken from an online fantasy game in which computer users, mainly children and teenagers, take on animated characters and move around an animated world buying, selling, chatting, making things, solving quests and so on. All contributions are typed and appear on the screen for all to see, although characters can choose to go with other characters into private areas.

In this excerpt there are several characters all milling around a public market area called the Grand Exchange, where online characters can exchange, buy and sell goods. I have given each character a letter for easy identification, and on the right I offer a 'translation' of what it means.

Turn	Player	Utterance	Translation
1	A:	selling death runes lowest in G>E	I am selling some 'death runes' at the lowest price in the Grand Exchange
2	B:	Ty	Thank you
3	C:	Np	No problem
4	D:	1 sec	1 second...
5	E:	Nty	No thank you
6	F:	Hmm nty	Hmm, no thank you

Gaming dialogue of this kind is notoriously difficult to follow for non-players, partly because of the unusual *turn-taking* pattern; it is not always clear who is talking to whom. In this example, one character, A, is offering something for sale (death runes are objects used for magic in the game) and claiming that his or her prices are the lowest in the Grand Exchange (G>E).

As with conversational texts, which we discussed in Chapter 6, a useful entry point for analysing this written text is the adjacency pair patterns. Drawing on our standard world schema of 'buying in a market place' it is possible to interpret line 1 as the start of an adjacency pair *offering* something. This anticipates a *second pair part* and in fact we get this from several characters, in lines 2, 5 and 6, and perhaps also 3.

Examining the adjacency pairs therefore allows some understanding of participants' turn-taking behaviour. However, another difficulty is the unusual jargon and abbreviations, similar to those used in text messaging. Unlike text messaging, which tends to draw on a fairly standard set of abbreviations and symbols, each individual online game to some extent develops its own lexis and terminology. In essence the only way for an analyst to come to understand this jargon is to act rather like an anthropologist in a new culture, either by immersing him or herself as a 'participant observer' (Spradley, 1980) and actually playing the game for a period of time, or by getting an 'informant' who knows the rules and conventions to interpret what is happening, as an anthropologist might do when studying a different culture.

An unusual aspect of turn-taking behaviour, which such an informant could help to elucidate, is the fact that several participants all 'talk' together, directing their comments at the character facing them, but the comments from *all* the characters within view appear on the screen together. This leads to complex exchanges such as this one below, a continuation of the one we have just seen. Whereas a player will know which thread he or she is following, and will ignore the others during the interaction, it is difficult for an analyst after the event to know which thread belongs to which participants. To help with the reading I offer a broad 'translation' of some of the jargon and abbreviations in the right hand column. While reading, try to identify:

a. which character is speaking to which other character(s);
b. what their main *aim* is in each case (the function of each utterance);
c. any *adjacency pairs* patterns.

After the initial offer and responses in lines 1–6, which we saw above, line 7 sees a new offer from a different character, this time wanting to buy a *d long* (a dragon long sword) for 102,000 of the game currency, and line 9 introduces yet another character wanting to buy a full set of *verac* (a type of armour in the game). A clue to the rest of the text is that several characters are simply trying to buy and sell, but one character is challenging another character to a fight.

	Characters	Text	Interpretation / translation
1	A:	selling death runes lowest in G>E	I'm selling 'death runes' – runes for magic, the cheapest in this 'Grand Exchange' marketplace
2	B:	Ty	Thank you
3	C:	Np	No problem

4	D:	1 sec	Wait 1 second…
5	E:	Nty	No, thank you
6	F:	Hmm nty	Hmm no, thank you
7	G:	Buying d long 102k	I want to buy a dragon long sword for 102,000
8	A:	sellin death runes lowest in G>E	I'm selling 'death runes'.
9	H:	Buying full verac	I want to buy a full suit of verac (a type of armour)
10	D:	Joe	Joe!
11	H:	Buying full verac	I want to buy a full suit of verac armour
12	Joe:	Get redy	Get ready!
13	D:	we r going pvp	We're going to the 'Player versus player' zone
14	L:	Hi ;)	*(New character enters)* Hi.
15	A:	sellin death runes lowest in G>E	I'm selling 'death runes'
16	D:	Not duel arena..	I don't want to go to the 'Duelling arena' *(because he can get a better advantage in another place)*
17	D:	Waste..	Let's go to the waste ground
18	Joe:	No	No
19	O:	Hi	*(New character enters, answers line 14)* Hi
20	N:	XD	*Smiley symbol:* XD = that's funny (X = closed/squinted eyes, D = the mouth)
21	D:	Yea..	Yes
22	H:	Buying full verac	I want to buy a full suit of verac armour
23	D:	You asked for a fight.	You asked for a fight
24	Joe:	No	No
25	O:	can you buy back ur logs ;)	Can you (L) please buy back the logs you sold me? (I need the money)
26	H:	Buying full verac	I want to buy a full suit of verac armour
27	D:	Thats pvp	That's the 'Player versus player' zone
28	Joe:	Dullin	I want to go to the 'Duelling arena'
29	D:	get food and pots	Get food and magic potions
30	D:	No u noob….	*(Refuses offer of Duelling arena)* – noob = noobie
31	D:	Rofl	Rofl = 'Rolling on floor laughing' (at Joe for being a scared 'noob' or newcomer)
32	D:	Scared now?	Scared now?

33	Joe:	Dullin	I want to go to the 'Duelling arena'
34	H:	Buying full verac	I want to buy a full suit of verac armour
35	B:	Buyuini whip max price	I'm buying a whip, maximum price
36	D:	4 lvls higher	You (Joe) are 4 levels higher in the game than me...
37	Joe:	No	No
38	D:	And ur scared	...and you are still scared to fight!
39	H:	Buying full verac	I want to buy a full suit of verac armour
40	Joe:	Dullin	I want to go to the 'Duelling arena'
41	D:	Scareddddd!!!!!!!!	You are scared!!!!!

The text is by no means easy to follow or understand. In essence, there are 4 characters (A, B, G, H) who are simply buying or selling, and make their offers throughout the exchange. Two other characters, L and O enter the Grand Exchange late and communicate only with each other, but several lines apart:

14.	L:	Hi ;)
19.	O:	Hi
25.	O:	can you buy back ur logs ;)

However, the main interaction in this long passage is between character D and character Joe. In this game if you fight and win you can get more points, so D wants to fight with Joe, not in the Duelling Arena, but somewhere else where he can get a better advantage, namely the Wasteland. The exchange is a classic example of a sustained attempt, through several adjacency moves, to persuade someone to do something, but with an equally clear resistance, albeit using few words, on the part of Joe. We can isolate this verbal interaction from the others and look just at these two participants' turns so as to follow it more easily:

	Characters	Text	Interpretation / translation
10.	D:	Joe	Joe!
12.	Joe:	Get redy	Get ready!
13.	D:	we r going pvp	We're going to the 'Player versus player' zone
16.	D:	Not duel arena..	I don't want to go to the 'Duelling arena' *(because he can get a better advantage in another place)*
17.	D:	Waste..	Let's go to the waste ground

18.	Joe:	No	No
21.	D:	Yea..	Yes
23.	D:	You asked for a fight.	You asked for a fight
24.	Joe:	No	No
27.	D:	Thats pvp	That's the 'Player versus player' zone
28.	Joe:	Dullin	I want to go to the 'Duelling arena'
29.	D:	get food and pots	Get food and magic potions
30.	D:	No u noob….	*(Refuses offer of Duelling arena)* – noob = noobie,
31.	D:	Rofl	Rofl = 'Rolling on floor laughing' (at Jo for being a scared 'noob' or newcomer)
32.	D:	Scared now?	Scared now?
33.	Joe:	Dullin	I want to go to the 'Duelling arena'
36.	D:	4 lvls higher	You (Joe) are 4 levels higher in the game than me…
37.	Joe:	No	No
38.	D:	And ur scared	…and you are still scared to fight!
40.	Joe:	Dullin	I want to go to the 'Duelling arena'
41.	D:	Scareddddd!!!!!!!!	You are scared!!!!!

This makes use of the *interacting* discourse mode, of course, so again a useful entry point is to analyse adjacency pair patterning and turn-taking. To start with, in line 10, D calls Joe by name. Joe responds indirectly in line 12 by opening a new adjacency pair move, an instruction to 'Get redy', showing his willingness. D then offers a *suggestion*, couched as a direct statement, proposing that they do not go to the Duelling arena, and offering an alternative in line 16. Joe refuses (line 18). In other words lines 13, 16 and 17, although three turns in the game, constitute a single *suggesting move*, and line 18 is the (dispreferred) response. This shows an interesting feature of online interaction, namely that discourse moves which would take one turn in real life might be broken up over several 'online turns'. It is also noticeable that the dispreferred response, unlike those in face-to-face conversations, has no mitigations or hesitations, but is a direct 'no', suggesting again an area in which online written adjacency pair use might differ in important ways from spoken interaction.

D does not accept Joe's refusal, countering in lines 21 and 23 with a *blaming* move (starting a new adjacency pair) as a way of applying pressure, and reinforces the pressure by taking two consecutive turns before allowing Joe to reply. Since Joe is still resisting (lines 24 and 28), D responds with 4 consecutive turns without waiting for a reply, first making a request (get food and potions) then refusing Joe's request to go to the duelling ground (line 28) with a mild insult 'No u noob', (a 'noob' being a novice or weak player) and then acting as if they are getting ready to go (line 29). Joe is still resisting, however, so D gets more aggressive, laughing at Joe (line 31), insulting him for being scared (lines 32, 38, 41), and then belittling him for the fact that, although he is at a higher game level than D, he refuses to fight.

The analysis here is only a sketch; a more detailed analysis of each turn and its function would undoubtedly reveal more complex and intricate aspects to the interaction. Nonetheless, it can be seen even from this brief discussion that participants in such forums can sustain quite elaborate and sustained interactions, very similar to face-to-face conversational exchanges, even while other participants all around them are 'talking' across them. They do this through a quite complex and developed code of abbreviations and symbols, as well as rapid turn-taking facilitated by very short messages. The communicative skill involved in such exchanges is impressive; each participant demonstrates an ability to achieve and negotiate communicative ends with a high degree of effectiveness and creativity, and with considerable economy of expression. However, there are some interesting differences between the turn-taking and adjacency pair activity in this online discourse as compared with face-to-face interaction.

8.6 Texting compared with online gaming interaction

Before leaving the topic of electronic communication it is useful to compare the discussion of text messaging in the previous section with the analysis of online gaming interaction here. It was noted that texting seems to be characterised by three main features, and all of them also apply to the language of online gaming:

(1) *brevity and speed*: messages are driven by the need to be brief and quick

(2) *paralinguistic restitution*: players use various devices such as exaggerated punctuation (*!!!??!*), emoticons and other symbols in order to overcome the absence of visual and auditory clues which body language, facial expression and intonation normally provide in face-to-face interaction

(3) *phonological approximation*: where the standard spelling is changed to fit closely with colloquial speech, e.g. 'gonna, 'bin', 'coz', 'girlz'

In line with the first of these, gaming interaction is typically brief and rapid. As for the second point, gaming of the kind we looked at offers more visual clues in the graphical elements than texting usually does, but is still restricted in terms of facial and phonological clues (the 'paralinguistic elements'). As a result, gaming language still includes a good deal of 'paralinguistic restitution', meaning the use of extensive punctuation, 'smileys', emoticons and the like to make up for the lack of facial and auditory clues. The third feature is also evident, with the use of similar types of phonological approximation, when participants alter their language so that it 'sounds' more like real speech. Examples in our text include 'redy', 'yea' and 'u'.

However, online gaming of the type discussed here evinces a number of significant differences from texting in terms of genre features. Four characteristic features of the genre of texting were identified above (adapting and expanding Thurlow and Poff, 2009:13):

(a) *the comparatively short length of text-messages*
(b) *the relative concentration of non-standard typographic markers*
(c) *their predominantly small-talk content and solidary orientation*
(d) *the use of the interacting discourse mode*

Three of these also apply to gaming language: messages are relatively short (a), there is a concentration of non-standard typographic markers (b), though arguably texting shows more of these than gaming language, and the discourse mode is *interacting* (d). However, the main difference between the two types of interaction is one of function (c). Certainly there is still an element of the *social solidarity* function in gaming, but unlike texting the main overall function in online gaming is obviously *play* (sometimes called the 'ludic function' from the Greek work *ludus* meaning a game). Texting also has its ludic element, of course (Crystal, 2008: 71), but it is plain that an online game, by definition, emphasises the ludic more than does text messaging.

The central difference between them is therefore in terms of their different functions. For these reasons we could characterise Online Gaming interaction of the kind we have been examining as consisting of:

Function
  (a) a predominantly ludic functional orientation

Features
  (b) comparatively short text-messages
  (c) a complex interweaving of turns and topic threads
  (d) a high concentration of non-standard typographic markers, aiming at paralinguistic restitution and phonological approximation

Finally, we noted the skill with which many players appear to engage with each other in order to achieve their purposes, adapting and modifying their language behaviour to suit different circumstances. Hult and Richins offer a good example of how one participant in their study switched from one register to another with apparent ease:

> Savvy communicators know how to bounce between genres and registers without much difficulty. In fact, in one of the observations of an IM'er [instant messenger] at work and play, the subject was simultaneously composing a rather formal letter to his grandparents (Dear Grandmother and Grandfather: Happy Anniversary! You have been such an inspiration and role model in my life) at the same time as he was IM'ing with a friend (hey, girl how are you?). (Hult and Richins 2006: n. p.)

This again demonstrates the fact that language users are able to adapt their behaviour to new media and contexts flexibly. In line with Crystal's point (see p. 153), that texting does not appear to be as harmful as some have suggested, online gaming discourse can also be seen as manifesting an impressive human ability to develop and utilise new linguistic and symbolic resources to suit new communicative environments. These abilities, rather than being negative or 'subtractive', can instead be viewed as potentially positive or 'adaptive and additive' (Thurlow, 2003), offering new ways of communicating to suit new forms of electronic media.

8.7 Summary

This chapter has examined a range of written genres, to complement our analysis of spoken genres in the previous chapters. In addition, the analyses in this chapter have highlighted the value of examining the following features of discourse:

1. *The structure of a piece of discourse:* analysing the structure of a piece of discourse can give insights into how it achieves its function. For example, a news article is often structured in a particular way to allow for efficient editing and maximum immediate impact. The discourse structure of a lonely hearts advertisement helps to achieve its function of attracting a partner.
2. *Event sequence*: the analysis of news reports made the point that analysing the sequence of events as presented in a text, and contrasting it with the actual historical sequence, can elucidate the impact of the text and perhaps the aims of the writer.
3. *Graphics and layout*: analysis of the news reports took into account the pictures which accompanied the text, their content and placement. This feature is an important part of many genres and examination of these

aspects, perhaps in a multimodal approach (Baldry and Thibault 2005), can be a useful tool when analysing certain texts and genres.

4. *Topic placement and 'topicalisation'*: writers often seek to control the *topic* and the *focus* of what they present, so as to focus attention on the area they see as important, at the same time perhaps drawing attention away from other issues.

5. *Content balance*: the analysis of the lonely hearts advertisements made the point that although both ads contained the same areas of content, the *balance of attention* given to each area shifted. This is linked to the previous point about topicalisation and focus, and shows how the *balance of content* can be manipulated to achieve certain effects, *foregrounding* certain elements and *backgrounding* others.

6. *Attribution:* we saw the value of examining different strategies among news reporters in *attributing* the information they are reporting, either vaguely or specifically.

7. *Sentence structure, syntax and lexis*: in each of the analyses of the above areas, aspects of the sentence structure, syntax and lexis helped to achieve the writer's effects. It is important in any discourse analysis to analyse the 'higher order' elements of organisation and content, and also the 'lower order' elements of linguistic syntax and lexis to see how the two aspects of any text work together to achieve the overall effect. Analysis of one without the other can be incomplete.

Political Oratory and Intertextuality

9

The last three chapters have examined a range of genres which draw on the discourse modes of *interacting, narrating, reporting* and *instructing*. This chapter considers one more genre, this time through the lens of *intertextuality*. Chapter 2 made the point that all texts draw in one way or another on other texts which went before, and that therefore they are all intertextual in one way or another. However, in some texts the intertextuality is more prominent and significant as a part of its impact and interpretation than in others. It is an example of this kind of text which will now be examined.

9.1 The role of intertextuality

In Chapter 2, the issue of intertextuality was raised through this example, a passage from the speech by Barack Obama when he was running for the US presidential nomination:

> It was the call of workers who organized, women who reached for the ballot, a president who chose the moon as our new frontier, and a king who took us to the mountaintop and pointed the way to the promised land: Yes, we can, to justice and equality.

It was argued there, with reference also to the 'Squirrel' text (p.15), that intertextual awareness is more than just references, but plays its part in the whole complex process of constructing texts and also in the process of interpreting and understanding them, and as such constitutes a key part of our discourse comprehension.

Allen (2000), in his major study of intertextuality, which includes a useful summary and discussion of its history and use in different fields, notes that: 'all utterances depend on or call to other utterances; no utterance itself is singular; all utterances are shot through with other, competing and conflicting voices (Allen, 2000:27). This metaphor of 'voice' had been used earlier by the writer and critic Bakhtin (1973), and by a number of other analysts. For example, Chouliaraki and Fairclough (1999:49) use the same metaphor: 'In the most general terms, intertextuality is the combination in my discourse of my voice and the voice of another.' However, as was argued in Chapter 2, this should not be taken to imply that intertextuality is purely a matter of 'quoting'. When we come as readers and analysts to interpret texts, we need to consider intertextuality not simply as a matter of visible references to other texts and genres (*products*) which we can then collect as we might pick out glittering diamonds from the mud, but as a far more pervasive *process*, whose effects on us might be less easy to see and more subtle, but all the more powerful for that reason.

The discussion can now turn to examine the speech by Barack Obama in greater detail, after which the issue of intertextuality can be revisited.

9.2 Political speeches and oratory

The heuristic in Chapter 5 proposed that a useful strategy for analysing a text might be to start with the question about function and impact (what is the text doing or seeking to do?) and then to consider how it does it. In the case of a Political Speech, the typical aim or function is of course to *persuade*. It is illuminating to see how a good orator can pull together a range of resources in order to achieve this function – the *features* of the speech, to which we can now turn.

This particular speech by Barack Obama was delivered in January 2008 after he had just lost a primary ballot in New Hampshire to Hilary Clinton, his rival for the Democratic nomination. The speech is not long – a mere thirteen minutes – but of all the speeches he made during his presidential campaign this one is arguably the most pivotal. It succeeded not only in rallying his supporters, but in setting a tone, identifying a theme and establishing a momentum which was eventually to carry him to presidential office. It was the first speech which established *'Yes we can'* as a creed or slogan. The phrase was immediately taken up and used in a host of songs and internet exchanges, which we will examine later, and was also revisited again, in a clear intertextual echo, in Obama's address in November 2008 after the election, when he accepted the presidency.

In terms of the *features* of the speech, and how they contributed to its impact, it will be useful now to examine the closing three minutes in the transcript reproduced on p. 166 below, to see how the slogan itself gains its power through Obama's use of emotive lexis, strong contrasts, clear rhythms and powerful repetitions, as well a host of intertextual echoes and other devices.

Classical means of persuasion: *logos, pathos* and *ethos*

Discourse serves to construct not only situations and other people (in ways discussed in Chapter 2) but also the character and personality of the speaker or writer. In politics this is crucial, if the speaker wants our votes. The way in which political discourse constructs the speaker has been studied for centuries, and such studies often refer back to the classical analysis offered by Aristotle in ancient Greece. For Aristotle, successful persuasion in oratory involves at least three main features, which are known by the terms *ethos, pathos* and *logos*. These categories are still of relevance to modern discourse analysis, since in effect they set out ways in which the discourse of a political speaker can construct the speaker and the situation in ways favourable to his or her cause.

The first of Aristotle's categories, *ethos* (related to the English word 'ethics') relates to 'the personal character of the speaker' (Aristotle, trans. Rhys Roberts, 1984:2155), and concerns the way in which the speaker puts his or her own character across to the audience in order to create a strong and trustworthy impression. '[Ethos] is not personality but moral character, that is the impression created through the speech that the speaker possesses qualities which invite trust and belief' (Carey, 2000:203). Political speakers can convey good *ethos* through the way they stand, the way they respond, body language, gestures, intonation and pitch and the way they take questions; all play their part in creating this sense of *ethos* and cause us to trust their judgement. When we consider Obama's speech in more detail we will see how he uses some of these strategies, consciously or instinctively, in order to create that sense of himself as someone we can believe and follow.

With respect to Aristotle's second element, *pathos* (related to the English word 'pathetic', to do with feelings), the speaker tries to induce *feelings* or *emotions* in the hearers which will make them support his or her point of view. This is appealing to the emotions by 'putting the audience into a certain frame of mind'. The reason for this is clear: '[P]ersuasion may come about through the hearers, when the speech stirs their emotions. Our judgements when we are pleased and friendly are not the same as when we are pained and hostile (Aristotle, trans. Rhys Roberts, 1984:2155). Political speakers make use of emotional means, such as fanning up nationalistic feelings, or hatred, or sympathy, perhaps by an anecdote, or perhaps by using emotive terms such as 'terrorist' or 'criminals' or 'victims'. Aristotle is understood to have considered this aspect of oratory as a relatively weak device, preferring instead the third element, *logos* (related to our word 'logic') by which he meant persuasion through logical argumentation. With this element, 'persuasion is effected through the speech itself when we have proved a truth or an apparent truth by means of the persuasive arguments suitable to the case in question' (Aristotle, trans. Rhys Roberts, 1984:2155).

These three general approaches to persuasion can be used all together, or at different times in the same speech. They can also, incidentally, help us to understand other genres – for example, news reports. The relevance of this analysis for Obama's speech is that at this point in the campaign he clearly needed to motivate his supporters and to show that he was resilient in the face of defeat, so the speech is strong on *ethos* and on *pathos*. This was not the moment for careful argumentation and debate, more the territory of *logos*, which come in a different kind of speech (and is considered more typical in forensic speeches, that is, speeches in the law courts). This was the moment to rally and stir up the audience to keep fighting, and this explains the style of speech which Obama then delivered.

Barack Obama's New Hampshire speech, January 2008

Here is a simplified transcript of the closing three minutes of the speech in question. (Video versions of it are available on the internet, and are useful to watch while reading the transcript and analysis below.)

In most transcripts, this speech is neatly divided into sections with gaps between them, giving the misleading impression that Obama paused after each sentence. This is untrue, and since his pausing and timing are crucial to the power of the speech (as will be considered in the analysis below), my transcript attempts to represent Obama's actual pausing and momentum strategies more exactly, his pauses timed in seconds. Responses of the crowd, which are also crucial to the impact of the whole, and also my comments, are marked in square brackets. Look out for elements of *pathos* and *ethos*, as well as ways in which Obama groups ideas and phrases rhythmically into *pairs* and groups of *three*:

(10 minutes, 9 seconds into the speech)
For when we have faced down impossible odds, when we've been told we're not ready or that we shouldn't try or that we can't, generations of Americans have responded with a simple creed that sums up the spirit of a people: Yes, we can. *[cheers begin]* Yes, we can. Yes, we can.
(10.38)

[cheers – strong crowd chanting repetition of 'Yes we can'. Obama says it once again.]

[13 second pause]

[Obama then raises his hand and continues]

(10.51)

It was a creed written into the founding documents that declared the destiny of a nation: Yes, we can.

[mild cheers, 1 second pause]

It was whispered by slaves and abolitionists as they blazed a trail towards freedom through the darkest of nights: Yes, we can. *[Mild cheers, but no significant pause]*. It was sung by immigrants as they struck out from distant shores and pioneers who pushed westward against an unforgiving wilderness: Yes, we can. *[Mild cheers, no pause]*. It was the call of workers who organized, women who reached for the ballot, a president who chose the moon as our new frontier, and a king who took us to the mountaintop and pointed the way to the promised land: Yes, we can...*[Cheers start]*...to justice and equality. *[Chant starts again 'yes, we can, yes we can']*

(11.41)

[21 second pause.Obama smiles, standing still.
Finally raises hand slightly and continues]

[Final section completed with no significant pauses, building to the climax]

(12.02)

Yes, we can, to opportunity and prosperity. Yes, we can heal this nation. Yes, we can repair this world. Yes, we can. And so, tomorrow, as we take the campaign south and west, as we learn that the struggles of the textile workers in Spartanburg are not so different than the plight of the dishwasher in Las Vegas, that the hopes of the little girl who goes to the crumbling school in Dillon are the same as the dreams of the boy who learns on the streets of L.A., we will remember that there is something happening in America, that we are not as divided as our politics suggest, that we are one people, *[Yeah]* we are one nation...and, together *[rising crescendo of cheers]*, we will begin the next great chapter in the American story, with three words that will ring from coast to coast, from sea to shining sea: Yes, we can.

[crowd start to repeat 'yes we can' but he continues]

Thank you, New Hampshire. Thank you. Thank you.

(13.09)

The power of this speech comes from many of its features, lexical, rhythmical, phonological, syntactical, intertextual amongst them, and in order to analyse some of these resources in more detail, I will take each aspect in turn. This will also allow me to make some wider points about how to analyse political speeches in general.

The lexis of political speeches

In terms of lexis we note in this part of the speech an impressive range of positive, emotive terms such as 'spirit', 'creed', 'destiny', 'freedom', 'promised land', 'justice', and 'equality'. Most of these words are general and vague – none of the *logos* of detailed policy – precisely because whereas other political speeches might aim to persuade through argument, the function of this speech is instead to persuade through motivation and inspiration, so it opts for the more emotional lexis of *pathos*. The nouns are deliberately *abstract*, of a kind which can carry emotive power largely through their emotional appeal to grand *ideologies* of the kind we discussed in Chapter 7. In this case, of course, many of them revolve around the idea of the American nation, constitution and political system, so they have the added effect of arousing patriotic, nationalistic emotions. Examples include phrases such as 'destiny of a nation', 'founding documents' (referring to the US founding constitutional documents), 'one nation', and 'one people'.

This accounts in part for the emotional effect of the lexical choices, but is there anything intertextual here? Later in the speech, as has already been noted, Obama explicitly signals a number of intertextual references when he alludes quite directly to a 'king' (meaning Martin Luther King) and 'president', President Kennedy, but an important point about intertextual power is that it can be more subtle and pervasive, precisely because it can be more indirect and obscure. For example, many of the words in Obama's speech themselves echo other phrases, concepts and texts intertextually in ways which the listeners will not consciously notice or identify – but their effect is all the more powerful for that. A good example is the word 'creed', implying something solid and ancient, which was used by Martin Luther King in his famous speech in the 1960s: 'I have a dream that one day this nation will rise up and live out the true meaning of its <u>creed</u>: "We hold these truths to be self-evident: that all men are created equal"' (King, 1963). No listener would make the lexical link directly and explicitly – the power of the word 'creed' comes rather from the general resonances it evokes, part of which is our distant memory of that earlier speech. Likewise the phrase 'one nation' echoes in a relatively subtle way the Pledge of Allegiance to the US flag: 'I pledge allegiance to the flag of the United States of America, and to the Republic for which it stands: <u>one Nation under God</u>, indivisible, with Liberty and Justice for all'. These could not be termed *deliberate* intertextual references, and most listeners would be unable to identify and place them specifically; the power of these words and phrases rather derives from resonances and echoes which are partly subconscious, part of the American listener's assumed *schema* of nationhood, with all the *ideologies* which that includes.

A third example is 'promised land', a phrase which alluded originally to the land given by God to the Jews, according to the Hebrew Bible (Genesis 15) but which in this speech – especially when it is paired with the idea of 'going to the mountaintop' – has an even stronger echo of the last speech by Martin Luther King, delivered on 3 April 1968, just one day before he was assassinated:

> I just want to do God's will. And He's allowed me <u>to go up to the mountain</u>. And I've looked over. And <u>I've seen the promised land</u>. I may not get there with you. But I want you to know tonight, that <u>we, as a people will get to the promised land.</u> And I'm happy, tonight. I'm not worried about anything. I'm not fearing any man. Mine eyes have seen the glory of the coming of the Lord. (King, 1963)

For this reason the phrase has a powerful resonance in US history and politics. In these ways intertextual forces can be subtle and pervasive; they can infuse and empower even single words and phrases in highly charged ways, without our being consciously aware of how they are doing so.

Pronouns

A final point related to lexis concerns Obama's use of *pronouns*, and specifically the pronoun 'we'. Discourse analysts have focussed frequently on the way in which pronouns are used in subtle ways to denote or enact power relations and solidarity relations. (A famous early discussion was that of Brown and Gilman in 1960, discussing second person pronouns.) The word 'us', for example, can include some people but exclude others. The pronouns 'they' and them' can also serve to marginalize and exclude, if used in particular ways. In this speech, of course, Barack Obama's intention is to generate solidarity with his audience of supporters and at the same time to generate a sense of unity with the country as a whole, so his use of 'we' – in 'Yes <u>we</u> can' and elsewhere – generates this sense of solidarity. But who are 'we'? The linking of the pronoun 'we' with 'Americans' is made explicit in the syntax: '... when <u>we</u>'ve been told <u>we</u>'re not ready or that <u>we</u> shouldn't try or that <u>we</u> can't, generations of <u>Americans</u>...' Pronouns can be deliberately vague, of course – 'we' might at other times mean the Democratic Party, or the whole world. That flexibility or ambiguity is part of their power. In certain texts, especially political texts, it can therefore be valuable to identify patterns of pronoun use and evaluate what effect those patterns might have.

Metaphor

One prominent area of discourse which not only reflects the world, but can play a part in constructing it, is that of *metaphor*. Chapman (2006) discusses the work of Lakoff and Johnson (1980) in particular, in which metaphor is considered to be an important element of a 'conceptual system underlying the manner in which we make sense of the world' (Chapman, 2006:113). Metaphor, which is in essence the use of a word or expression from one domain in a new and unexpected domain in order to achieve particular effects, can therefore be a potentially powerful feature of discourse, as has been recognised, for example, in Charteris-Black's (2006) study of metaphor in political speeches, including those of Martin Luther King. In fact a straightforward example of such metaphors and their power comes from Martin Luther King's speech, quoted previously, concerning the journey to the promised land: 'And He's allowed me <u>to go up to the mountain</u>. And I've looked over. And <u>I've seen the promised land</u>. I may not get there with you.'

The use of this metaphor *projects* and *constructs* the political process as a difficult journey, divinely inspired, towards a place which is positive, and promised as a right. It also constructs the audience as being with him on that journey, therefore achieving empathy with them, as well as drawing on the full intertextual force of the biblical parallel and the resonance of the biblical language.

Obama's speech does not have a single metaphor at its heart, but offers what has been termed 'metaphorical framing' (Bloor and Bloor, 2007:75), which basically sets up a general position of 'we' (America, his supporters, Obama, the audience) – struggling against a range of problems and difficulties, but doing so with hope and optimism. This larger picture is then given visual, metaphorical force with a series of images which all push in the same direction.

Phrase	Possible metaphorical associations
For when we have *faced down* impossible odds	FIGHT metaphor

It was whispered by slaves and abolitionists as they *blazed a trail* towards freedom through the darkest of nights...	PIONEER / TOUGH JOURNEY metaphor
It was sung by immigrants as they *struck out* from distant shores	JOURNEY TO SAFETY / TOUGH JOURNEY metaphor
...and pioneers who *pushed* westward against an unforgiving wilderness	PIONEER / TOUGH JOURNEY metaphor
It was the *call* of workers who organized	part of a STRUGGLE FOR RIGHTS metaphor
...women who *reached* for the ballot	part of a STRUGGLE FOR RIGHTS metaphor
a president who *chose* the moon as our new frontier	PIONEER / TOUGH JOURNEY metaphor
and a king who *took us* to the mountaintop and pointed the way to the promised land	TOUGH JOURNEY metaphor

The result of these choices, expressed through lexis but essentially metaphorical in nature, is a flood of images associated with struggling for what is right, journeying through difficult landscapes, reaching your goal by working together and seeking justice, always with a sense of hope, all communicated in part through the choice of active verbs implying free choice and determination, such as 'struck out', 'pushed', 'sung', reached', 'chose', took'. The force of the lexis, in short, is complemented by the strength of these striking interwoven metaphors, acting subliminally to reinforce the nexus of messages which Obama wishes to convey.

The patterning of political rhetoric: repetition, parallelism, doubling and tripling

Besides the lexical choices, including pronouns and metaphors, another significant feature of the speech is the way its ideas are organised, patterned and structured. My analysis will concentrate essentially on patterns at clause and sentence level.

Patterning in Obama's speech is extensive; we can witness it even in the first sentence of the excerpt:

PROBLEM   [1] For when we have faced down impossible odds,
               [2] when we've been told

               [2a] we're not ready
               [2b] or that we shouldn't try
               [2c] or that we can't,

SOLUTION or   [3] generations of Americans have responded with a simple
RESPONSE   creed that sums up the spirit of a people:

               [3a] Yes, we can. *[cheers begin]*
               [3b] Yes, we can.
               [3c] Yes, we can.

Segments 1 and 2 together constitute a pair of ideas, both of them setting up the *problem* part of the sentence, which is later to be *answered* by segment 3. At once we can appreciate that if Obama had omitted segment 2 altogether then the sentence would have been substantially weaker, as follows:

[1] For when we have faced down impossible odds,
[3] generations of Americans have responded with a simple creed that sums up the spirit of a people:

By adding in segment 2, in other words, he has dramatically strengthened and reinforced the problem expressed in segment 1. The result of this, of course, is that when segment 3 eventually provides the *answer* or *resolution* to the problem, the effect is all the more resounding.

This device is a form of *parallelism*, which means making two or more statements which are parallel or equivalent to each other and can give a sense of strength and balance. All kinds of repetition are clearly effective means of strengthening. *Parallelism*, one particular type of repetition which sets up matching pairs and groups, is particularly effective as a powerful rhetorical device, and is central to Obama's style. Parallelism can consist of at least these types:

a) Simple repetition of the same word or phrase: 'Yes we can, Yes we can.'
b) Use of a synonym or near synonym: 'the struggles' 'the plight'.
c) Repetition of a syntactic structure: 'It was…It was…'
d) Other pairs and trios, to be considered below.

In this particular case the parallel is achieved by *doubling*, here achieved by means of a second 'when' clause to reinforce the first. Some orators usually make use of a doubling technique to make a *contrast*, one clause deliberately contrasting with another, which is sometimes called a *contrastive pair*. An example of this from British politics is offered by Atkinson:

> The truth is beginning to dawn on our people that there are two Conservative parties in this election.
>
> <u>One</u> is offering the continuation of the policies we've had for the last five years...
>
> <u>And the other</u> is offering a return to the policies of forty years ago!
>
> *(Audience laughs and claps)*
>
> (adapted from Atkinson, 1984: 74)

Such uses of doubling to highlight a contrast are quite common in political speeches, and we also see the device in well-known phrases, such as 'To be or not to be, that is the question' from Shakespeare's *Hamlet*. Here however, Obama uses this device of doubling to give a sense of *reinforcement* and *strengthening* rather than contrast. But what makes Obama's phrasing even stronger and more memorable is that inside the doubled phrases we also see another parallelism, this time a form of *tripling*, in a device which is sometimes called the 'list of three' or 'rule of three'. This is a well-known rhetorical device in which the speaker uses three elements one after the other in order to make an effect or to draw applause. Here, Obama uses the 'list of three' technique twice in the same sentence, in a neat parallel:

    [2] when we've been told
        [2a] we're not ready
        [2b] or that we shouldn't try
        [2c] or that we can't,
        ...
        [3a] Yes, we can. *[cheers begin]*
        [3b] Yes, we can.
        [3c] Yes, we can. *[Applause]*

Atkinson, in his well-known book on political speeches (1984: 57), explains the importance of these lists of three as follows: 'One of the main attractions of three-part lists is that they have an air of unity or completeness about them. Lists comprising only two items tend to appear inadequate or incomplete'. If Obama had said simply 'Yes we can. Yes we can', it would obviously have been less resonant. We can also see the importance of such triads in other aspects of communication, for example the tripling of characters in fairy stories (The Three Little Pigs, Goldilocks and the Three Bears, Three Billy Goats Gruff), and the tripling of phrases in children's stories:

'I'll huff and I'll puff and I'll blow your house in!' The device also appears in numerous set phrases (for example, 'ready, steady, GO!', 'Father, Son and Holy Ghost', 'well, well, well'), and we have already seen that it has a place in jokes. In short, the device can occur in a wide range of linguistic contexts to great effect. Using the device himself, Atkinson notes that the three part list serves 'to strengthen, underline or amplify almost any kind of message' (Atkinson, 1984: 60).

Analysis of Obama's speech shows that parallelism, and in particular this doubling and tripling, is a key part of its impact. In the first sentence we see two types of triplet, the first being a list of three joined by '...or...or...' and the second a direct three-fold use of the key phrase 'Yes we can.' The importance of this second triplet is that it introduces for the first time the driving motif of the whole speech, which is then taken up again and again right through to the speech's climax. In the second section, now that the motif of 'Yes we can' has been introduced, Obama sets up a new syntactic parallel pattern which is then repeated four times, each unit ending with the main 'Yes we can' motif:

> It was a creed...Yes we can.
> It was whispered...Yes we can.
> It was sung...Yes we can.
> It was the call of...Yes we can to justice and equality.

The parallelism is therefore clear to see; even within some of the sentences themselves we have other syntactic parallels and repetitions, for example the structure *noun + who*:

> 'It was the call of <u>workers who</u> organized, <u>women who</u> reached for the ballot, <u>a president who</u> chose the moon as our new frontier, and <u>a king who</u> took us to the mountaintop and pointed the way to the promised land.'

The whole section is therefore an intricate series of balances and repetitions. But what is the effect of this? In essence, the main framing structure, the repeated syntactical device 'It was', alerts the audience – already primed by hearing other speakers using such devices over the years – to expect a series of items. Obama does not disappoint, offering three sentences with the same basic structure, each followed by the now established motif 'Yes we can.' The list is then followed by a fourth clause, but the fact that this one ends differently (with a longer motif: 'Yes we can to justice and equality') signals to the audience that this is the conclusion of a section of the speech and that it is time to respond. In terms of *warranting* this interpretation (see Chapter 6, p. 108) it is significant to our analysis that the audience recognises the cue and does begin to cheer and chant. Obama, for his part, acknowledges this by allowing a pause of 21 seconds. The analysis of the discourse structures is therefore corroborated or *warranted* with reference to the observed behaviour of the crowd, and also to the behaviour of the speaker himself.

It was argued earlier that the metaphorical patterning suggested motifs of journeying against the odds. It is fitting therefore that Obama now, as he comes to the climax of the speech, constructs 'we' as ourselves embarking on a journey, 'as we take the campaign south and west', and takes up again some of the metaphors of *struggle* and *plight*. He does so with a resounding set of new parallelisms, building towards the impressive rhetorical climax. We can set out these parallels and repetitions as follows. It is remarkable how many pairs and repeated structures are combined within such a short passage:

SITUATION	as we take the campaign south and west,	*south and west* is a balanced pair
	as we learn that	repeats and balances the previous structure: *as we ...*
	The struggles of the textile workers in Spartanburg are not so different than the plight of the dishwasher in Las Vegas,	*struggles* and *plight* are a matched pair, as are the two types of workers, and the two places – a neat balance
	that the hopes of the little girl who goes to the crumbling school in Dillon are the same as the dreams of the boy who learns on the streets of L.A.,	*hopes* pairs with *dreams*, the *girl* pairs with the *boy*, *Dillon* pairs with *LA* (Los Angeles)
RESPONSE	we will remember that there is something happening in America,	syntactic repetition of *that* ... – three-part pattern
	that we are not as divided as our politics suggest,	
	that we are one people, *[Yeah]*	
	we are one nation ...	one people pairs with one nation
	...and, together, *[rising crescendo of cheers]* we will begin the next great chapter in the American story, with three words that will ring from coast to coast, from sea to shining sea: Yes, we can.	Balanced pairs: *coast to coast, sea to shining sea*

From this brief analysis the importance of the device of parallelism can be appreciated, in the form here of elegant *repetition* – repeating phrases and structures in a creative way. This is used in conjunction with other features, as when his closing passage offers further examples of lexis with special intertextual resonance (for example, 'sea to shining sea' alludes to a well-known patriotic song, *America the Beautiful*); there are examples of *alliteration* – repetition of certain sounds – which add to the auditory impact of the oratory (for example, the /s/ sound in the phrase 'responded with a simple creed that sums up the spirit of a people', or the pattern of /k/ and /s/ in 'coast to coast...sea to shining sea'). Other devices, too numerous to discuss here in detail, such as his delivery, the rhythm, stress and body language, also play their part, all contributing to what is surely one of the most powerful political speeches of its generation.

Encouraging, accepting and refusing applause

It is important in examining the speech not to forget Obama's audience; in a speech of this type they represent an important part of the *context* of the discourse. The effectiveness of any political speech depends on the way it engages and interacts with the audience. If the speaker can successfully motivate and lead the listeners, then that interaction can give the speech 'a feeling of shared purpose and identity' (Charteris-Black, 2006:63). It is of value, then, to turn to consideration of the ways in which Obama 'manages' the audience and its responses.

In his enthralling book on political speeches, Atkinson (1984) discusses devices which he calls 'claptraps', defined as mechanisms employed by a speaker in order to get the audience to applaud at key points of the speech. Two of these 'claptraps' are the pairs and triplets which we have mentioned already – combined, of course, with modulation of tone, pitch and loudness, and pauses at the right moments. Body language, head movement and 'gaze' can also serve as part of 'claptraps', signalling to the audience the moment to respond (in an interesting type of 'turn-giving'). The way a speaker uses position, stance, eye movement and gaze, as Goodwin (1981; 2007) has pointed out, can significantly impact on the effect of the language elements.

In this light it is noteworthy that Obama does indeed, after his first triple use of 'Yes we can' delivered with appropriate intonation, gaze and body language, receive significant applause. His 'claptrap' was effective. It is also interesting that he allows the applause and chanting from the crowd to continue for a full 13 seconds, himself saying the phrase a fourth time in chorus with them. In this way he leads the crowd into interacting with him, so that they become partners in the discourse.

What is curious about this case, however, is the way in which Obama appears slightly uneasy about the crowd chanting – he does not encourage it, but seems to tolerate it benevolently. When he is ready to start again he signals the fact by raising his arm slightly and then continues over the crowd as the chanting subsides. Atkinson notes the importance of a political speaker giving an impression of seriousness by appearing to want to continue *despite* the crowd. By seeming to refuse the applause, even talking over the cheering, an orator can give the impression of determination and seriousness, and even of modesty in declining the implied praise. This of course is a key part of the creation of Aristotelian *ethos*, the sense of a strong and serious person who deserves our respect and does not want praise, a sense created both by pushing on with the speech, and also by body language, posture and tone of voice.

I noted earlier that some transcripts of this speech set out each idea separately, as if Obama paused regularly. This is highly misleading, as was noted, and shows the importance of analysing not only the transcript but the delivery itself whenever possible, so as to evaluate properly a speaker's pacing. Here, at 11 minutes and 41 seconds, the crowd start chanting for a second time and Obama allows a full 21-second pause, but again he shows restraint rather than enthusiasm, offering only a brief smile before raising his hand slightly and continuing over the cheers and chanting, which then subside. He goes on to complete the final minute or so of his speech with scarcely a pause, as we can see from the transcript.

This is not to say that he rushes the conclusion; he takes the speech rhythmically and steadily to its climax, not even waiting for audience response before his final, quite quick 'Thank you, New Hampshire. Thank you. Thank you'. In this way he follows the theatrical actor's maxim of 'leaving the crowd wanting more', rather than letting them cheer themselves to a stop. Some commentators criticised him afterwards for what they saw as a low-key ending, but in their analysis they fail to appreciate that his aim was to blend the *pathos*, the emotional impact, with the *ethos*, the strong, calm image of himself as a reliable leader, in which he was surely fully successful.

Key features of the political speech

Political speeches, then, have persuasion as their main function, and can achieve that function through a wide range of resources or features. These can now be summarised as follows:

1. *Lexical resources*, including the choice of *verb and noun types* to motivate or argue, the use of *metaphor* and the use of *pronouns*.

2. A speaker can structure his or her ideas through the use of *parallelisms,* perhaps simple *repetition*, or use of *synonyms*, or other pairs, sometimes embedded inside each other. We also saw examples of repeated syntactic structures used as *discourse signals* to tell an audience to expect a set of linked points.

3. The *'list of three'* is one of the devices which speakers can use to generate applause (a 'claptrap' as Atkinson called it), and more generally to guide and manage audience response. This is important because although oratory appears to consist of one lengthy 'turn' from only one speaker, it relies for its success on its ability to interact with the audience, and therefore draws on the *interacting* discourse mode, in a way particular to the genre.

4. Other features include *intonation, rhythm* and *stress*, or such phonological devices as *alliteration*.

5. *Audience management*: discourse always tries to manage the audience. In the case of speeches we saw the use of linguistic devices, but also the use of body language, gestures, 'gaze', position and stance (Goodwin, 1981; 2007).

6. *Pausing and flow strategies:* the use of pausing and flow is important in speeches, but also in other forms of *interacting* discourse.

7. In many areas of the speech part of the impact comes from *allusions* and references, explicit or implicit, to other texts or people or events in an *intertextual* way.

As was noted before, one of the indicators of the success of Obama's speech was the fact that it was taken up intertextually by others. It is to this interesting intertextual dimension that our discussion can now return.

'Yes we can': imitations and parodies

Obama's New Hampshire speech generated enormous public attention, for example on the internet in the form of art, music and comment. The most well-known tribute is the song launched by the musician *will.i.am* with the group *Black Eyed Peas* along with a number of well-known actors and singers in a collective called 'WeCan08'. Their song, which has been viewed by millions on the website Youtube, skilfully harnesses the rhythms of Obama's original delivery, using the words of his speech only slightly modified ('I want change' and 'we want change' are not in the original speech), and shows him speaking in a frame in black and white, with other singers and other artists sometimes appearing instead of, or alongside him. Obama's own voice, his rhythm and intonation as he delivers the speech, are set alongside other voices singing and saying the same words in harmony. The speech itself has been cut and reordered in a new sequence, and we can also hear the cheering of the New Hampshire audience mixed and repeated. The rhetorician's 'rule' or 'list of three' is replaced by the musicians' chorus, so that at one point Obama's voicing of 'Yes we can' is copied and repeated nine consecutive times in harmony with the singers. On screen we sometimes see the words YES, WE CAN and HOPE.

This is prototypically intertextual, of course, since it is one text referring deliberately to another. Or rather, taking a broader perspective on intertextuality, this song is operating *intersemiotically*, alluding not only to the linguistic text of the speech but rather to the *whole event* of the New Hampshire oration, with all of its visual, social, political and historical semiotic resonances (for the concept of *intersemiosis* see (Lemke, 1992; Kress, 2000; Bax, 2004). The fact that with modern media the second text, the song, can actually include the first text in video format within it, and then add to it and embellish it musically and visually, adds hugely to its intertextual impact, because no longer do we need to *remember* an older event or speech – as we might have to remember Martin Luther King's or Kennedy's speeches – we can actually experience that original text within the new text itself. This technological innovation, of course, gives a whole new power to intertextual and intersemiotic creativity, redoubling the impact of the allusion.

What can we call this kind of borrowing? If it is imitation for humour or mockery, we tend to call it parody, pastiche or spoof. Here however, there is no mockery intended, so we might consider it a 'tribute' or 'homage'. However, other artists have followed a more satirical, less reverent route. In Britain the phrase 'Yes we can' was already well-known as part of a children's song from a cartoon series about a character called 'Bob the Builder', who could fix anything, and asked in music 'Can we fix it? Yes we can'. This led immediately to a series of spoofs and parodies on the song in Britain, which also appeared on the internet (see YouTube.com). Some of these aim to be merely humorous, but others are satirical and use the parody to critique Obama. For example one called 'Barack the Builder', by an artist called Sarcastic Truth, critiques Obama's socialism and calls him a Trojan Horse (an interesting intersemiotic reference in itself) attempting to bring in socialist ideas, 'brainwashing children to a socialist view'. These are instances of what have been called 'intertextual chains' (Fairclough 1993), in which a text builds on an earlier text, which in turn builds on an earlier text and so on. They also serve to demonstrate how such parodies can have markedly different intentions and functions, ranging from simplistic humour to biting critique.

9.3 Summary

This chapter has discussed political speeches and identified numerous features which can contribute to the effect of such oratory (summarised on p. 177). In more general terms, the discussion has also brought out the role of intertextuality as an important feature in certain texts, contributing powerfully, alongside other features, to achieving the function of texts. It has aimed to raise awareness of how intertextuality can, either in direct or more subtle ways, contribute significantly to the effect of a text on the reader or listener. For this reason intertextual analysis is an important part of the analyst's toolkit, full discussion of which we can consider in the final chapter.

CHAPTER

Doing Discourse Analysis

10

This chapter aims to bring together the techniques, approaches and strategies for analysing texts described in earlier chapters. The larger purpose of this is to build upon and extend the broad heuristic approach to discourse analysis outlined in Chapter 5, and also to offer further demonstrations of how this general approach can be implemented in practice.

So far the focus in this book has been on individual texts. However, attention will now move onto bigger study projects, involving corpora rather than individual texts, since it is frequently the focus of discourse analysis research to consider larger patterns of discourse extending over more than one piece of textual data. This will also allow for the fuller discussion of questions such as the quantity of data needed for a typical corpus, as well as issues of data collection and ethics. This means that the three basic questions which have framed the approach so far, namely *what* the text does or aims to do, *how* it does it, and *why*, will be set within the wider context of larger research studies, and embedded within a set of other questions, to give eight in total, as follows:

Structure of a Discourse Analysis research project

Question 1: Research question
What do I want to find out?
Question 2: Research literature
What have other people said about my topic?
Question 3: Data
What data do I need, and how can I get it?
Question 4: *WHAT*
What is this text (or corpus) doing?
Question 5: *HOW*
How does this text/corpus do what it does?

purpose ≠ reason

Question 6: *WHY*

Why does this text/corpus do what it does?

Reason?
plotivation
Ontology/ worldview

Question 7: *WHAT ELSE*

How else could this research be conducted?

Question 8: Presentation and writing up

How can I present it? Writing up the study

This scheme therefore builds on and extends the heuristic presented in Chapter 5, whose main elements can be discerned in three of the eight questions. As the scheme is discussed through this chapter, the principles and issues in question will be illustrated with reference to two small-scale discourse analysis studies carried out as part of their postgraduate studies by Aya Ikuma (Ikuma, 2008) from Japan and Ilaria Moscheni (Moscheni, 2008) from Italy. I am grateful to Aya and Ilaria for permission to quote their work. These two studies examine different kinds of data and use markedly different approaches. Aya's study examines patterns of spoken and written discourse in a corpus of data collected during a period of ethnographic observation in an educational setting, whereas Ilaria's concerns the analysis of a corpus of newspaper texts reporting on a particular criminal case. The difference between the two studies allows us to see how contrasting approaches to discourse analysis projects can deal with a variety of methodological challenges and issues.

10.1 Question 1: Research question

A useful first step for any research project in discourse analysis is to consider what stimulates the analyst's own interest. Analysts might have a personal interest in a particular genre or a particular topic, for example in race and racism (see van Dijk, 1987b; 1991), discourse and gender (Jeffries, 2007), food and food production (Cook, 2004), war reporting (Bax, 2006) or similar. A study might focus on something with a personal resonance, to do with the analyst's own environment or identity, or on perceived social problems or injustices. It might equally focus on more conventional or perhaps smaller areas of discourse, such as the discourse of an online game, or of chat rooms, or text messages.

Mobile Phones

Any students caught using a mobile phone will have their name
and details taken. Disciplinary action will be taken.
Thank you.

In Aya's case, she had noticed that in a university library there were certain patterns of written and spoken discourse, stimulated by her observation of signs such as the one illustrated, which reflected an interesting 'power rela-tionship between the library staff and the students' (Ikuma, 2008:2), and which at the same time had a 'politeness' dimension. She was interested in understanding this better. For her part, Ilaria had come across newspaper reports about a man in Austria who had allegedly locked his daughter in a basement for many years and abused her, and what caught her attention was the different ways in which each newspaper represented the man and other elements of the story. To examine further the issue of *representation* in the press, she wanted to study the news reports to see if she could identify patterns.

Any investigation is likely to be fully productive only if it is *systematic*. This means that both of these two researchers needed to think about the research perspective (Flick, 2008), and then try to refine a topic into a *research question*. This is useful even if the research is small in scale, as it focuses the analyst's attention and sets the boundaries for the study.

10.2 Question 2: Research literature

Once a topic of interest has been established and set out as a workable research question, it is important to see what other writers and researchers have said about it. If this is not done thoroughly, there is always a danger that the study will simply repeat research that has already been done.

A useful first step is to make use of internet search engines, if they are avail-able. A simple search on the Google search engine for example (at http://www.google.com) for 'chat room messages discourse', comes up with articles relating to cohesion and reference in chat room discourse, conversational endings in chat room discourse and various others. When the same search terms are entered into the specialist academic search engine Google Scholar (at http://scholar.google.com) it yields even more scholarly references to similar and related topics, as well as links to research studies. A search on Google Books (http://books.google.com) also gives a wide range of scholarly books which mention these precise terms. Using search engines in this way can therefore be a quick and effective starting point for a research study, allowing the researcher to see the range of related areas which have already been investigated, and obtain a range of references to be explored. The result is almost always a refining and sharpening of the research focus and research question.

Such internet searches can never be a substitute for more careful and lengthier library research aiming at the same thing, but they offer an effective way of gauging whether or not a project has been covered before, and how. However, the internet should be used cautiously and critically. An attractive article in the Wikipedia online encyclopaedia for example (www.wikipedia. org) may not be accurate, or complete, or confirmed by good research. This is not to say that such sites are not valuable, but – as always in academic research – we need to treat them critically and be circumspect. Once these sources have been investigated, a full library search will allow the more complete picture to emerge concerning what has already been discovered about the chosen topic, as well as different methods for researching it and analysing the data.

10.3 Question 3: Data

In the case of Aya's small-scale study, she chose to gather part of her data ethnographically by observing the interactions, including language use, in the environment of the university library. To help her explain to her readers what she was aiming at, she cited Brewer's description of ethnography: 'the study of people in naturally occurring settings or "fields" by means of methods which capture their social meanings and ordinary activities' (Brewer, 2000:6). In her written study she set out a detailed table explaining systematically when and where she had observed, over several days, and identified the focus of each observation. In addition she gathered other forms of data such as written notices and leaflets, and took her own observation notes and made drawings relating to signs and symbols, as well as other aspects which seemed to relate to the issues of power and politeness. She then itemised these in detail in an appendix. For example, among many others she copied down the sign reproduced above, relating to the use of mobile phones. It is apparent that this sign raises interesting questions of control and punishment, on the one hand, in contrast with other aspects of politeness ('Thank you') on the other.

Ilaria's study, by contrast, concerned a corpus of written texts. Again, her work was a piece of small-scale research, so she decided to carry out an *intensive* analysis rather than an *extensive* one, and limited her corpus to ten reports on the same story, taken from different English language newspapers. She explained clearly how she had made her selection and why, and why it was relatively limited in size, and then in her appendix she itemised the articles, with her sources.

How to gather data and how much you need

We can see from these examples that decisions on how to gather data, and how much data to gather, will depend on the approach to be adopted, and what kind of data suits the research question. It is of course important to gather enough data to have something to say, but not so much as to be overwhelmed – and it is up to the researcher to strike the balance. A central issue is whether there is enough data to support the findings claimed. An effective way of gauging how much data is necessary, and how to obtain it, is to read a wide variety of other research studies in the same area, so as to compare the intended data set with the sets which other researchers have used. The analyst will then need to make a judgement as to how much and what types of data to choose, drawing partly on the work of other research-ers as a guide.

Triangulation can be a useful concept at this stage, since – as the name sug-gests – it means in simple terms looking at the topic from more than one angle. A danger in research is that if we look at something from one direc-tion only we may not see all its facets, so it may be of value to use more than one approach and source of data, as Aya did in her study, since that can give different perspectives on what you are studying. Triangulation is in essence '[t]he combination of different methods, theories, data and/or researchers in the study of one issue' (Flick, 2008:120), which not only allows the researcher to feel that the study is more 'rounded', it also helps to convince the reader that what is claimed at the end of the research is likely to be more valid, because, to put it simply, several of the sources of data are saying the same sort of thing. This means that the researcher might, at the stage of planning the methodology, seek other sources of data which might give insight into the issue. Of course, as Wood and Kroger (2000:176) note, referring to the importance of warranting an analysis: '[t]riangulation in itself is not a crite-rion of warrantability; rather, it can contribute to the likelihood that work will be seen as warranted'.

Ethics in discourse research

The issue of ethics in research has become more important in recent years as it is appreciated that some research in the past treated human subjects in ways which we would now consider unacceptable. In fact the word 'sub-jects' itself ironically tends to construct people as 'objects', and nowadays we would probably use the term 'participants' instead. Whenever research involves human participants, of course, care needs to be taken with the ethi-cal dimension. Two useful rules of thumb are these: 'Your research should not cause any harm or distress, either psychological or physical, to anyone taking part in it', and 'Anyone taking part in the research should be aware that they are taking part in research, understand what the research is about and consent to take part in it' (Rapley, 2007:32).

It is ultimately the responsibility of each researcher, of course, to be sure that their research follows such guidelines.

Informed consent and observation

In cases such as Ilaria's, informed consent is not an issue, and this may be true for many studies of public written discourse. However, with spoken discourse these ethical considerations often mean getting 'prior informed consent' for any data collection. In this light, what of observational research in public spaces, such as Aya's, which involves many strangers in public settings? In such cases, ethical guidelines are available from some of the relevant professional bodies. An example is these, from the American Sociological Association, specifically addressing the issue of such research in public spaces. These 'guidelines' accept that such research can ethically be carried out, so long as: '(1) the research involves no more than minimal risk for research participants, and (2) the research could not practicably be carried out were informed consent to be required', and furthermore 'Sociologists may conduct research in public places or use publicly available information about individuals (e.g., naturalistic observations in public places, analysis of public records, or archival research) without obtaining consent' (http://www.asanet.org: Ethics section 12.01). It is important that any researcher aiming to collect spoken data should examine and observe such guidelines fully, and then in the written study explain how the ethical dimension was managed.

Reflexivity: thinking about your own role

Another important dimension of data gathering is to take account of your own position as a researcher. In Ilaria's case, for example, she needed to consider her own position as a reader and as a person, and take account of any such aspects which might affect her research. In Aya's case this was even more crucial, since she had to consider her own role and perspective as a researcher in that setting, but also whether her physical presence in the setting she was observing might actually change the very elements she was trying to observe.

This is sometimes called the Observer's Paradox (Labov, 1972; Trask and Stockwell, 2007). It is a paradox because, in essence, an observer can only hope to understand a social setting by becoming involved in it, at least by entering it. However, by the very act of entering it the setting is disturbed, and does not therefore constitute the 'pure' version which the researcher aimed to study. One possible solution to this is, at the very least, to be *reflexive*, which means 'reflecting upon and understanding our own personal, political and intellectual autobiographies as researchers and making explicit where we are located in relation to our research respondents. Reflexivity also means acknowledging the critical role we play in creating, interpreting and theorizing data' (Mauthner and Doucet, 1998:121).

In other words we need to be aware of, and acknowledge, our own place in the research, as well as dealing with the possible effect which our own presence in the setting might have on our findings. For this reason many research studies include a section in which the researcher demonstrates awareness of his/her own role and impact, and explains how s/he dealt with the issue.

10.4 Question 4: *What* – what is this text doing?

Assuming that the researcher has gathered sufficient data, the question arises as to how to approach the data for the purpose of analysis. This question, addressed in Chapter 5 as part of the heuristic, can now be revisited.

Analysts cannot escape the fact that they are first and foremost readers and listeners, and that their interpretation must to some extent depend on that fact. Although this seems obvious, discourse analysts appear at times determined to obscure their own subjective involvement by hiding behind a battery of apparently objective techniques and measures. However, the subjective element cannot be eradicated completely.

A position adopted by a number of qualitative researchers is that instead of insisting on the 'false notion of scientific objectivity' (Okely, 1996:23), it is methodologically more satisfactory to acknowledge the subjective dimension, and even to place it at the heart of the research endeavour. In discourse analysis this would mean starting with this question, when analysing a text: *what effect does it have on me as a reader/listener?* In essence, this is the position assumed by the heuristic in Chapter 5, of which this is one of the first questions. However, in delineating the heuristic it was also made clear that in addition to his or her personal response to a text or texts, the analyst should also take measures to corroborate, substantiate or revise any element of subjectivity.

In a refreshingly practical approach, McGregor (2003) suggests two stages which aim to draw on our inevitably subjective interpretations and then to go beyond them. The first stage in her discussion is to read or listen in a relatively uncritical way, acting as far as possible as we would when reading or listening naturally. The second step is then to read or listen again (where possible) in a more critical way, asking ourselves questions concerning the genre, layout, pictures, focus, prominent lexis, context and so on. In a sense this blends the *what* question into the *why* question (to be considered shortly), and it helps to make the point that although we can attempt to start as a 'normal' reader and listener, it is then important to review the text in a more careful, considered and critical way. A number of readings, looking for different aspects, may give different perspectives on the text.

Besides approaching texts through this kind of systematic reading or listening process, it may also be possible for the researcher to investigate what effect or impact the texts might have on other people. In a larger study this might involve the type of audience research which is well-established in the field of media studies (see, for example, Schrøder *et al.,* 2003). Reader or listener responses might also be investigated on a smaller scale, for example through focus groups or interviews, to gauge the ways in which other people interpret the discourse (as discussed in Krueger and Casey, 2000, for example).

A further approach might be to examine the wider impact of the text in question. This might operate on a relatively large scale, such as looking at critical responses to a novel or film, but it could also operate on a smaller scale. For example Aya in her research observed what effect the notices in the library had on the behaviour of users. Another way might be to look for any intertextual borrowing of the text by other texts – if many people cite Obama's or Martin Luther King's speeches then this is an *index* of the impact of those speeches. These are samples of strategies which again allow a form of *triangulation*, complementing the starting point which is the analyst's own response.

It is not always possible to corroborate one's own interpretation in these ways, of course. Ilaria in her particular study could not in practice get other readers' interpretations (although had she had more time she might perhaps have used a focus group) so she needed to *warrant* her interpretation and analysis in other ways to be considered below. Nonetheless, it is always worth considering ways of obtaining evidence of other views and reactions to any text, though these will always be complementary to our own interpretation and cannot substitute for it. The point is to make efforts to get alternative perspectives as far as possible, using multiple methods and triangulation as appropriate.

10.5 Question 5: *How* – how does this text do what it does?

The kind of critical reading described above begins in effect also to answer the second core question, namely *how* the text achieves its impact. This is the heart of any discourse analysis, so it will here be considered in some detail.

Techniques and approaches to analysis

The heuristic approach presented in Chapter 5 offers one way of approaching the analysis of discourse. In essence, having examined the *what* question by considering the texts in context, so as to identify their impact or effect in broad terms, the heuristic moves to consider *how* this impact or function is achieved, by examining the many *features* of the texts.

A significant feature of a text is how it draws on *genre knowledge* to achieve particular effects. Since many texts follow genres closely, it is useful for the analyst to consider genre features early in any analysis, so as to identify the text's function as well as significant textual features. A second feature which can be important in the impact of a text is the broad *discourse mode* which it employs, for example it may use *narrating* mode or *describing* mode as part of its impact on the reader or listener in important ways. For the reason that the genre and discourse mode of a text are relatively regular, and can be studied relatively systematically, it makes sense for any approach to discourse analysis to devote considerable attention to them, which explains their prominence in this book. They represent useful initial perspectives from which to start to 'interrogate' a text in its context so as to see how it achieves its impact.

The analysis of spoken and written texts in previous chapters demonstrates the wide range of features which can be involved in achieving a text's function. It is therefore helpful if the analyst can borrow or draw inspiration from research approaches which have been tried and described by other researchers. To help with this, I now list the main approaches we have seen in the book so far, along with the main discourse mode they relate to, with reference to examples from earlier chapters (see Table 10.1). If an analyst has identified the *genre, discourse mode, function* and salient *features*, especially any emerging patterns, in each text in a corpus, it will be possible to choose from this list an approach which might be of value in the fuller analysis. I have divided the list into three broad parts, relating to higher-order elements, lower-order elements, and non-linguistic elements. A convincing analysis will probably examine higher-order elements and lower-order and/or paralinguistic elements together, in order to demonstrate how the text uses different lexical, phonological and syntactical features to achieve its functions and impact. In other words, it is not likely that an analysis will choose only one of the elements in the list; it will almost certainly need to show evidence from lower-order elements (for example, lexis, syntax and phonology) and to consider higher-order elements, as well as non-linguistic elements where relevant, so as to explain how its effects are achieved by all elements working together.

Table 10.1 Summary of selected approaches to discourse

A *Higher order elements*

Technique or approach	Discussed in Chapter	Genres and types of texts where this approach might be of value
1 Analysis of *adjacency pairs*	4, 6, 7, 8	All texts in *interacting* mode
2 Analysis of *patterns of turn-taking and turn-giving*	4, 6, 7, 8	All texts in *interacting* mode
3 Analysis of *repair strategies*	6	All texts in *interacting* mode
4 Analysis of *topic placement,* 'topicalisation' or 'topic control'	4, 6, 7, 8	All texts in *interacting* mode
5 Analysis of *question patterns*	7	All texts in *interacting* mode
6 Analysis of *exchange analysis* which involves categorising classes and then trying to identify them in subsequent discourse	6	All texts in *interacting* mode
7 Analysis and evaluation of *discourse structure*	8	All texts, e.g. Lonely hearts advertisements, News reports
8 Analysis of *narrative structure*	4,6	Texts in narrating mode, including Jokes, News reports, Advertisements, novels and other fiction
9 Analysis of *event structure*	4, 6	e.g. Jokes, News reports, novels and other fiction
10 Analysis of *content focus*	8, 9	e.g. News reports, Lonely hearts ads, Political speeches
11 Analysis of *content balance*	8	e.g. Lonely hearts ads, News reports, Political speeches
12 Analysis of the *style* of a text (and assessment of how it relates to the overall function)	6, 7, 9	e.g. Job interviews, Conversation, Cross-examination, Political speeches
13 Analysis of *audience management*	7, 9	All texts in interacting mode, particularly with persuasive functions, such as TV adverts, Political speeches
14 Analysis of intertextuality: -specific intertextual references -possible less direct allusions and echoes -genre and genre mixing -other intertextual effects and influences	2, 4, 9	All discourse modes and texts

B Lower order elements: cohesion, lexis, syntax

> *Technique or approach*

15   Analysis of patterns of cohesion

16   Analysis of *lexical choices*

     -abstract or concrete?

     -jargon?

17   Analysis of *pronoun choices*

18   Analysis of *metaphor*

19   Analysis of *parallelism*

     -repetition pairs

     -contrasting and reinforcing

     -three-part structures

     -semantic parallelism

20   Analysis of *verb tense choices* and patterns

21   Analysis of *pausing and flow strategies*

22   Analysis of *intonation, stress patterns, accent features,* etc.

C Non-linguistic elements

23   Analysis of graphics, layout, and so on

24   Analysis of gaze, *position, stance and attitude* (cf. Goodwin, 1981; 2007)

25   Analysis of *the use of body language and gesture*

Context revisited

For reasons discussed in Chapter 2 (see p.21) and set out here by Gee, context is central to the analysis of discourse:

> discourse analysis is always a movement from context to language and from language to context. We gain information about a context in which a piece of language has been used and use this information to form hypotheses about what that piece of language means and is doing. In turn, we closely study the piece of language and ask ourselves what we can learn about the context in which the language was used and how that context was construed (interpreted) by the speaker/writer and listener(s)/reader(s). (Gee, 2005:14)

In this way, if Aya wishes to explain the sign which told users that 'any students caught using a mobile phone will have their name and details taken', she must take account of the contextual dimensions, but must understand context to mean not merely the physical context in itself. As was noted earlier, '[c]ontext is not an external set of circumstances but a selection of them internally represented in the mind' (Widdowson, 2007:20). The point, then is not simply to notice aspects of the physical context, but to try to understand how they are assimilated by the various users of the library and how they impact on their understandings and behaviour. Aya could do this not only by taking note of what she observes about the position of the sign in relation to other elements of the context, but by observing how users, both staff and students, responded to it, how she herself (as a participant observer) reacted to it, and how it coincided with or contradicted other aspects of her research data. She might, if conditions allowed and if it were among her research aims, obtain data directly about participants' own views and responses to such signs. In broad terms, a researcher needs to take account of the full implications of such data as part of a wider context.

Choosing an appropriate approach for analysis

After she had gathered her data, Aya started to analyse it, and began to notice certain *patterns*. She noticed for example that when staff in the library asked students to be quiet, they used particular indirect speech acts (Searle, 1969), and quiet, calm voicing, and in addition they acted immediately. However, when a student asked another student to be quiet, they tended to wait for several minutes before speaking, to use a more direct speech act, and higher pitch. She then considered how this contributed to a larger picture of politeness / authority / control / status relationships, and was able to demonstrate with useful examples, argumentation and numerical evidence the ways in which the language and other physical and behavioural aspects operated together.

Aya's approach was relatively inductive; she gathered data from observation and elsewhere, and then analysed it to discover patterns. Ilaria by contrast adopted a more deductive approach. Her aim was to examine a corpus of newspaper articles from different newspapers in order to discover linguistic patterns in the representation and reporting of particular events. She started with a set of categories (and that is why her work is more deductive) drawn from Fairclough (2003), to include elements such as direct reporting, indirect reporting with active verbs, indirect reporting with passive verbs, reporting through speech acts (for example, 'she admitted that...'), and other reporting devices. After devising an analytical grid on the basis of these categories, she analysed each sentence of each news article in detail, aiming to identify similarities and differences between the various types of newspaper.

In these different ways, the two analysts followed systematic and well-supported processes of analysis so as to identify patterns in the discourse. Another way of doing this, particularly with documentary data, is to adopt the Constant Comparative Method described in detail in, for example, Maykut and Morehouse (1994). The aim of this is also to identify 'units of meaning', in other words groups of data which seem together to be pointing towards the same findings. Maykut and Morehouse recommend that with documentary data the analyst can physically cut and group pieces together. Other approaches, for example that adopted by Ilaria, involve colour coding as part of the annotation process. No matter which approach is adopted, this is the stage where the mass of relatively 'messy' data starts to take shape into fewer meaningful main findings, as a broad pattern emerges.

Warranting your findings

Discourse analysis is arguably a largely qualitative, interpretive area of study. However, like all research it also has a *persuasive* element, since a good analysis is one which convinces its readers that it has identified patterns which serve to explain what is happening. To succeed in this attempt at persuasion, the analyst needs to be able to show that any statements are grounded in the *evidence* of the data itself. It is therefore important to demonstrate with close reference to the data, perhaps with statistical or numerical support, that these patterns are genuine. This point was made also in Chapter 6 (see p. 108) with reference to *warranting* any claims through close reference to the transcript (in the case of CA research), but the point applies equally to other sources of data in other research traditions.

Being persuasive does not mean arguing for one side or another. On the contrary, part of being persuasive in an academic medium is demonstrating balance and close reference to the data. Gee has argued that in some examples within the Critical Discourse Analysis (CDA) framework, researchers have failed to do this: 'sometimes [some discourse analysis] seems to amount to proselytizing for one's own politics in the absence of any close study of oral or written language' (Gee, 2004:20). The danger of this is that the analysis then fails to be credible. A strong analysis will make a point and then support it with specific evidence in the data, preferably drawing on several sources of data (in a sort of triangulation). An analysis of newspaper reporting, say, such as the one in Chapter 8, could refer to elements of the lexis, sentence structure, topicalisation, graphics (for example, the choice of photos) to make a point about how the paper represents the matter at hand. If the researcher demonstrates that several sources of evidence point in the same direction, then the analysis will tend to be more persuasive.

Lincoln and Guba (1985) highlight the danger in qualitative research of looking only for data which confirms the researcher's viewpoint and suggest that at times a full 'negative case analysis' will be useful. The aim of seeking and then taking full account of negative data, *discrepancies* or *counter-examples*, is to ensure balance and demonstrate neutrality. This can contribute to the strength of the overall *theory* which the researcher is aiming to offer: '[t]he theory that is being developed becomes more robust if it addresses negative cases, for it sets the boundaries to the theory; it modifies the theory, it sets parameters to the applicability of the theory' (Cohen *et al.*, 2007:185).

10.6 Question 6: *Why* – why does this text do what it does?

It was noted in Chapter 5 that the central questions to be asked in the heuristic need not be asked in a particular sequence. In the case of the *why* question, concerning the wider socio-political dimensions of the text, the question could be asked at the start of the process, or later. Since this question has been taken by some to be at the heart of the whole endeavour of discourse analysis, it is worth digressing here to consider how these wider socio-political issues impact on the field as a whole.

Mention has been made in several earlier chapters of the approach to discourse known as Critical Discourse Analysis or CDA. This approach has gained moment in recent years and proponents sometimes suggest that they are going beyond what 'standard' discourse analysis has done in the past. Here is an argument which leads eventually to this kind of claim:

> much of the discourse analysis of the twentieth century was essentially non-critical, which is to say that it did not present a critique of social practices.
>
> It had three main purposes: (1) to identify and describe how people use language to communicate; (2) to develop methods of analysis that help to reveal the categories (or varieties) of discourse and the essential features of each; and (3) to build theories about how communication takes place. (Bloor and Bloor, 2007:12)

These writers then contrast this more 'traditional' position with a CDA viewpoint:

> Although these questions are important, there have always been some discourse analysts with a broader agenda, and gradually their number

has increased. They see discourse both as a product of society and also as a dynamic and changing force that is constantly influencing and re-constructing social practices and values, either positively or negatively. In order to approach this broader agenda, they need to address and analyse discourse practices in critical ways, questioning the texts and processes that they study. This requires commitment to social concerns. (Bloor and Bloor, 2007:12)

Bloor and Bloor then go on to offer a cogent account of CDA's main objectives:

- to analyse discourse practices that reflect or construct social problems;
- to investigate how ideologies can become frozen in language and find ways to break the ice;
- to increase awareness of how to apply these objectives to specific cases of injustice, prejudice, and misuse of power.

To these practical objectives, we can add the more theoretical aims that have been proposed for the subject:

- to demonstrate the significance of language in the social relations of power;
- to investigate how meaning is created in context;
- to investigate the role of speaker/writer <u>purpose</u> and authorial <u>stance</u> in the construction of discourse.

                         (Bloor and Bloor, 2007:12–13, emphasis in original)

The approach to discourse analysis adopted in this book has attempted to take account of both the 'traditional' and the more critical perspective, in Bloor and Bloor's terms. In terms of the traditional framework, the book has analysed examples of real discourse, considered different methods of analysis, and considered what this tells us about wider issues about communication and interpretation. However, it has also adopted a more critical perspective, suggesting in Chapter 2 and elsewhere that two central aspects of discourse analysis are a concern with

- the ways in which discourse can serve to *construct and reinforce ideology and viewpoint*, and
- the *socio-political implications and consequences* of this kind of ideological construction.

This reflects the fact that, partly because of work in CDA, no account of discourse analysis can nowadays completely ignore critical perspectives.

However, that is not to say that all analyses of discourse will necessarily adopt the precise aims which Bloor and Bloor have listed, since there may be perfectly valid discourse studies from other points of view. Furthermore, a number of prominent critics have expressed their unease at some of the products and workings of CDA. Gee, for example, was quoted in the last section critiquing certain CDA attitudes to warranting. Blommaert was cited on p.22 critiquing aspects of the CDA approach to context. Widdowson, in a sustained critique (2004:173), concludes that CDA 'has, by academic standards, serious shortcomings as an approach to discourse analysis – shortcomings, furthermore, which actually compromise the very cause which motivates it.'

For this reason any discourse analyst must approach Critical Discourse approaches critically, so to speak, and appreciate the fact that discourse analysis which does not adopt a CDA position can still, of course, be valuable and interesting.

Nonetheless, returning to the focus of this section, I have taken as axiomatic the view that a thorough discourse analysis will need at some point to ask the *why* question when analysing texts. This in essence seeks to examine the implications of the text in its wider socio-political context, on the understanding that discourse – as discussed several times – is a 'loaded weapon'. The analyst needs therefore to consider who might have loaded it, why, and what their target might be.

In terms of Aya's research, this would lead her to ask not only *what* the impact of the discourse in the library was doing, and *how* exactly it operated. Consideration of the *why* question would raise bigger issues for her, concerning, for example the socio-political relationship which the authorities were seeking to establish in relation to library users, the ways in which power and authority were conceived by those authorities, and then accepted or resisted by users, and even how this approach to students and other library users reflected wider views about social roles, authority and education.

In the case of Ilaria's research, she might ask why different newspapers represented different aspects of the case in different ways, which could lead for example to larger questions about political bias, cultural stereotyping, the representation of gender, of fatherhood, and so on. In short, in these and other examples, the *why* question could open out a number of the issues which Bloor and Bloor cited as being central to CDA, including questions of injustice, ideology, power, misuse of power, inequality, and prejudice.

It is taken as useful, then, to ask the wider question about a text's socio-political implications in each discourse analysis project. Of course, what the researcher then discovers will depend on the nature of the texts under study.

10.7 Question 7: *What* else – how could it be done differently?

There are always a variety of ways of approaching a text or corpus. It makes sense, therefore, that at the end of the research process the analyst should reflect in retrospect on how the research could have been carried out differently or how further research could extend the insights gained. In longer studies, for example at PhD level, there is frequently a section on 'avenues for future research' and also discussion of how the research was less effective than it might have been, or of how it could have been carried out differently. The point, once again, is not to pretend that the research was perfect, but to acknowledge openly that there are always shortcomings in any project, and to build on them.

10.8 Question 8: Presentation and writing up

Having completed the project itself, the researcher usually needs to present it in written form in an academic context. A useful principle here is to 'show the workings' in ways discussed in Chapter 5 (see p. 97), so that the reader can appreciate the rigour, system and care behind the research at all points. The reader should be given enough information so as to be convinced by the review of the literature (that it was sufficient and well-targeted), by the data collection (that it was systematic, thorough, and sufficient in quantity), by the analytical procedure (that it was systematic and balanced) and by the findings (that they are supported by the evidence). Academic writing, as I said above, is in part a matter of persuading the reader of the rigour of the researcher's procedure and approach.

10.9 Endnote

This chapter has developed a set of guidelines for carrying out a discourse analysis project based on the three main questions posed in the introduction, *what*, *how* and *why*, along with five other questions related to the research process itself. In the process it has attempted to bring together the threads of the book as a whole. An important part of this is the summary of selected approaches to discourse presented in Table 10.1, which for ease of reference itemises each of the techniques discussed in the preceding chapters. The researcher aiming to analyse a text or corpus can make use of that summary to identify which approach or approaches might be most suitable, and then re-read the relevant section in the earlier part of the book, as well as following up the references to read the more specialist literature on each approach.

Discourse is all around us and affects us all. It can at times seem like a loaded weapon ready to be aimed and fired. My hope is that this book has made a small contribution to raising awareness of how discourse can achieve some of its power, as well as outlining a variety of approaches to investigating diverse forms of discourse in a variety of contexts systematically and thoroughly. The book will have served its main purpose, however, if it also stimulates and facilitates further research into the host of fascinating texts which impact on our lives, so as to elucidate more fully the complex but intriguing relationship between language behaviour and the social domains in which it operates.

Bibliography

Abbs, B., V. Cook and M. Underwood, *Realistic English Dialogues* (Oxford: Oxford University Press, 1979).

Alexander, R., *Aspects of Verbal Humour in English* (Gunter Narr Verlag, 1997).

Allen, G., *Intertextuality* (London: Routledge, 2000).

Almasi, J., *Teaching Strategic Processes in Reading: Solving Problems in the Teaching of Literacy* (New York: Guilford Press, 2002).

Aristotle, *Poetics*, in *The Classical Greek Reader*, ed., K. Atchity (Oxford: Oxford University Press, 1988),209–16.

Aristotle, 'Rhetoric', (trans. Rhys Roberts, W.) in *Aristotle Complete Works: the Revised Oxford Translation*, Vol. 2, ed. J. Barnes (Princeton: Princeton University Press, 1984).

Atkinson, M., *Our Masters' Voices: The Language and Body Language of Politics* (New York: London: Routledge, 1984).

Auer, P., 'Introduction: John Gumperz' approach to contextualization', in *The Contextualization of Language*, ed. Peter Auer and Aldo DiLuzio (Amsterdam: John Benjamins, 1992), 1–37.

Austin, J., *How to do things with Words: The William James Lectures delivered at Harvard University in 1955*, ed. J. O. Urmson (Oxford: Clarendon, 1962).

Bain, A., *English Composition and Rhetoric* (London: Longman, Green & Company, 1877).

Bakhtin, M., *Problems of Dostoevsky's Poetics* (tr. R.W. Rotsel) (Ann Arbor, Mich.: Ardis, 1973).

Baldry, A. and P. Thibault, *Multimodal Transcription and Text Analysis* (London: Equinox Publishing, 2005).

Bamberg, M., *Narrative Development: Six Approaches* (London: Routledge, 1997).

Barnett, M., *More than Meets the Eye: Foreign Language Learner Reading* (Englewood Cliffs, NJ: Prentice-Hall, 1989).

Bartlett, F., *Remembering: An Experimental and Social Study* (Cambridge: Cambridge University Press, 1932).

Bax, S., *Researching Intertextual Reference and Intertextual Reading*, PhD dissertation, University of Kent, 2004.

Bax, S., 'Beware the press in times of war', *British Journalism Review*, Vol. 17, No. 2, June 2006, 53–8.

Bell, A., *The Language of News Media* (Oxford: Blackwell, 1991).

Bell, A., 'The discourse structure of news stories', in *Approaches to Media Discourse*, ed. Bell, A. and P. Garrett (Malden: Oxford, 1998) 65–103.

Bellack, A., H. Kliebard, R. Hyman and F. Smith, *The Language of the Classroom* (New York: Teachers College Press, 1966).

Berger, P. and T. Luckmann , *The Social Construction of Reality: A Treatise in the Sociology of Knowledge* (Garden City, NY: Anchor Books, 1966).

Berry, M., 'Systemic linguistics and discourse analysis: a multi-layered approach to exchange structure' in *Studies in Discourse Analysis*, ed. M. Coulthard and M. Montgomery (London: Routledge & Kegan Paul, 1981), 120–45.

Bhatia, V., 'Applied genre analysis: analytical advances and pedagogical procedures', in *Genre in the Classroom*, ed. A. Johns (Mahwah, NJ: Lawrence Erlbaum, 2002), 279–83.

Bhatia, V., *Worlds of Written Discourse* (London: Continuum International Publishing Group, 2004).

Blommaert, J., *Discourse: A Critical Introduction* (Cambridge, Cambridge University Press, 2005).

Bloor, T. and M. Bloor, *The Functional Analysis of English* (London: Hodder Arnold, 2004).

Bloor, M. and T. Bloor, *The Practice of Critical Discourse Analysis: An Introduction* (London: Hodder Arnold, 2007).

Bolinger, D., *Language, the Loaded Weapon: The Use and Abuse of Language Today* (Longman, 1980).

Bransford, J. D. and Johnson, M. K., 'Contextual prerequisites for understanding: some investigations of comprehension and recall', *Journal of Verbal Learning and Verbal Behavior*, 11, (1972), 717–26.

Bregman, A. and Haythornthwaite, C., 'Radicals of Presentation in Persistent Conversation', Proceedings of the 34th Annual Hawaii International Conference on System Sciences (HICSS-34)-Volume 4 Maui, Hawai January 3–6, 2001, available from http://www.visi.com/~snowfall/HICSS_PC_History.html [Accessed 19/11/08]

Brewer, J., *Ethnography* (Buckingham: Open University Press, 2000).

Brooks, C. and R. Warren, *Modern Rhetoric*, 3rd edn (New York: Harcourt Brace Jovanovich, 1972).

Brown, R. and A. Gilman, 'The pronouns of power and solidarity', in *Style in Language*, ed. Sebeok, T. (New York: MIT, 1960), 253–76.

Bruner, J., *Actual Minds, Possible Worlds* (Cambridge, MA: Harvard University Press, 1986).

Bruner, J., *Acts of Meaning* (Cambridge, MA: Harvard University Press, 1990).

Buck, G., *Assessing Listening* (Cambridge: CUP, 2001).

Cameron, D., *Working with Spoken Discourse* (London: Sage, 2001).

Carey, C., 'Observers of speeches and hearers of action: the Athenian orators', in *Literature in the Greek and Roman Worlds: A New Perspective*, ed. O. Taplin (Oxford: Oxford University Press, 2000),192–216.

Carrell, P., 'Some issues in studying the role of schemata, or background knowledge in second language comprehension', *Reading in a Foreign Language*, 1 (1983), 81–92.

Carrell, P., J. Devine and D. Eskey, *Interactive Approaches to Second Language Reading* (Cambridge: Cambridge University Press, 1988).

Chapman, S., *Thinking about Language: Theories of English* (Basingstoke: Palgrave Macmillan, 2006).

Charteris-Black, J. *Politicians and Rhetoric: The Persuasive Power of Metaphor* (Basingstoke & New York: Palgrave Macmillan, 2006).

Chatman, S., *Story and Discourse: Narrative Structure in Fiction and Film* (Cornell University Press, 1989).

Cheepen, C., *The Predictability of Informal Conversation* (London: Pinter Publishers, 1988).

Cheng, W., *Intercultural Conversation* (Amsterdam: John Benjamins Publishing Company, 2003).

Cherry, C., *On Human Communication* (Cambridge Mass.: MIT Press, 1957).

Chilton, P., *Analysing Political Discourse: Theory and Practice* (London: Routledge, 2004).

Chomsky, N. *Aspects of the Theory of Syntax* (Boston, MA: MIT Press, 1965).

Chouliaraki, L. and N. Fairclough, *Discourse in Late Modernity* (Edinburgh: Edinburgh University Press, 1999).

Clark. H., *Using Language* (Cambridge: Cambridge University Press, 1996).

Clark, U., *Studying Language: English in Action* (Basingstoke: Palgrave Macmillan, 2007).

Clift, R., P. Drew and I. Hutchby, 'Conversation Analysis', in *The Pragmatics of Interaction*, Volume 4 of *Handbook of Pragmatics Highlights*, ed.S. D'hondt., J. Östman and J. Verschueren (Amsterdam:John Benjamins, 2009), 40–55.

Cohen, L., L. Manion and K. Morrison, *Research Methods in Education* (London: Routledge, 2007).

Cook, G. *Discourse* (Oxford: Oxford University Press, 1989).

Cook, G. *Genetically Modified Language: The Discourse of Arguments for GM Crops and Food* (London: Routledge, 2004).

Coulthard, M. 'Whose text is it? On the linguistic investigation of authorship', in S. Sarangi and R.M. Coulthard (eds), *Discourse and Social Life* (London: Longman, 2000) 270–87.

Coulthard, M. and A. Johnson, *An Introduction to Forensic Linguistics: Language in Evidence* (London: Routledge, 2007).

Crane, J. and J. Michie Ino, 'A Discourse of Despair: The Semiology of Lonely-Hearts Language', *Sociological Perspectives*, Vol. 30, No. 3 (July 1987), 227–44.

Crystal, D. *txtng – the gr8 db8* (Oxford: Oxford University Press, 2008).

Cutting, J. *Pragmatics and Discourse: A Resource Book for Students* (London: Routledge, 2002).

de Beaugrande, R. *A New Introduction to the Study of Text and Discourse* http://www.beaugrande.com/ [Accessed 27/3/1008]

de Beaugrande, R. and Dressler, W., *Introduction to Text Linguistics* (London: Longman, 1981).

Delin, J., *The Language of Everyday Life: An Introduction* (London: Sage, 2000).

Duranti, A. *Linguistic Anthropology* (Cambridge: Cambridge University Press, 1997).

Emmott, C. *Narrative Comprehension: A Discourse Perspective* (Oxford: Oxford University Press, 1997).

Eysenck, M. and M. Keane, *Cognitive Psychology: A Student's Handbook*, 4th edn (London: Taylor & Francis, 2000).

Fairclough, N., *New Labour, New Language?* (London: Routledge, 2000).

Fairclough, N., *Analysing Discourse* (London: Routledge, 2003).

Fairclough, N., *Discourse and Social Change* (Oxford: Wiley-Blackwell, 1993).

Field, J., *Psycholinguistics: A Resource Book for Students* (London: Routledge, 2003).

Flick, U., *Designing Qualitative Research* (London: Sage, 2008).

Fowler, R., *Language in the News: Discourse and Ideology in the Press* (London: Routledge, 1991).

Fowler, R., Hodge, B., Kress, G. and Trew, T. *Language and Control* (London: Routledge & Kegan Paul, 1979).

Frow, J., *Genre* (London: Taylor & Francis, 2006).

Garfinkel, H., *Studies in Ethnomethodology* (Malden, MA: Polity Press/Blackwell Publishing, 1984 [originally 1967]).

Garfinkel, H., *Ethnomethodology's Program* (New York: Rowman & Littlefield, 2002).

Gee, J., *An Introduction to Discourse Analysis*, 1st edn (London: Routledge, 1999).

Gee, J., 'Discourse Analysis: What Makes It Critical?', in *An Introduction to Critical Discourse Analysis in Education*, ed., R. Rogers (Mahwa, NJ: Lawrence Erlbaum Associates, 2004), 19–50.

Gee, J., *An Introduction to Discourse Analysis,* 2nd edn (London: Routledge, 2005).

Gee, J., 'Discourse Analysis: what makes it critical?' in *An Introduction to Critical Discourse Analysis in Education,* ed. R. Rogers (Mahwa, NJ: Lawrence Erlbaum Associates, 2005), 19–50.

George, A., *The Epic of Gilgamesh: The Babylonian Epic Poem and Other Texts in Akkadian and Sumerian* (Harmondsworth: Penguin Books, 2003).

Gibbons, J., *Forensic Linguistics* (Oxford, Blackwell, 2003).

Goodman, K., 'Reading: A psycholinguistic guessing game', *Journal of the Reading Specialist*, 6: 126–35 (1967).

Goodman, K., 'Psycholinguistic Universals in the Reading Process', in *Psycholinguistics and Reading,* ed.F. Smith. (New York: Holt, Rinehart & Winston, 1973), 21–9.

Goodwin, C., *Conversational Organization: Interaction between Speakers and Hearers* (New York: Academic Press, 1981).

Goodwin, C., 'Interactive footing', in *Reporting Talk: Reported Speech in Interaction,* ed. E. Holt and R. Clift (Cambridge: Cambridge University Press, 2007) 16–46.

Gough, P., 'One second of reading', in *Language by Ear and by Eye* , ed. J. Kavenaugh and I. Mattingly (Cambridge. MA: MIT, 1972), 331–58.

Grabe, W., 'Developments in reading research and their implications for computer-adaptive reading assessment', in *Issues in computer-adaptive testing of reading proficiency Volume 10 of Studies in Language Testing,* ed. M. Chalhoub-Deville (Cambridge: Cambridge University Press, 1999), 11–47.

Grabe, W., 'Narrative and Expository Macro-Genres', in *Genre in the Classroom,* ed. Johns, A. (Mahwah, NJ: Lawrence Erlbaum, 2002), 249–67.

Grabe, W. and F. Stoller, *Teaching and Researching Reading* (Harlow: Pearson, 2002).

Gregoriou, C., *English Literary Stylistics* (Basingstoke: Palgrave Macmillan, 2009).

Grice, H., 'Logic and Conversation', in *Syntax and Semantics,* Vol. 3, ed. P. Cole and J. Morgan (New York: Academic Press), 41–58.

Gumperz, J., *Discourse Strategies* (Cambridge: Cambridge University Press, 1982).

Gumperz, J., 'Contextualization revisited' in *The Contextualization of Language, ed.,* P. Auer and A. DiLuzio (Amsterdam: John Benjamins, 1992), 39–53.

Halford, G., *Children's Understanding: The Development of Mental Models* (Mahwah, NJ: Lawrence Erlbaum Associates, 1993).

Halliday, M., 'Part A' in *Language, Context and Text: Aspects of Language in a Social–Semiotic Perspective,* ed. M. Halliday and R. Hasan (Oxford: Oxford University Press, 1989), 1–49.

Halliday, M. and Hasan, R., *Cohesion in English* (Harlow: Longman, 1976).

Halliday, M. and R. Hasan, *Language, Context and Text: Aspects of Language in a Social-Semiotic Perspective* (Oxford: Oxford University Press, 1985).

Harris, P., *Reading in the Primary School Years* (London:Thomson Learning Nelson, 2005).

Heritage, J., *Garfinkel and Ethnomethodology* (Oxford: Blackwell, 1984).

Herring, S., 'Computer-mediated discourse analysis: An approach to researching online behaviour', in *Designing for Virtual Communities in the Service of Learning,* ed., S.A. Barab, R. Kling, and J.H. Gray (New York: Cambridge University Press, 2004), 338–76.

Heydon, G., *The Language of Police Interviewing* (Basingstoke: Palgrave Macmillan, 2005).

Hicks, D., 'Discourse teaching and learning' in Goodman, S., T. Lillisand J. Maybin *Language, Literacy and Education: A Reader* (Stoke on Trent: Trentham Books, 2003), 3–24.

Hoey, M., *Textual Interaction* (London, Routledge. 2001).

Holliday, A., 'Six lessons: cultural continuity in communicative language teaching', *Language Teaching Research September 1/3,* 1997, 212–38.

Holliday, A., *Doing and Writing Qualitative Research* (London: Sage, 2002).

Holmes, J., *An Introduction to Sociolinguistics,* 3rd edn (London: Longman, 2008).

Hult, C. and R. Richins, 'The rhetoric and discourse of instant messaging' *Computers and Composition Online, Theory into Practice,* Spring 2006 http://www.bgsu.edu/cconline/hultrichins_im/hultrichins_im.htm.

Hutchby, I., *Conversation and Technology: From the Telephone to the Internet* (Oxford: Blackwell, 2001).

Hutchby, I. and R. Wooffitt, *Conversation Analysis: Principles, Practices and Applications* (Cambridge: Polity Press, 1998).

Hyon, S., 'Genre in Three Traditions: Implications for ESL', *TESOL Quarterly*, Vol. 30, No. 4 (Winter, 1996), 693–722.

Ikuma, A., *Language in Use,* Unpublished Research Paper, MA TESOL (Canterbury: Christ Church University, 2008).

Jeffries, L., *Discovering Language: The Structure of Modern English* (Basingstoke: Palgrave Macmillan, 2006).

Jeffries, L., *Textual Construction of the Female Body: A Critical Discourse Approach* (Basingstoke: Palgrave Macmillan, 2007).

Jeffries, L. and McIntyre, D., *Stylistics* (Cambridge: Cambridge University Press, 2010).

Johns, A., 'Genre awareness for the novice academic student: An ongoing quest' , *Language Teaching* (2008) 41:2, 237–52.

Johnstone, B., *Discourse Analysis* (Oxford, Blackwell, 2002).

Jones, K. and J. Stilwell Peccei, 'Language and Politics' in *Language, Society and Power: An Introduction* by L. Thomas, I. Singh, J. Stilwell Peccei, J. Jones (London: Routledge, 2004), chapter 3, 35–53.

Jupp, V., *The Sage Dictionary of Social Research Methods* (London: Sage Publications, 2006).

Khalifa, H. and C. Weir, *Examining Reading: Research and Practice in Assessing Second Language Reading* (Cambridge: Cambridge University Press, 2009).

King, M., 'I have a dream' speech, 1963, http://www.stanford.edu/ group/King// publications/speeches/address_at_march_on_washington.pdf. Also at http://www. mlkonline.ne

Kress, G., 'Text as the punctuation of semiosis: pulling at some of the threads', in *Intertextuality and the Media: From Genre to Everyday Life,* ed.U. Meinhoff. and J. Smith (Manchester: Manchester University Press, 2000), 132–54.

Krueger, R. and M. Casey, *Focus Groups: A Practical Guide for Applied Research* (London: Sage, 2000).

Labov, W., *Language in the Inner City* (Philadelphia: University of Pennsylvania Press, 1972).

Labov, W. and J.Waletzky, 'Narrative analysis' in *Essays on the Verbal and Visual Arts,* ed. J. Helm (Seattle: University of Washington Press, 1967), 12–44.

Lakoff, G. and M. Johnson, *Metaphors We Live By* (Chicago: University of Chicago Press, 1980).

Lemke, J., 'Intertextuality and educational research', *Linguistics and Education,* 4 (1992), 257–67.

Levinson, S., *Pragmatics* (Cambridge: Cambridge University, 1983).

Lincoln, Y. and E. Guba, *Naturalistic Inquiry* (Beverly Hills, CA: Sage, 1985).

Martin J. R., *Factual Writing: Exploring and Challenging Social Reality,* Deakin University, Victoria, Australia: Deakin University Press, 1985 (also published in 1989 by Oxford University Press).

Martin, J., 'Language, register and genre', in *Analysing English in a Global Context: A Reader,* ed. A. Burns and C. Coffin (London: Routledge, The Open University, 2001), 149–66.

Martin, J. and D. Rose, *Working with Discourse* (London: Continuum, 2003).

Martin, J. and D. Rose, *Genre Relations: Mapping Culture* (London: Equinox, 2008).

Matoesian, G., *Reproducing Rape: Domination through Talk in the Courtroom* (Chicago: University of Chicago Press, 1993).

Mauthner, N. and Doucet, A. 'Reflections on a vice centred relational method', in *Feminist Dilemmas in Qualitative Research,* ed.,J. Ribbens. and Edwards, R. (London: Sage, 1998).

Maxwell Atkinson, J., and J. Heritage, *Structures of Social Action: Studies in Conversation Analysis* (Cambridge: Cambridge University Press, 1984).

Maykut, P. and R. Morehouse, *Beginning Qualitative Research: A Philosophic and Practical Guide* (London: The Falmer Press, 1994).

McGregor, S., 'Critical Discourse Analysis – A Primer', *Kappa Omicron Nu FORUM Critical Science and Critical Discourse Analysis*, Vol. 15, No. 1 Available at: http://www.kon.org/archives/forum/15–1/mcgregorcda.html (2003).

Merritt, M., 'Distributing and Directing Attention in Primary Classrooms', in *Communicating in the Classroom*, ed. L.C. Wilkinson (New York: Academic Press, 1982), 223–44.

Metro 'Nescafe ad 'most romantic' of all time' http://www.metro.co.uk/ 11 February 2008.

Miller, C., 'Genre as social action', *Quarterly Journal of Speech*, 70, (1984) 151–67.

Moscheni, I., *Language in Use*, Unpublished Research Paper, MA TESOL (Canterbury: Christ Church University, 2008).

Mulholland, J., 'E-mail: uses, issues and problems in an institutional setting', in *Writing Business: Genres, Media and Discourses*, ed. F. Bargiela-Chiappini and C. Nickerson (Harlow: Longman, 1999), 57–84.

Okely, J., *Own or Other Culture* (London: Routledge, 1996).

Orwell, G., *1984* (London: Signet Classics [1948] 1981).

Paltridge, B., *Genre and the Language Learning Classroom* (Ann Arbor: University of Michigan Press, 2001).

Paltridge, B., *Discourse Analysis: an Introduction* (Continuum: London, 2006).

Parker, I. and the Bolton Discourse Network, *Critical Textwork* (Buckingham: Open University Press, 1999).

Pomerantz, A., 'Compliment Responses: Notes on the Co-Operation of Multiple Constraints', in *Studies in the Organization of Conversational Interaction*, ed. J. Schenkein (New York: Academic Press, 1978), 79–112.

Potter, J., 'Discourse analysis as a way of analysing naturally occurring talk', in *Qualitative Research: Theory, Method and Practice*, ed. D. Silverman (London: Sage, 1997), 200–20.

Pridham, F., *The Language of Conversation* (London: Routledge, 2001).

Propp, V., *The Morphology of the Folk Tale* (Austin: University of Texas Press, 1968, originally published in Russian, 1928).

Rapley, T., *Doing Conversation, Discourse and Document Analysis* (London: Sage, 2007).

Renkema, J., *Discourse Studies: An Introductory Textbook* (Amsterdam: John Benjamin Publishing Company, 1993).

Ricouer, P., *Time and Narrative*, Volume 1 (Chicago: University of Chicago Press, 1990).

Rock, F., *Communicating Rights: The Language of Arrest and Detention* (Basingstoke: Palgrave Macmillan, 2007).

Rogers, R., (ed.) *An Introduction to Critical Discourse Analysis in Education* (Mahwah, NJ: Lawrence Erlbaum Associates, 2004).

Rosch, E., `Principles of categorization', in Rosch, E. and Lloyd, B. (1978), 27–48.

Rosch, E. and Lloyd, B. (eds) *Cognition and Categorization* (Mahwah, NJ: Lawrence Erlbaum Associates 1978).

Rowan, C., 'Informing and Explaining Skills: Theory and Research on Informative Communication', in *Handbook of Communication and Social Interaction Skills*, ed. John O. Greene. and Brant R. Burleson (Mahwah, NJ and London: Lawrence Erlbaum Associates, 2003), chapter 10: 403–38.

Rumelhart, D., 'Toward an Interactive Model of Reading', in *Theoretical Models and Processes of Reading,* ed. H. Singer and R. Ruddell (Newark, Delaware: International Reading Association, 1985), 722–51.

Sacks, H., *Lectures on Conversation* (2 vols), ed. by Gail Jefferson (Oxford: Wiley-Blackwell, [1961–72] 1995).

Sacks, H., Schegloff. E. and Jefferson, G., 'A simplest systematics for the organization of turn-taking for conversation', *Language 50,* (1974) 696–735.

Samuels, S. and M. Kamil, 'Models of the Reading Process', in *Handbook of Reading Research,* Volume 1, ed. P. Pearson R.. Barr, M. Kamil and P. Mosenthal (1984) (New York: Longman) 185–225.

Schank, R.C. and Abelson, R., *Scripts, Plans, Goals, and Understanding* (Hillsdale, NJ: Earlbaum Associates., 1977).

Schegloff, E., 'Sequencing in conversational openings', in *Directions in Sociolinguistics,* ed. J.J. Gumperz and D. H. Hymes (New York: Holt, Rinehart & Winston, 1972), 346–80.

Schegloff, E., *Sequence Organization in Interaction* (Cambridge: Cambridge University Press, 2007).

Schegloff, E., Jefferson, G. and Sacks, H., 'The preference for self-correction in the organisation of repair in conversation', *Language,* 53 (1977), 361–82.

Schiffman, H., *Linguistic Culture and Language Policy* (London: Routledge, 1996).

Schrøder K., K. Drotner, S. Kline and C. Murray *Researching Audiences* (London: Arnold, 2003).

Schulze-Wenke, S., 'Form and function of "first verbs" in talk-in-interaction', in *Syntax and Lexis in Conversation: Studies on the Use of Linguistic Resources in Talk-in-Interaction,* ed. Auli Hakulinen and Margret Selting (Amsterdam: John Benjamins, 2005), 319–48.

Scott, L. and R. Batra, *Persuasive Imagery: A Consumer Response Perspective* (Mahwah, NJ:Lawrence Erlbaum Associates, 2003).

Searle, J., *Speech Acts: An Essay in the Philosophy of Language* (Cambridge: Cambridge University Press, 1969).

Seedhouse, P., 'Classroom interaction: possibilities and impossibilities', *ELTJ,* 50/1 (1996), 16–24.

Silverman, D., *Harvey Sacks: Social Science and Conversation Analysis* (US: Oxford University Press, 1998).

Simpson, P.. *Language, Ideology and Point of View* (London: Routledge, 1993).

Sinclair, J. and Coulthard, M., *Toward an Analysis of Discourse: the English Used by Teachers and Pupils* (Oxford: Oxford University Press, 1975).

Skemp, R., *Intelligence, Learning and Action* (Chichester: John Wiley , 1979).

Smith, C., *Modes of Discourse: The Local Structure of Texts* (Cambridge: Cambridge University Press, 2003).

Sperber, D. and D. Wilson, *Relevance: Communication and Cognition* (Oxford: Blackwell, 1968).

Spradley, J., *Participant Observation* (New York: Holt, Rinehart & Winston, 1980).

Stockwell, P., *Cognitive Poetics* (London: Routledge, 2002).

Stubbs, M., *Discourse Analysis* (Oxford: Basil Blackwell, 1983).

Swales, J., *Genre Analysis: English in Academic and Research Settings* (Cambridge: Cambridge University Press 1990).

ten Have, P., *Doing Conversation Analysis* (London: Sage, 1999).

Thornbury, S., *Beyond the Sentence: Introducing Discourse Analysis* (London: Macmillan, 2005).

Thurlow, C., 'Generation Txt? The sociolinguistics of young people's text-messaging' (2003) http://extra.shu.ac.uk/daol/articles/v1/n1/a3/thurlow2002003-paper.html.

Thurlow, C. and M. Poff, 'Text-messaging', http://faculty.washington.edu/thurlow/papers/thurlow&poff (2009).pdf. To appear (in press) in S. C. Herring, D. Stein and T. Virtanen (eds), *Handbook of the Pragmatics of CMC* (Berlin and New York: Mouton de Gruyter).

Thwaites, T., L. Davis and W. Mules, *Tools for Cultural Studies: An Introduction* (South Melbourne: Macmillan, 1994).

Todorov, T., *The Poetics of Prose*, trans. R. Howard (Cornell, Cornell University Press, 1977 [1971]).

Todorov, T., *Genres in Discourse*, trans. Catherine Porter (Cambridge: Cambridge University Press, 1990 [1978]).

Toolan, M., *Narrative: A Critical Linguistic Introduction* (London: Routledge, 2001).

Trask, R. and P. Stockwell, *Language and Linguistics: The Key Concepts* (London: Routledge, 2007).

Unger, C., *Genre, Relevance and Global Coherence: The Pragmatics of Discourse Type* (Basingstoke and New York: Palgrave Macmillan, 2006).

Urquhart, S. and Weir, C., *Reading in a Second Language: Process, Product and Practice* (New York: Longman, 1998).

van Dijk, T., 'Episodic models in discourse processing', in *Comprehending Oral and Written Language*, ed. R. Horowitz and S. Samuels (New York: Academic Press, 1984).

van Dijk, T., 'Structures of news in the press', in *Discourse and Communication*, ed.T. Van Dijk (Berlin: De Gruyter, 1985), 69—93.

van Dijk, T., *Discourse Studies: A Multidisciplinary Introduction* (London, Sage, 1987a).

van Dijk, T., *Communicating Racism. Ethnic Prejudice in Thought and Talk* (Newbury Park, CA: Sage, 1987b).

van Dijk, T., *Racism and the Press* (London: Routledge, 1991).

van Dijk, T., 'Opinions and ideologies in the press', in *Approaches to Media Discourse*, ed. A. Bell. and P. Garrett (Malden: Oxford, 1998), 21–63.

Wallace, C., *Reading* (Oxford: Oxford University Press, 1992).

Werlich, E., *A Text Grammar of English* (Heidelberg: Quelle & Meyer, 1976).

Widdowson, H. G., 'Discourse analysis: a critical view', *Language and Literature*, 4(3) (1995), 157–2.

Widdowson, H., 'Discourse analysis: a critical view', in *Controversies in Applied Linguistics*, ed. B.Seidlhofer (Oxford: Oxford University Press, 2003), 132–45.

Widdowson, H., *Text, Context, Pretext: Critical Issues in Discourse Analysis* (Oxford: Blackwell , 2004).

Widdowson, H., *Discourse Analysis* (Oxford: Oxford University Press, 2007).

Wood, L. and R. Kroger, *Doing Discourse Analysis: Methods for Studying Action in Talk and Text* (London: Sage, 2000).

Yule, G., *Pragmatics* (Oxford: Oxford University Press, 1996).

Index

Note: **bold** font indicates the main pages where the entry is discussed or defined.